No Spiritual Investment in the World

signale
modern german letters, cultures, and thought

Series editor: Peter Uwe Hohendahl, Cornell University

Signale: Modern German Letters, Cultures, and Thought publishes new English-language books in literary studies, criticism, cultural studies, and intellectual history pertaining to the German-speaking world, as well as translations of important German-language works. *Signale* construes "modern" in the broadest terms: the series covers topics ranging from the early modern period to the present. *Signale* books are published under a joint imprint of Cornell University Press and Cornell University Library in electronic and print formats. Please see http://signale.cornell.edu/.

No Spiritual Investment
in the World

Gnosticism and Postwar German Philosophy

Willem Styfhals

A Signale Book

Cornell University Press and Cornell University Library
Ithaca and London

Cornell University Press and Cornell University Library gratefully acknowledge the College of Arts & Sciences, Cornell University, for support of the Signale series.

First published 2019 by Cornell University Press and Cornell University Library

Library of Congress Cataloging-in-Publication Data

Names: Styfhals, Willem, 1988– author.
Title: No spiritual investment in the world : gnosticism and postwar
    German philosophy / Willem Styfhals.
Description: Ithaca, NY : Cornell University Press : Cornell University
    Library, 2019. | Series: A Signale book | Includes bibliographical
    references and index.
Identifiers: LCCN 2018057107 (print) | LCCN 2019001553 (ebook) |
    ISBN 9781501731013 (pdf) | ISBN 9781501731020 (epub/mobi) |
    ISBN 9781501730993 | ISBN 9781501730993 (cloth) |
    ISBN 9781501731006 (pbk.)
Subjects: LCSH: Philosophy, German—20th century. | Gnosticism. |
    Germany—Intellectual life—20th century.
Classification: LCC B3181 (ebook) | LCC B3181 .S825 2019 (print) |
    DDC 193—dc23
LC record available at https://lccn.loc.gov/2018057107

CONTENTS

Acknowledgments

Although the cover of this book mentions only my name, I have not written this book alone. The words may be mine, but the book's content reflects the countless conversations I had with friends, family, and colleagues. And even the words could not have been where they are right now without their support and confidence. The cover is too small anyway to list all the people who directly or indirectly contributed to this book. Therefore, I gladly take the opportunity to name those people here.

Before naming names, however, I owe thanks to many institutions and organizations for their material support as well: first and foremost, the Institute of Philosophy and KULeuven, but also the Research Foundation—Flanders (FWO) and the Belgian American Educational Foundation (BAEF). I would also like to thank several universities where I was able to present work in progress or spend time as a visiting scholar. I am pleased to thank the University of Antwerp for the stimulating collaborations; Columbia University, the University of Iceland, and Loyola University Chicago for welcoming me as a visiting scholar; the Zentrum für Literatur- und Kulturforschung in Berlin for inviting me to present my work and do research in Jacob Taubes's archives, and finally Yale University for giving me the opportunity to finish this book during my stay as a postdoctoral fellow.

This book is based on research I conducted at KULeuven (Belgium). Studying Gnosticism at an institute with roots in neo-Scholasticism, and reading less canonical German philosophers like Odo Marquard, Jacob Taubes, and Hans Blumenberg in a department with a long tradition in Husserl's and Heidegger's phenomenology, made me feel like some kind of a modern heretic. Admittedly, I liked this status. This is probably what attracted me, like Jacob Taubes, to the topic of Gnosticism in the first place. But even for a self-professed heretic the intellectual environment at the Institute of Philosophy in Leuven could not have been more open and more stimulating. I owe special thanks to my colleagues and my lifelong friends from Leuven: Gerbert Faure, Simon Truwant, Wolter Hartog, Vincent Caudron, Dries Simons, and Laurens Dhaenens. Without their intellectual support and friendship this book would simply not have been possible. More than just conversation partners or readers of my manuscript, they are the reason I could write this book in the first place. I also want to thank some of my professors from Leuven for their advice and for their comments on earlier drafts of the chapters in this book: Karin de Boer, Toon Breackman, Paul Cortois, Roland Breeur, Paul Moyaert, Nicolas de Warren, and Guy Vanheeswijck. The latter has the dubious honor of having read almost every word I have ever written. I would like to thank him for his generosity and his continuing interest in my work.

André Cloots and Stéphane Symons deserve to be thanked here separately. Not only did they support my writing this book from the very beginning to the end, but they have also been my two mentors over the past few years. André Cloots introduced me to philosophy when was I was eighteen years old, and supported me until I obtained my doctoral degree almost ten years later. I cannot even begin to express how much I owe to him both personally and academically. The same is true of Stéphane Symons. If André Cloots was my Doktorvater, Stéphane Symons was my older Doktorbruder. He helped me with the most annoying practical problems of this book as well as the most difficult philosophical issues (often concerning Walter Benjamin whose work he knows like few others). But, most importantly, he became one of my closest friends along the way.

Obviously, this book was not written in Leuven alone. In many ways, I have followed the journeys of the main figures I studied. With the exception of Hans Blumenberg and Odo Marquard, none of the thinkers discussed in this book stayed in Germany for long periods of time. Jacob Taubes, in particular, traveled his entire life between Berlin, New York, Paris, and Jerusalem, never finding a real home in any of these cities. In my attempt to follow Taubes, I have studied like him at Columbia University in New York and done research in Berlin for several months, stopping along the way in Paris, Jerusalem, Chicago, New Haven, and even Reykjavik. Among all the people I have met, two deserve special thanks. Martin Treml invited me to Berlin and gave me access to Taubes's letters. I am thankful for his feedback and generous support. More importantly, he is one of the warmest, funniest, and most sympathetic academicians I have ever met. Kirk Wetters invited me to join the German Department at Yale for a year as a visiting scholar. It was there that I finished this book, and it is mainly thanks to his intellectual, personal, and material support that I was able to achieve that. In addition to these people, I warmly thank friends and colleagues from all over the world for their advice and for the fascinating discussions about my research: Stijn Latré, Herbert De Vriese, Jonathan Sozek, Samuel Moyn, Mark Lilla, Daniel Steinmetz-Jenkins, Hannes Bajohr, Jerry Muller, Benjamin Lazier, Felix Steilen, Jeffrey Barash, Michaël Foessel, Agata Bielik-Robson, Herbert Kopp-Oberstebrink, Daniel Weidner, Nitzan Lebovic, Sigrid Weigel, Adam Stern, Björn Thorsteinsson, Colby Dickinson, Egon Bauwelinck, Thomas Meyer, Peter Gordon, Jonathon Catlin, Paul North, Noreen Khawaja, Katharina Kreuzpaintner, Terrence Renaud, Rüdiger Campe, Marcel Schmidt, and Asaf Angermann.

Parts of the book and specific arguments I develop in the chapters have already been published elsewhere. An earlier and shorter version of chapter 2 was published as "Evil in History: Karl Löwith and Jacob Taubes on Modern Eschatology," *Journal of the History of Ideas* 76, no. 2 (2015). The discussion of Jacob Taubes and Gershom Scholem in chapter 3 was published as "Deconstructing Orthodoxy: A Failed Dialogue between Gershom Scholem and Jacob Taubes," *New German Critique* 45, no. 1 (2018). Some fragments of chapter 6 were published in "Modernity as Theodicy: Odo Marquard Reads Hans Blumenberg's *The Legitimacy of the Modern Age*," *Journal of the History of Ideas* 80, no. 1 (2019). I thank the editors of both journals for permission to reprint the material here.

Thanks is also due to Marian Rogers, who helped me prepare the manuscript, to Kizer Walker, the managing editor of the Signale series, and to the series editor, Peter Hohendahl, for patiently guiding me through the complex process of publishing a first book.

I am also very grateful to those who helped me find and access the sources I needed to write this book and to the many libraries and archives where I pursued my research. In particular, I would like to thank Steven Spileers and the staff of the Philosophy Library at KULeuven for their help and advice. I also want to thank the Zentrum für Literatur- und Kulturforschung in Berlin for giving me access to Jacob Taubes's letter archive (Martin Treml and Herbert Kopp-Oberstrebrink, in particular) and the Deutsche Literatur Archiv in Marbach for allowing me to do research in Hans Blumenberg's Nachlass. I thank Bettina Blumenberg for her permission to quote from her father's unpublished writings.

I would like to thank my family too: my parents, Marijke and Jan; my sister, Margot; and my wife, Mariske. Because their contribution to this book is perhaps the least tangible, it is all the more profound. Without their encouragement, I would not even have undertaken the project of writing a book. Finally, I could not be more thankful to Mariske for joining me on my intellectual and physical journeys to follow these weird German philosophers.

No Spiritual Investment in the World

INTRODUCTION

Jacob Taubes and the German Gnosticism Debates

"I have no spiritual investment in the world as it is," claimed Jacob Taubes, a Jewish philosopher of religion, in a short note on Nazi jurist Carl Schmitt.[1] The message this statement tried to convey initially remains enigmatic, even ambiguous. Did Taubes claim to be a modern atheistic materialist, a nihilist perhaps, who denied the world any spiritual value? Or was this actually a deeply religious statement from someone who rejected his attachment to this world in favor of another world to come? Paradoxically, both can be the case.

---

1. Jacob Taubes, "Die Geschichte Jacob Taubes-Carl Schmitt," in *Apokalypse und Politik: Aufsätze, Kritiken und kleinere Schriften,* ed. Herbert Kopp-Oberstebrink and Martin Treml (Munich: Wilhelm Fink, 2017), 305 (emphasis original; appears in English in the original German text).

On the one hand, this claim epitomized the religious worldview of Apocalypticism and Gnosticism. Taubes made this very explicit: "I can imagine as an apocalyptic: let it all go down."[2] Someone who believes that the end of time is imminent does not care for the world and certainly does not want to invest in it or legitimate it as it is. Such an apocalyptic worldview can even entail the radical degradation of the meaning of the world that was characteristic of the ancient Christian heresy of Gnosticism. Indeed, the Gnostics considered the world to be an evil, fallen, godless, demonic, meaningless, or inferior place in comparison to the fullness of a radically transcendent divine meaning. In this view, reality appeared as a world prison that humanity had to be redeemed from rather than as a positive life-world that we can become spiritually attached to. Indeed, it would be plainly absurd to have any investment in such a Gnostic world at all.

On the other hand, Taubes's claim to have no spiritual investment in the world could also be a decidedly modern or secular one. More is at stake here than a naïve religious belief in the end of time or the depravity of the present. Or, at least, the implications of such apocalyptic and Gnostic claims reach beyond the domain of religion proper. The Gnostic-apocalyptic lack of spiritual investment in the world survives in the attitude of the modern nihilist, who could not care less for the world, or in that of the revolutionary, who is deeply unsatisfied with the current state of things and wants to destroy reality in order to change it. On this point, Taubes contrasted his own position with Schmitt's whom he also considered an apocalyptic thinker but one who wanted to restrain rather than attain the Apocalypse. In Taubes's view, Schmitt wanted to save the world from its end. While Taubes, as a modern Gnostic, delegitimized the world, Schmitt, as a jurist, "has to legitimate the world as it is."[3] In contradistinction to the modern revolutionary

---

2. Taubes, "Die Geschichte Jacob Taubes-Carl Schmitt," 305; English translation: Jacob Taubes, "Appendix A: The Jacob Taubes-Carl Schmitt Story," in *The Political Theology of Paul*, trans. Dana Hollander (Stanford: Stanford University Press, 2004), 103.
3. Taubes, "The Jacob Taubes-Carl Schmitt Story," 103.

or to the ancient Gnostic and apocalyptic who typically opposed the political status quo, the jurist has to avoid chaos at all costs and make sure that the state remains. Indeed, Schmitt considered the state to be an apocalyptic force in its own right to the extent that it functions as a restrainer—Schmitt referred here to Saint Paul's concept of the *katechon*—holding back the end of the world, and thus making political legitimacy and immanent existence possible.[4]

The strange affinity across the ages between ancient Gnosticism and modern thought, implied in Taubes's idiosyncratic claim, is the object of study in this book. Taubes was indeed not the only thinker to connect the Gnostic mind-set to modern phenomena. Many of his contemporaries such as Eric Voegelin, Hans Blumenberg, Hans Jonas, Odo Marquard, and Gershom Scholem were even more explicit on this point. This book focuses on these twentieth-century German intellectuals who at some point made use of the concept of Gnosticism to make sense of philosophical or political modernity. They did so from very different disciplinary backgrounds, making use of conflicting historical sources, and with incommensurable philosophical agendas. Taubes was the one who tried to bring their different positions together into a unified debate. He created connections between the theories of modern Gnosticism where their respective authors saw none; and he triggered discussions even where the envisioned debaters themselves shunned the debate. Taubes's own position was hardly the most original or profound, but his mediating role in these "Gnosticism debates" was essential. He knew Voegelin, Blumenberg, Jonas, Marquard, and Scholem personally, corresponded with them extensively, and attempted to put them in contact with each other to discuss their positions on Gnosticism and modernity. Admittedly, Taubes's attempts often failed. To a certain extent, the Gnosticism debates existed in his mind more so than in reality. Insofar as this book aims to reconstruct historically the postwar German debates on modern Gnosticism, inevitably it relies on the way Taubes first constructed them.

---

4. See Carl Schmitt, *The Nomos of the Earth in the International Law of Jus Publicum Europaeum*, trans. G.L. Ulmen (New York: Telos Press Publishing), 59–62.

In order to bring the different positions of Voegelin, Blumenberg, Jonas, Marquard, and Scholem together, this book takes Taubes's position as its point of departure. It argues accordingly that all these thinkers shared the conviction, for better or worse, that modern thought was lacking *spiritual investment in the world as it is*. For some, this modern-Gnostic loss of spiritual investment was a sign of cultural crisis and intellectual decay. Modernity or specific modern evolutions implied for thinkers like Voegelin, Jonas, and Marquard a spiritual crisis that could be resolved only through a return to the systems of meaning of ancient Greek philosophy or myth. Not unlike Schmitt, these thinkers ultimately wanted to legitimize the world as it is. For others, such as Scholem and Taubes himself, the modern revival of Gnosticism and the loss of spiritual investment were primarily a source of intellectual fascination as they surprisingly linked secular modernity to the rich but forgotten history of heresy and religious dissent. In view of their Jewish messianism, moreover, Scholem and Taubes were hardly concerned with the spiritual legitimacy of the world as it is. Still others, such as Blumenberg, agreed that modernity had made spiritual investment in the world problematic but added that, in response to this return of Gnosticism, modern thought promoted new kinds of investment in the world as it is. For Blumenberg, these modern investments in the world did not presuppose any spiritual or divine meaning of reality. On the contrary, the world gained meaning only insofar as it had significance for human self-assertion—that is, insofar as human beings invested in it or even changed it to realize their own existence.

The concern with the meaning and legitimacy of the world was a crucial one for the thinkers discussed in this book. What ultimately motivated Taubes's, Voegelin's, Blumenberg's, Jonas's, Marquard's and Scholem's analyses of modern Gnosticism was the question of how to make sense of a world whose immediate spiritual meaning was at risk or even fundamentally lost. Modern thought shared this predicament with ancient Gnosticism, although the latter unequivocally solved the problem by extracting every possible meaning from this world and transposing it into the world beyond. For all these thinkers alike, the meaning and legitimacy of the world had been radically challenged in modern times—be it by the disenchanted worldview of modern science; by radical philosophical movements as diverse as nihilism, pessimism, progressivism, and atheism; by the sociocultural evolution of secularization; or by unprecedented political events such as the rise of totalitarianism and the Holocaust. All these cases implied a withdrawal of the divine from the world and, accordingly, an erosion of its spiritual meaning. In a world where the divine is radically absent, any spiritual investment in the world is rendered problematic. Again, modernity shared this withdrawal of the divine with Gnosticism's conception of divine absence, although Gnosticism's mythological and cosmological explanation could not have been more different from its modern counterpart.

The confrontation with the Holocaust was one reason why God could be portrayed as absent from the world in the twentieth century. The Holocaust challenged both Jewish and Christian views of God and left theologians wondering how faith in God could persist after Auschwitz. The thinkers discussed in this book were not so much concerned with these theological speculations but rather with the implications of these challenged conceptions of God for understanding the world. If God traditionally guaranteed the order and meaning of the world, his nonexistence, absence, or impotence during the Holocaust obviously challenged the understanding of our world and ourselves. Thus, the Holocaust not only challenged the traditional concept of God but also the traditional concept of the world itself. Many of the intellectuals that are studied here were Germans with Jewish roots who lived and wrote just after the end of the Second World War. In this regard, one could ask whether it was still possible for them to naïvely accept or even legitimize and spiritually invest in a world that had made the Holocaust possible.

The issue of the world and God's absence from it obviously went beyond the legacy of the Second World War. God's absence had been discussed prior to Holocaust theology in interwar Protestant theology of crisis. The death of God had already been proclaimed several times from the nineteenth century onward. Prior to the two world wars, God had already lost his age-old function as the ultimate guarantee of the meaning of reality. With God's death, the modern world had become a nihilistic and disenchanted universe. This modern loss of meaning obviously challenged the possibility of spiritual investment in the world. For how could we be spiritually invested in a disenchanted world that does not care for us and is to be understood as dead materiality? The retreat of the divine from the world coincided with the sociopolitical process of secularization that designates the decreasing role of religion in political society and the declining legitimacy of religious traditions. These evolutions form the broad intellectual context of the debates on modern Gnosticism. What was ultimately at stake, however, was neither God's death nor his absence, neither disenchantment nor secularization, but rather the status of a world from which the divine had withdrawn, and of the human beings that lived in it. What concerned Taubes, Voegelin, Blumenberg, Jonas, Marquard, and Scholem is exactly the realization that any immediate, spiritual investment in the world had become impossible in modern times.

The crucial question then remains, how does one make sense of the world after the divine has withdrawn from it and, in the wake of this withdrawal, has made the spiritual investment in the world problematic. It is only from the point of view of this shared question that the differences between Taubes, Voegelin, Blumenberg, Jonas, Marquard, and Scholem can be assessed. Should a disenchanted, nihilistic, de-divinized world be abolished altogether, as the Gnostic maintained? This position was epitomized in Taubes's Gnostic-apocalyptic attitude and was shared by Scholem's messianism. Or can one conceive of ways to reestablish the world's meaning and dignity? If so, can this be done either by retrieving the lost sources of meaning or by constructing new values from within this nihilistic predicament? The former was the strategy employed by Voegelin, Jonas, and Marquard; the latter was Blumenberg's. In spite of the vast historical separation between Gnosticism and modernity, these philosophical concerns could be discovered in ancient Gnosticism as well. Nonetheless, the question remains, why have so many thinkers specifically wanted to use the concept of

Gnosticism to diagnose modernity's lack of spiritual investment in the world as it is? Certainly, there are other, more evident ways to address the problems of cultural crisis, nihilism, and meaninglessness than making reference to a religious movement that disappeared more than a millennium ago. The parallels between Gnosticism and specific modern phenomena are fascinating, but they are hardly convincing enough for the idiosyncratic comparison to be self-explanatory. Accordingly, it should be inquired why these thinkers could specifically make this surprising conceptual connection.

A History of Gnosticism in Modern Times

An important explanation for the idiosyncratic use of Gnosticism is the simple fact that ancient Gnostic sources and indeed the concept of Gnosticism itself became more widely available around the beginning of the twentieth century. Because of the prominence of the study of Gnosticism in theological, historical, literary, and philosophical circles during the first half of the twentieth century, Taubes, Voegelin, Blumenberg, Jonas, Marquard, and Scholem could make use of this fashionable concept in order to address more contemporary issues. Moreover, the concept of Gnosticism has a certain vagueness that allowed for the proliferation of its meanings. Precisely because Gnosticism is not and has never been a category that signifies a well-defined historical phenomenon, these thinkers could apply it to a virtually infinite range of seemingly unrelated modern or secular phenomena.

Gnosticism was certainly not a unified religion with an elaborate doctrine or an organized church. Rather, Gnosticism is a collective name for a range of religious movements that arose either as predecessors of Christianity or as early Christian heresies. The theological unity of these Gnostic religions was attributed to them in retrospect, arguably as late the nineteenth century. Gnostic heresies had obviously already been studied in antiquity by the church fathers—Irenaeus's *On the Detection and Overthrow of the*

So-Called Gnosis, commonly called *Adversus Haereses* (*Against Heresies*), being the most important example. However, the possible doctrinal or historical unity of different Gnostic sects such as Valentinianism, Hermeticism, Marcionism, Mandaeism, and Manichaeism never came up for discussion in these early heresiological texts. Rather, these religious movements were lumped together under the general heading of "heresy," as they supposedly shared some heretical conception of mystical knowledge (gnosis). Although the notion of gnosis was used in antiquity, the historical and theological concept of Gnosticism itself is a modern invention, commonly traced back to Henry Moore, who coined the term in 1669. In other words, the study of Gnosticism as an autonomous religious phenomenon that is not immediately to be dismissed as derivative Christianity did not exist before the end of the seventeenth century. In fact, the study of Gnosticism did not gain prominence until the nineteenth century and the rise of a Romantic fascination with oriental, exotic, and forgotten spiritualities.

The more serious scientific studies of Gnosticism arose only around the end of the nineteenth century in Germany with the work of liberal theologian and church historian Adolf von Harnack and the history of religions school. Harnack discussed Gnosticism at length in his multivolume *Dogmengeschichte* of 1885. His later *Marcion: Das Evangelium vom Fremden Gott* was even one of the key sources for Blumenberg's discussion of Gnosticism.[5] The history of religions school also did pioneering work in the scientific study of the history of early Christianity, but scholars such as Richard Reitzenstein and Wilhelm Bousset no longer considered Gnosticism a Christian heresy. Their discoveries of its oriental and pre-Christian roots led them to the conclusion that Gnosticism was an independent and autonomous religious phenomenon that potentially even influenced the rise of Christianity itself.

The beginning of the twentieth century witnessed a sprawling increase of historical publications on Gnosticism. Bulky introductions to ancient Gnosticism were written, among which Hans

---

5. Adolf von Harnack, *Marcion: Das Evangelium vom Fremden Gott* (Leipzig: J.C. Hinrichssche Buchhandlung, 1924).

Leisegang's *Die Gnosis* was one of the most influential.[6] Moreover, historical reconstructions of Gnostic texts were compiled in
large anthologies. The fact that Franz Kafka, Walter Benjamin,
and Georges Bataille all owned such an anthology (i.e., Wolfgang
Schultz's *Dokumente der Gnosis*) is a telling example of the interest in Gnosticism among the intelligentsia at the time.[7] At the
turn of the century, Gnosticism became an important source of
inspiration for writers, theologians, psychoanalysts, philosophers,
and political theorists alike. This appeal of Gnosticism confined
itself initially to the German intellectual world and German literature. Gnostic inspirations can be traced in the novels of Franz
Kafka, Hermann Hesse (*Steppenwolf*), and Thomas Mann (*Doctor
Faustus*).[8] Similarly, the George-Kreis, the German literary group
centered on Stefan George, has often been associated with Gnosticism; and Hugo Ball even called Dadaism a "Gnostic sect."[9] In
addition, Gnosticism became a defensible theological position—
for example, in the work of the German Protestant theologians of
crisis Karl Barth and Friedrich Gogarten or in Gershom Scholem's
historical reflections on Jewish mysticism. Carl Jung's psychoana-
lytic work was also influenced by his readings of ancient Gnostic
texts; he even wrote his own Gnostic hymn, entitled *Septem Ser-
mones ad Mortuos* (*Seven Sermons to the Dead*).[10] Furthermore,
Ernst Bloch's mystical-Marxist philosophy was highly influenced
by Gnostic speculations, as was Ludwig Klages's philosophy of
life and Georg Lukács's *The Theory of the Novel*.[11] Finally, Carl
Schmitt connected his infamous distinction between the friend and

6. Hans Leisegang, *Die Gnosis* (Leipzig: A. Kröner, 1924).

7. Wolfgang Schultz, *Dokumente der Gnosis* (Jena: Eugen Diedrichs, 1910).

8. See Stanley Corngold, *Lambent Traces: Franz Kafka* (Princeton: Princeton University Press, 2004); Kirsten J. Grimstad, *The Modern Revival of Gnosticism and Thomas Mann's "Doktor Faustus"* (Rochester: Camden House, 2002).

9. Hugo Ball, *Flight out of Time: A Dada Diary,* trans. Ann Raimes and ed. John Elderfield (Berkeley: University of California Press, 1996), 66.

10. Carl G. Jung, *The Gnostic Jung,* ed. Robert A. Segal (London: Routledge, 1992).

11. See Ernst Bloch, *Geist der Utopie* (Munich: Verlag von Duncker und Humblot, 1918); Georg Lukács, *Die Theorie des Romans: Ein geschichtsphiloso-phischer Versuch über die Formen der großen Epik* (Berlin: Cassirer, 1920).

the enemy, which circumscribes the nature of the political, to the Gnostic, theological enmity between God and the devil.[12]

The single most influential piece of Gnosticism scholarship in the first half of the twentieth century was undoubtedly Jonas's monumental *Gnosis und spätantiker Geist* (*Gnosticism and the Spirit of Late Antiquity*).[13] This work, the first volume of which was published in 1934, was considered the standard introduction to Gnosticism until the publication of the Nag Hammadi codices that were discovered in Egypt in 1945. From the 1960s onward, the discovery of these new Gnostic texts would revolutionize the historical study of early Christianity in general and would even challenge the very definition of Gnosticism. More important than its significance for the historical study of Gnosticism, however, *Gnosticism and the Spirit of Late Antiquity* contained a profound philosophical discussion of Gnosticism. Jonas was the first to develop a typological understanding of Gnosticism that allowed him to understand the deeper existential motivation behind this religious phenomenon rather than merely focus on its concrete historical manifestations. Gnosticism's most important characteristics according to Jonas were its dualism and its existential sense of alienation. Gnostic dualism consisted in an ontological separation between God and the world, where God is radically absent from and alien to the world. To put it in Manichaean terms, the cosmos is the evil realm of darkness; God is the realm of light and goodness. This dualism subsequently implied a separation between God and human beings, who are radically alienated from the evil world they inhabit and from the divine they cannot reach.

For Jonas, Gnosticism became a philosophical concept that could ultimately be understood and applied independently of its traditional historical delineations. In this regard, it is hardly a coincidence that the thinkers who made use of the notion of Gnosticism

---

12. Carl Schmitt, *Political Theology II: The Myth of the Closure of Any Political Theology*, trans. Michael Hoelzl and Graham Ward (Cambridge: Polity Press, 2008), 123.

13. Hans Jonas, *Gnosis und spätantiker Geist*, vol. 1, *Die mythologische Gnosis* (Göttingen: Vandenhoeck und Ruprecht, 1934).

to make sense of the modern condition all relied on Jonas's interpretation. Taubes, Blumenberg, Voegelin, Marquard, and Scholem
indeed cited Jonas as their most important source. The concept
of Gnosticism that is used throughout this book is therefore also
Jonas's. The book basically understands Gnosticism in terms of
dualism, designating both divine absence and worldly nihilism.
The choice of Jonas's dualistic concept of Gnosticism implies
neither that there are no other interpretations of Gnosticism nor
that Jonas's is the only correct one.[14] Although this conception of
Gnosticism is admittedly narrow and contestable, its use is justified insofar as this interpretation had the greatest currency in the
postwar German Gnosticism debates.[15] The centrality of Jonas's
conception of Gnosticism in these debates can also be explained by
the fact that Jonas himself had already announced the possible connection between Gnosticism and modernity in *Gnosticism and the
Spirit of Late Antiquity*. He used his teacher Martin Heidegger's
philosophical framework to determine Gnosticism's existential
motivation (*Daseinshaltung*), but he also used his own insights into
the nature of Gnosticism to assess the nihilistic and existentialist
aspects of twentieth-century thought, including Heidegger's own
philosophy.

This strange combination of an objective scientific study of
Gnosticism with more contemporary and normative interests is
hardly unusual. In a comprehensive overview of the modern study
of Gnosticism, *What Is Gnosticism?* Karen King convincingly

---

14. An important aspect of Gnosticism that is almost entirely ignored throughout the book is its intellectualism and elitism, which Max Weber emphasized in his
sociology of religion: Max Weber, *Gesammelte Aufsätze zur Religionssoziologie*
(Tübingen: J.C.B. Mohr, 1920–21).

15. Recent scholarship has problematized Jonas's typological understanding
of Gnosticism, arguing that defining Gnosticism in such general terms misrepre-
sents the essential heterogeneity of Gnostic speculations. Taking this recent scholarship into account, however, would be anachronistic, as it would misrepresent
what Gnosticism actually meant for Taubes, Blumenberg, Voegelin, Marquard,
and Scholem. See Karen L. King, *What Is Gnosticism?* (Cambridge, MA: Harvard University Press, 2003); Michael A. Williams, *Rethinking "Gnosticism": An
Argument for Dismantling a Dubious Category* (Princeton: Princeton University
Press, 1999).

argued that modern scholarship tended to present Gnosticism as the heretical other that circumscribes genuine, orthodox Christianity. She argued that ancient Gnosticism is rarely researched for its own sake but has primarily been studied to address indirectly "the normative identity of Christianity."[16] In many ways, this book goes along with King's claim that the study of Gnosticism has almost always been subordinated to other concerns; however, this book wants to take this idea one step further. It argues that the twentieth-century study of Gnosticism has been indirectly concerned not only with the normative identity of Christianity, but also with the normative identity of secular modernity. From the outset, the historical scholarship on ancient Gnosticism was preoccupied with the potential survival of Gnosticism in modern times. In *Die christliche Gnosis* (1835), theologian Ferdinand C. Baur had already made the connection between Gnosticism and German idealism. In the last part of his book, Baur explicitly discussed the Gnostic aspects of Böhme's, Schelling's, Schleiermacher's, and Hegel's philosophies of religion.[17] Eugen Schmitt even dedicated the entire second volume of his Gnosticism book (1907) to *die Gnosis des Mittelalters und der Neuzeit*.[18] Not unlike Gnosticism itself, the nature of secular modernity has almost always been defined in opposition to Christianity. For this reason, Voegelin was able to use the concept of Gnosticism to characterize modern secular politics, thereby opposing it to Christian politics. In this view, Gnosticism and secular modernity can be connected as the structural counterparts of Christianity. What was at stake for many thinkers in their discussions of modern Gnosticism was exactly the relation between Christianity and modernity, and hence the issue of secularization.

Given this intertwinement of the scientific study of Gnosticism with other, more contemporary motivations, it becomes

---

16. King, *What Is Gnosticism?* 2–3.

17. Ferdinand C. Baur, *Die christliche Gnosis: oder, die christliche Religionsphilosophie in ihrer geschichtlichen Entwicklung* (Tübingen: Verlag von Osiander, 1835).

18. Eugen H. Schmitt, *Die Gnosis: Grundlagen der Weltanschauung einer edleren Kultur*, vol. 2, *Die Gnosis des Mitteralters und der Neuzeit* (Jena: Eugen Dietrichs, 1907).

increasingly difficult to make a clear methodological separation between modern Gnosticism scholarship, the modern revivals of Gnosticism, and the philosophical studies that used the concept of Gnosticism to define or criticize modernity. The work of Bousset and Reitzenstein clearly falls under the first category. The second category then contains modern thinkers and movements that either considered themselves Gnostic or have been called so by others. The most obvious examples would be Bloch, Jung, and Jonas's Heidegger. Voegelin, Blumenberg, and Marquard would fall under the third category because they associated certain modern trends with Gnosticism but without identifying themselves with it. However, the classification becomes less evident for figures such as Jonas, Scholem, and Taubes. Jonas is both a modern scholar of Gnosticism and someone who uses Gnosticism as a philosophical concept for making sense of the modern condition. Scholem's and Taubes's work arguably falls under all three categories at the same time, because they are interested in Gnosticism as a historical phenomenon, they identify themselves to some extent as modern Gnostics, and they study the modern legacy of Gnosticism. However artificial the distinction between these three categories might appear, it is useful to delineate methodologically the scope of this book. For the main focus will be on the third category—Gnosticism as a critical concept that is used to understand the modern condition.

This third dimension of the German debates on modern Gnosticism, in particular, gained prominence in the 1950s and 1960s in the work of Taubes, Voegelin, Blumenberg, Jonas, Marquard, and Scholem. These postwar debates obviously had their intellectual roots in the pre- and interwar contexts that have been mentioned. Much has already been written on the role of Gnosticism in the interbellum period, but a systematic and extensive overview of the postwar debates, as is attempted here, is lacking.[19] The relation between Gnosticism and early twentieth-century philosophers like

---

19. For a concise overview of the debate on modern Gnosticism in postwar German thought, see Yotam Hotam, "Gnosis and Modernity: A Postwar German Intellectual Debate on Secularisation, Religion, and 'Overcoming' the Past," *Totalitarian Movements and Political Religions* 8, nos. 3–4 (2007): 591–608.

Bloch, Heidegger, and Klages has been studied extensively; and
Benjamin Lazier's *God Interrupted: Heresy and European Imagination between the World Wars* even developed a brilliant intellectual history of heresy and Gnosticism in interwar German thought,
mainly focusing on the thought of Hans Jonas, Leo Strauss, and
Gershom Scholem.[20] The current book can be read as a sequel to
Lazier's *God Interrupted,* continuing his historical reconstruction
of the debates on modern Gnosticism by focusing now on the evolution of these debates after the Second World War. To the extent
that the Gnosticism debates started long before the war, the focus
on the postwar debate risks entering the discussion in medias res,
especially because some of the debaters, like Jonas and Scholem,
already wrote extensively on Gnosticism in the 1930s. In order
to avoid this, chapter 1 introduces some of the interwar contexts
in more detail. However, the postwar debate can be studied as a
separate episode in its own right, as the Second World War and
the Holocaust were an important caesura in the Gnosticism debates. Among other reasons, the evaluation of Gnosticism radically
shifted after the war from a rather positive approach to an explicitly negative one.

   Although the debate on modern Gnosticism was a paradigmatically German one, similar issues were also discussed in France
around the same time. Pierre Klossowski, for example, referred
to the Marquis de Sade as a Gnostic; Albert Camus, in *L'homme
revolté,* associated the modern revolutionary spirit with ancient
Gnosticism; and Raymond Ruyer discussed the mystical and "neo-
gnostic" tendencies of twentieth-century sciences in his *La gnose
de Princeton.*[21] There was no clear historical affinity between the

   20. See Michael Pauen, *Dithyrambiker des Untergangs: Gnostizismus in
Ästhetik und Philosophie der Moderne* (Berlin: Akademie, 1994); Yotam Hotam,
*Modern Gnosis and Zionism: The Crisis of Culture, Life Philosophy, and Jewish
National Thought* (London: Routledge, 2009); Benjamin Lazier, *God Interrupted:
Heresy and the European Imagination between the World Wars* (Princeton:
Princeton University Press, 2008).
   21. See Pierre Klossowski, *Sade mon prochain* (Paris: Seuil, 2002); Albert
Camus, *L'homme revolté* (Paris: Gallimard, 1951); Raymond Ruyer, *La gnose de
Princeton: Des savants à la recherche d'une religion* (Paris: Fayard, 1974).

German debates and Klossowski's, Camus's, or Ruyer's claims, although Camus knew Jacob Taubes's wife, Susan, personally. Susan Taubes lived in Paris for several years and was also interested in the Gnostic features of modern thought.[22] However, France had its own scholarly tradition of Gnosticism research that Camus and Klossowski could rely on. Henri-Charles Puech's *En quête de la gnose* is one of the most important historical works on Gnosticism written in French, but Gnosticism was also discussed in more philosophical contexts, by Georges Bataille.[23]

The alleged return of Gnosticism in modern times has also been defended in more recent scholarship. In line with Voegelin's work, some American conservative Catholic thinkers such as Cyril O'Regan and Philip Lee have associated modern thought or modern Protestantism with a return of Gnosticism.[24] More nuanced scholarship on modern Gnosticism has mainly appeared in German. Studies by Micha Brumlik, Michael Pauen, Richard Faber, and Yotam Hotam combine a historical overview of the German Gnosticism debates with their own Gnostic readings of modernity.[25] Finally, a whole range of New Age esoteric spiritualities have considered themselves as reviving Gnosticism or relying explicitly on the mystical notion of gnosis. These positions have become even more idiosyncratic today than they already were half a century ago. The publication of the Nag Hammadi manuscripts essentially testified to the heterogeneity of Gnostic speculations. Defining Gnosticism in general philosophical terms as in Jonas's

---

22. See Susan Taubes, "The Gnostic Foundations of Heidegger's Nihilism," *Journal of Religion* 34, no. 3 (1954): 155–72.

23. See Henri-Charles Puech, *En quête de la gnose* (Paris: Gallimard, 1978); Georges Bataille, "Le bas matérialisme et la gnose," in *Oeuvres complètes I, Premiers écrits 1922–1940* (Paris: Gallimard, 1970), 220–27.

24. See Cyril O'Regan, *Gnostic Return in Modernity* (Albany: SUNY Press, 2001); Philip J. Lee, *Against the Protestant Gnostics* (Oxford: Oxford University Press, 1993).

25. See Micha Brumlik, *Die Gnostiker: Der Traum von der Selbsterlösung des Menschen* (Frankfurt am Main: Eichborn, 1992); Pauen, *Dithyrambiker des Untergangs*; Richard Faber, *Politische Dämonologie: Über modernen Marcionismus* (Würzburg: Königshausen und Neumann, 2007); Hotam, *Modern Gnosis and Zionism*.

concept of dualism is no longer convincing today. The notion of Gnosticism is either limited to a narrowly defined historical phenomenon or even dismissed altogether. Accordingly, its application to structurally related modern phenomena is much more problematic than ever.

Toward a Metaphorology of Gnosticism in Postwar German Thought

The overview of Gnosticism's role in twentieth-century thought has shown that there is hardly any consensus about the nature of Gnosticism. For this reason, there is even less consensus about the nature of the modern return of Gnosticism. At first glance, it is not at all clear what exactly is said about modernity when it is called Gnostic. Gnosticism scholar Ioan Culianu caricatured this situation beautifully:

> Once I believed that Gnosticism was a well-defined phenomenon belonging to the religious history of late antiquity. . . . I was to learn soon, however, that I was naïf indeed. Not only Gnosis was gnostic, but the catholic authors were gnostic, the neo-platonic too, Reformation was gnostic, Communism was gnostic, Nazism was gnostic, liberalism, existentialism and psychoanalysis were gnostic too, modern biology was gnostic, Blake, Yeats, Kafka, Rilke, Proust, Joyce, Musil, Hesse and Thomas Mann were Gnostic. From very authoritative interpreters of Gnosis, I learned further that science is gnostic and superstition is gnostic; power, counter-power, and lack of power are gnostic; left is gnostic and right is gnostic; Hegel is gnostic and Marx is gnostic, Freud is gnostic and Jung is gnostic; all things and their opposite are equally Gnostic. . . . The more I learn, the more I understand that the Gnostics have already taken hold of the whole world, and we are not aware of it. It is a mixed feeling of high anxiety and admiration, since I cannot refrain myself from thinking that these alien body-snatchers have done a very remarkable job indeed.[26]

Culianu was absolutely right that at a certain moment everything could be called Gnostic. Voegelin's theories were exemplary in this

---

26. Ioan Culianu, "The Gnostic Revenge: Gnosticism and Romantic Literature," in *Gnosis und Politik*, ed. Jacob Taubes (Munich: Wilhelm Fink, 1984), 290.

respect. In Voegelin's work, almost every modern thinker or political movement was associated with Gnosticism at some point. To make Culianu's ludicrous list even longer, Voegelin also called Nietzsche, Hobbes, Joachim of Fiore, and modern liberalism Gnostic. To make matters worse, other thinkers either completely disagreed with Voegelin's claims and applied the concept of Gnosticism to even different phenomena, or they called the same thinkers Gnostic but did so for different reasons, relying on incompatible definitions of Gnosticism itself. For some, Gnosticism implied some kind of nihilism that is akin to modern nihilism; for others it just meant dualism, which could structurally return in Protestant theology or early modern thought; still others focused on the mystical notion of gnosis and its alleged afterlife in modern science and totalitarian politics.

In this perspective, Gnosticism increasingly appeared as an empty notion without fixed conceptual meaning. Culianu even called it a "sick sign" that "can accommodate with different contexts, in which it acquires different meanings."[27] Accordingly, Gnosticism as such can hardly tell us anything about modernity. Strictly speaking, there is also no demonstrable historical connection between ancient Gnosticism and any modern phenomenon. There is no historical proof whatsoever that specific ancient heresies secretly survived during the Middle Ages, resurfaced in early modernity, and had an epochal significance for modern politics or philosophy.

Although Gnosticism does not tell us anything about the nature of modernity as such, it could definitely tell something about the thinkers that have made use of the concept to make sense of modernity. If Gnosticism were nothing more than a fashionable topic in German thought, one could at least try to gain insight into these topical references to Gnosticism. Accordingly, this book explores what these thinkers conceptually achieved by making use of the concept of Gnosticism: What exactly did they have in mind when they connected Gnosticism to modernity? And what mark did these idiosyncratic references to Gnosticism leave on their thinking?

---

27. Culianu, "Gnostic Revenge," 91.

From this perspective, this book does not want to agree or disagree with the claim that there is a connection between Gnosticism and the modern age; and it is even less interested in defending Taubes's, Voegelin's, Blumenberg's, Jonas's, Marquard's, or Scholem's philosophical positions. This book is therefore not a philosophical exploration of the Gnostic aspects of modern thought—too many books have already attempted this. Rather, it is a historical study of the discourse on Gnosticism in postwar German philosophy.[28] Accordingly, the book's method is that of intellectual history— developing a history of the idea (*Ideeengeschichte*) or, if you will, a history of the concept (*Begriffsgeschichte*) of Gnosticism.

Although Gnosticism is invoked as a historical or philosophical concept in German thought, Culianu convincingly showed that Gnosticism did not function as a real concept in these discourses. This observation obviously challenges the possibility of doing a conceptual history of Gnosticism. Culianu called Gnosticism a sick sign, an empty notion void of a univocal conceptual meaning. Gnosticism seemed to function as a concept, but actually it was a pseudoconcept. Because many thinkers had a completely different understanding of Gnosticism or at least applied it very differently, there is no single or general conceptual explanation for the meaning of the notion of Gnosticism in postwar German thought. Moreover, these different understandings are seldom compatible within a well-defined debate. Although Taubes, Voegelin, Blumenberg, Jonas, Marquard, and Scholem all referred to Gnosticism, they hardly shared each other's philosophical concerns. For example, something rather different was at stake in Blumenberg's concept of Gnosticism than in Voegelin's: Blumenberg associated Gnostic dualism with the late medieval emphasis on divine absence and God's radical transcendence, while Voegelin rather showed how the mystical notion of gnosis implied a radical immanentism that

---

28. This book distances itself from the methodology applied by Brumlik, Pauen, Faber, and Hotam (see note 25). Although their books rely on nuanced historical scholarship, they ultimately present just another interpretation of Gnostic return in modernity instead of a historical overview of the Gnosticism debates. The methodology that is applied here is more in tune with Lazier's *God Interrupted*.

he considered characteristic of modern thought. Unsurprisingly, Voegelin and Blumenberg never debated their different interpretations of Gnosticism and Gnostic return. They were only later played off against each other by Taubes.[29] An actual debate never existed because a unified concept of Gnosticism was lacking. Such a concept of Gnosticism arose only in Taubes's post factum attempt to construe the debate. In other words, the debate itself arose in the reception of the different positions on modern Gnosticism. From this perspective, the book could be read as a history of reception of the postwar German Gnosticism debate, challenging a more straightforward conceptual history. Nonetheless, it is possible to uncover certain recurring motifs in the use of Gnosticism in postwar German philosophy independent of its conceptualization in Taubes's reception. The mere fact that Taubes, Voegelin, Blumenberg, Jonas, Marquard, and Scholem all used the same notion inevitably forced them to make similar associations. Although Gnosticism did not have a well-defined conceptual content that returned in all these thinkers, the notion had certain connotations that simply could not be dismissed. These connotations cannot be conceptualized, as they were essentially metaphorical.

The observation that Gnosticism had no real conceptual but only metaphorical meaning in this discourse does not imply that it could simply mean anything. Unlike a concept, which typically has one well-defined meaning, a metaphor can stand for many different meanings. However, a specific word cannot be used as a metaphor for just anything. For example, if someone is called metaphorically a pig, it can be taken to mean that he is dumb, that he eats too much or too fast, that he is fat, and so on, but the word "pig" simply cannot be used to call someone gentle or sophisticated. The same held true for Gnosticism in postwar German thought. The notion had been used to convey a range of different ideas, but this range was not infinite. In this regard, Culianu's conviction that Gnosticism is an empty notion that can be accommodated to every possible context is incorrect. If someone wanted to make use

---

29. See Jacob Taubes, ed., *Gnosis und Politik* (Munich: Wilhelm Fink, 1984).

of Gnosticism, one had a limited range of connotations at one's disposal. One was free to emphasize some of these connotations that were not as important to others, and to dismiss other connotations that were significant for others, but one could not invent new connotations out of the blue. Although the thinker's interpretative freedom was relative to certain meanings that were metaphorically associated with Gnosticism, such a freedom would not be possible at all with regard to a concept.

Blumenberg called the study of the role of metaphor in theoretical contexts metaphorology.[30] To the extent that this book can be read as a metaphorology of Gnosticism, Blumenberg's methodology for studying intellectual history is applied to his own work. This could sound like a dubious strategy, if it were not for the fact that Blumenberg had applied his metaphorological method in *Die Legitimität der Neuzeit (The Legitimacy of the Modern Age)* to assess the German secularization debates that formed the intellectual background of the debates on Gnosticism and modernity.[31] In twentieth-century German theories of modernity, the concept of secularization counted as the default category to make sense of the nature and genesis of modern thought. Two of the most renowned examples of what Blumenberg termed the secularization theorem were Carl Schmitt's claim that "all significant concepts of the modern theory of the state are secularized theological concepts,"[32] and Karl Löwith's analysis of modern progress as secularized Christian eschatology.[33] If the concept of secularization implied the continuity between theology and secular politics or modern science, the discovery of the genealogical relations

---

30. See Hans Blumenberg, *Paradigmen zu einer Metaphorologie* (Frankfurt am Main: Suhrkamp, 1997); English translation: Hans Blumenberg, *Paradigms for a Metaphorology,* trans. Robert Savage (Ithaca: Cornell University Press, 2010).

31. See Hans Blumenberg, *Die Legitimität der Neuzeit,* 2nd rev. ed. (Frankfurt am Main: Suhrkamp, 1976), pt. 1; English translation: Hans Blumenberg, *The Legitimacy of the Modern Age,* trans. Robert Wallace (Cambridge, MA: MIT Press, 1983).

32. Carl Schmitt, *Political Theology: Four Chapters on the Concept of Sovereignty,* trans. George Schwab (Chicago: University of Chicago Press, 1985), 36.

33. See Karl Löwith, *Meaning in History: The Theological Implications of the Philosophy of History* (Chicago: University of Chicago Press, 1949), 2, 60.

between Gnosticism and modernity could be understood as a specific variant of the secularization thesis. Accordingly, the debates on Gnosticism and modernity not only coincided historically but also presupposed structurally and metaphorically the German secularization debate. As a result of his metaphorological study of the concept, Blumenberg fiercely rejected secularization as a category that could adequately define the nature of modernity. For much the same reasons, he rejected the continuity between Gnosticism and modern thought. Nonetheless, Blumenberg still defined modernity in relation to Gnosticism, albeit in a negative way. In opposition to Voegelin's claim that Gnosticism is "the nature of modernity,"[34] Blumenberg understood the modern age as the "second overcoming of Gnosticism."[35]

The fact that Blumenberg himself used Gnosticism in this way highlights a potential problem with the metaphorical strategy in studying Gnosticism. Indeed, neither Blumenberg himself nor any other thinkers used Gnosticism as a metaphor.[36] Nonetheless, this

---

34. Eric Voegelin, *The New Science of Politics: An Introduction* (Chicago: University of Chicago Press, 1952), 107.

35. Blumenberg, *Legitimacy*, 126.

36. This problem with my metaphorological reading could also be solved by approaching the pseudoconcept of Gnosticism as a signature, in Giorgio Agamben's sense. In *The Kingdom and the Glory*, Agamben problematized the concept of secularization not by calling it a metaphor, as Blumenberg did, but by approaching it as a signature: "In other words, secularization is not a concept but a signature . . . , that is, something that in a sign or concept marks and exceeds such a sign or concept referring it back to a determinate interpretation or field, without for this reason leaving the semiotic to constitute a new meaning or a new concept. Signatures move and displace concepts and signs from one field to another . . . without redefining them semantically. Many pseudoconcepts belonging to the philosophical tradition are, in this sense, signatures that . . . carry out a vital and strategic function, giving a lasting orientation to the interpretation of signs." Giorgio Agamben, *The Kingdom and the Glory: For a Theological Genealogy of Economy and Government*, trans. Lorenzo Chiesa (Stanford: Stanford University Press, 2011), 4. Just as this book applied Blumenberg's metaphorology of secularization to the notion of Gnosticism, Agamben's approach of secularization as a signature could be applied to Gnosticism as well. As a signature, Gnosticism would be displaced from the field of history (Gnosticism as a concept that describes an ancient religion) to that of philosophy (Gnosticism as a pseudoconcept that makes sense of the nature of modernity) without being redefined semantically.

book shows how Gnosticism actually functioned as a metaphor in the postwar German debates on modern Gnosticism. Gnosticism was no longer used as a well-defined historical concept but was increasingly used as a metaphor for more contemporary issues. Although initially a real concept, Gnosticism was metaphorized, and its metaphorics operated in the background of pseudo-conceptual uses.[37] If Gnosticism's role in the German debates on modern Gnosticism is metaphorical rather than conceptual, the crucial question is what this metaphor actually stood for. What kind of ideas did the metaphor of Gnosticism represent that could not be expressed in conceptual language? Additionally, why can these issues not be known, discussed, or approached conceptually? These are the central questions that this book tries to answer. The point of answering these questions is to gain insights into the deeper philosophical stakes of the debates on modern Gnosticism, which often appear as nonsensical to the contemporary reader. This can be done by translating the metaphor of Gnosticism back into a language that is understandable to the reader and by trying to uncover the metaphorical associations thinkers made when using the concept of Gnosticism—or, as Blumenberg put it, by "entering into the author's imaginative horizon and reconstructing his translation."[38] The point is not to render Gnosticism's metaphorical function into pure conceptual language but to open up the imaginative spaces in which the philosophical significance of the notion of Gnosticism becomes clear.

Gnostic Motifs

In line with the metaphorological approach just outlined, the six chapters of this book all explore one possible reference of the metaphor of Gnosticism. They all deal with a specific metaphorical connotation of Gnosticism that implicitly structured the debates on the

---

37. For Blumenberg on metaphorization and background metaphorics, see the conclusion to this book.
38. Blumenberg, *Paradigms*, 62.

nature of modern thought. In other words, the chapters do not pre-suppose a clear conceptual definition of Gnosticism. The different problems with defining Gnosticism and with applying such a defi-nition to the debates on modern Gnosticism have already been in-dicated. Instead, each chapter focuses on a certain idea or discourse that has been associated with Gnosticism more loosely. If Gnosti-cism was used as a metaphor for a range of philosophical concerns or problems, each chapter uncovers and explores one of these con-cerns. In *Weltrevolution der Seele,* cultural theorist Thomas Macho and philosopher Peter Sloterdijk presented a relatively exhaustive overview of the imaginative or metaphorical horizons that can be connected to Gnosticism. They did so by compiling a range of lit-erary, philosophical, and theological texts that explicitly or implic-itly addressed these Gnostic themes.[39] Macho and Sloterdijk took both ancient and "modern" Gnostic sources into account. Inter-estingly, they did not classify these texts according to well-defined conceptual characteristics of Gnosticism—such as its dualism or its concept of mystical knowledge. Rather, they relied on certain themes and motifs that either recurred in Gnostic mythology or that have been associated with it later on—such as "the attempted creation" (*die versuchte Schöpfung*), "revaluation of values" (*Um-wertung der Werte*), and "the Fall and salvation" (*Sündenfälle und Erlösungen*).

In an attempt to make sense of the role of Gnosticism in postwar German thought, this book selects and discusses some of Macho and Sloterdijk's "Gnostic motifs" (*Motive der Gnosis*), focusing on those that are most relevant to the debate on Gnosticism and modernity. In addition, some other motifs that they did not men-tion are discussed. Each chapter revolves around one such motif and its specific role in the theoretical reflections on modern thought and politics. Precisely because Gnosticism did not function in these debates as a univocal concept with well-defined characteristics, different thinkers emphasized different motifs or connotations of

---

39. See Thomas Macho and Peter Sloterdijk, eds., *Weltrevolution der Seele: Ein Lese- und Arbeitsbuch der Gnosis von der Spätantike bis zu der Gegenwart* (Lahnau: Artemis und Winkler, 1991), vol. 2.

Gnosticism. Accordingly, each chapter approaches the same topic of Gnostic return in modernity from a radically different thematic perspective. These perspectives are hardly ever compatible but to the extent that some thinkers did allude to the same Gnostic motifs it is possible to play them off against each other. This approach retains the essentially dialogical nature of the German Gnosticism debates and avoids studying the different theories of modern Gnosticism in isolation, while at the same time it accounts for the fundamental incompatibilities of these theories. The sequence of the chapters is chronological—starting with Jonas's reflections from the 1930s on Gnosticism (chapter 1); continuing with Taubes's debates with Löwith (chapter 2) and with Scholem (chapters 3 and 4), both of which began around the end of the 1940s; and finishing with Voegelin's theory of modern Gnosticism, which he introduced in the early 1950s (chapter 5), and Blumenberg's and Marquard's counter-positions (chapter 6), which took shape in the 1960s and were further discussed in the 1970s.

In the first chapter, "Crisis: Gnostic Dualism in Late Modernity," Gnosticism is approached as a category of both cultural and metaphysical crisis. The chapter introduces some crucial interwar contexts in which Gnosticism was used to make sense of the modern condition. Thus, it presents the prehistory of the postwar Gnosticism debates. The chapter focuses first on the so-called theology of crisis and on the role of Gnosticism in the work of Protestant theologians Karl Barth, Friedrich Gogarten, and Rudolf Bultmann. The chapter then turns to Oswald Spengler's and Hans Jonas's interpretation of Gnosticism's role in the crisis of late antiquity, and concludes with Jonas's interpretation of the relation between Gnosticism and modernity. Gnosticism functioned in Jonas's thought as a concept that diagnosed the crises of twentieth-century modernity.

The second chapter, "Eschaton: Gnostic Evil in History," focuses on the relation between the debates on modern Gnosticism and the contemporaneous discourses on the secularization of eschatology, homing in on the work of Taubes and Löwith. Although the debates on secularized eschatology are as idiosyncratic and problematic as those on Gnosticism, the chapter shows that the same metaphorical and imaginative horizons are present in both discourses. Since eschatology is the theological discipline that speculates about salvation at the end of history, it is a crucial aspect of every Gnostic speculation. If Gnosticism presupposed that the world is radically depraved, fallen, or evil, the redemption from this world is an absolutely crucial concern for the Gnostic. Accordingly, the role of Gnosticism in the reflections on modernity relied on some of the associations that the discourse on secularized eschatology also made. Both discourses reflected on the modern afterlife of the theological categories of salvation, the Fall, evil, and the Apocalypse. In this sense, the second chapter explores Macho and Sloterdijk's Gnostic motif of "the Fall and salvation."

The third chapter, "Subversion: Heresy and Its Modern Afterlives," explores the role of heresy, antinomianism, and subversion in the thought of Scholem and Taubes. The scope of the chapter coincides to a large extent with Macho and Sloterdijk's motif of "libertine Gnosticism" (*Die libertinistische Gnosis*). First, it will show that the concept of Gnosticism has often been used as a metaphor for heresy. Associating Gnosticism with heresy and subversion almost necessarily entails a rejection of Gnosticism and its possible survival in the modern age. However, Taubes and Scholem had a strange fascination with heresy and even identified themselves with the heretical imperative. For them, heresy could even function as a model for understanding and dealing with modernity. In this regard, they approached modern secularization as a peculiar kind of Jewish heresy.

In the German debates on modern gnosis, Gnosticism was oftentimes considered to be nihilistic. Nihilism was indeed a crucial category in Jonas's, Taubes's, and Scholem's understanding of Gnosticism. Chapter 4, "Nothingness: Dialectics of Religious Nihilism," elaborates on this nihilistic connotation of Gnosticism. In this regard, Gnosticism was often understood as the historical precursor of modern nihilism. Some Jewish thinkers, such as Taubes, Scholem, and Walter Benjamin, even used religious nihilism as a category to make sense of the world and of human agency after the "death of god." For these three thinkers, a meaningful comportment to a world that had become void of divine meaning necessitated an inversion of the order of immanence. The central Gnostic motif of this chapter therefore corresponds to Macho and Sloterdijk's "revaluation of values." Scholem, Benjamin, and Taubes elaborated on a dialectical relation between an initial religious rejection of the meaning of the world (passive nihilism) and an antinomian investment in this world that subverts its immanent logic (active nihilism).

Chapter 5, "Epoch: The Gnostic Age," explores how the concept of Gnosticism was used not only to make sense of specific modern phenomena but also to understand the modern age as such. This epochal connotation is completely absent from Gnosticism's historical meaning but is all the more pertinent in the debates on modern Gnosticism. The chapter's main focus is on Voegelin's interpretation of modernity as "the Gnostic age." His interpretation was both the most explicit and most far-reaching Gnostic reading of modernity, as he subsumed virtually every modern thinker or idea under the heading of Gnosticism. For this reason, Voegelin's theory of modernity is also the most contestable, and was opposed explicitly by Blumenberg. However, Blumenberg also connected Gnosticism to the modern age but reversed Voegelin's interpretation, claiming that modernity is the overcoming of Gnosticism. In an attempt to make sense of these wide-ranging and unusual understandings of the modern epoch, this chapter seeks to find some common ground between Voegelin's and Blumenberg's opposed views.

Finally, chapter 6, "Theodicy: Overcoming Gnosticism, Embracing the World," mainly deals with Blumenberg's understanding of modernity as the overcoming of Gnosticism and with Marquard's interpretation of this enigmatic definition. The role of theodicy in early modern thought is used here as a key to understanding Blumenberg's interpretation of Gnosticism. For both Blumenberg and Marquard, the philosophical project of theodicy was structurally opposed to Gnosticism. While Gnosticism rejected the world as fundamentally depraved, modern theodicy embraced the world by rationally proving that evil could not fundamentally corrupt reality. Accordingly, theodicy is not so much a Gnostic but rather an anti-Gnostic motif. In Blumenberg's perspective, theodicy was one of the concrete means through which modernity overcame Gnosticism. In contrast to Taubes's interpretation of modern thought as Gnostic world-negation, Blumenberg and Marquard ultimately believed that modernity implied a modest affirmation of the here and now.

Since these Gnostic motifs that respectively structure the six chapters of the book—crisis, eschaton, subversion, nothingness, epoch, and theodicy—often presuppose incompatible metaphorical and conceptual perspectives, they cannot be brought together into a general or comprehensive explanation of the role of Gnosticism in postwar German thought. Although the metaphorics of Gnosticism cannot be traced back to one conceptual meaning, asking a different question could offer a more comprehensive picture. Instead of asking what imaginative, metaphorical, and conceptual spaces were opened up by the notion of Gnosticism, one could ask why these spaces could not be entered more conceptually. In other words, why did thinkers like Taubes, Voegelin, Blumenberg, Jonas, Marquard, and Scholem needed this long detour over the history of early Christian heresy to confront issues that sometimes appeared to be very urgent and contemporary? The conclusion to this book shows that conceptual thought actually failed to address these issues directly, so that the metaphor of Gnosticism had to stand in for it. Many reasons can be given for why conceptual thought failed at exactly this moment to make sense of exactly these issues. One of them could be the experience of the Holocaust, which failed to be conceptualized in the traditional philosophical and ethical categories. However, the thinkers discussed in this book were confronted not only with concepts failing to make sense of specific issues and events but also with the possible modern failures of conceptual thought itself to make sense of the world. In one way or another, they were all dealing with the legacy of nihilism and disenchantment, and with modern philosophy's inability to conceptualize the intrinsic meaning of the world. In view of these philosophical issues, the question that took center stage for these thinkers was whether and how *spiritual investment in the world as it is* was possible in modern times.

1

CRISIS

Gnostic Dualism in Late Modernity

Gnosticism is a category of crisis. Richard Reitzenstein, the historian of early Christianity, indeed claimed that Gnosticism arose in antiquity "under the pressure of terrible times."[1] For Hans Jonas, Gnosticism was the central force in the epochal crisis of late antiquity that led to the rise of Christian and medieval culture. He even considered Gnosticism to be the very "spirit of late antiquity."[2] From a different perspective, the German theologian Adolf von Harnack also understood Catholicism and the rise of the medieval paradigm as a reaction to (Marcionite) Gnosticism and as a resolution of the historical crisis it represented.[3] Gnosticism, in this view, represents an explosive historical situation that demands resolution through a sudden change to a new epoch. This historical situation, from which Gnosticism supposedly arose and whose crisis it came

1. Richard Reitzenstein, *Die hellenistischen Mysterienreligionen: Nach ihren Grundgedanken und Wirkungen* (Stuttgart: B.G. Teubner, 1927), 5.

2. See Hans Jonas, *Gnosis und spätantiker Geist*, vol. 1, *Die mythologische Gnosis* (Göttingen: Vandenhoeck und Ruprecht, 1934); Jonas, *Gnosis und spätantiker Geist*, vol. 2, *Von der Mythologie zur mystischen Philosophie* (Göttingen: Vandenhoeck und Ruprecht, 1954). My discussion of these books is largely based on Michael Waldstein, "Hans Jonas' Construct 'Gnosticism': Analysis and Critique," *Journal of Early Christian Studies* 8 (2000): 341–72.

3. See Adolf von Harnack, *Marcion: Das Evangelium vom Fremden Gott* (Leipzig: J.C. Hinrichssche Buchhandlung, 1924).

to represent, is also reflected in Gnostic theology. Gnosticism's characteristic dualism implies a strict separation (*Krisis*) between transcendence and immanence. Radically separated from the divine, human beings accordingly find themselves in a crisis situation that can be resolved only in salvation and in the mystical knowledge of God (gnosis). Although it is debatable whether Gnosticism historically arose in times of crisis, the concept of Gnosticism definitely functioned in twentieth-century scholarship as a category of crisis—either as a diagnosis of crisis or as cure for it. Insofar as the phenomenon of Gnosticism was representative of the crisis of late antiquity for scholars like Reitzenstein, Harnack, and Jonas, their contemporaries increasingly applied it to the crisis of modernity as well. As one commentator notes, the twentieth-century interest in Gnosticism cannot be understood without taking into account the *Kulturkrise* that dominated early twentieth-century cultural life in Germany.[4] In order to understand how Gnosticism came to be associated with crisis and how it developed after the Second World War into a metaphor for the crisis of Western modernity as such, it is therefore necessary to return to the pre- and interwar contexts in which Gnosticism first became a source of intellectual fascination.

Generally speaking, the attraction of Gnosticism in the early twentieth century was related to the increasing discontent with the Enlightenment and with the perceived crisis of the modern conception of rationality. Insofar as gnosis represented a mystical knowledge that has access to a truth transcending the world and human reason, Gnosticism could inject the "iron cage" of modern rationality with a theological, esoteric, heretic, and apocalyptic inspiration. This inspiration did not depend on an orthodox religious tradition that increasingly lost its legitimacy in the modern world but sprang from the heretical undercurrents of Western monotheism. Thus, it could become an intellectual resource for modern Christian and Jewish thinkers alike—for, among others, radical Protestant theologians like Karl Barth, Friedrich Gogarten, and Rudolf Bultmann, who will be discussed in the current chapter, and Jewish messianists like Ernst Bloch, Gershom Scholem, and

---

4. See Yotam Hotam, *Modern Gnosis and Zionism: The Crisis of Culture, Life Philosophy, and Jewish National Thought* (London: Routledge, 2009), 15–32.

Walter Benjamin, who will be discussed in the next chapters. The obvious danger of appealing to an ancient and forgotten religion to adjust secular modernity is that this strategy could easily amount to replacing modern rationality with sheer irrationality and world-negation. Instead of complementing modern rationality and solving its crisis, the appeal to Gnosticism could just as well destabilize modernity from within and bring the crisis to a head. While Gnosticism initially served as an antidote to modern rationality, it was soon viewed as the very cause of the crisis of modernity. The role of Gnosticism in twentieth-century German thought was indeed deeply ambiguous. Gnosis was a source of both horror and fascination. Modern Gnosticism was a *pharmakon,* in the Greek sense of the word, being both poison and medicine at the same time. While a small dose of Gnosticism could possibly cure modernity of its illnesses of rationalism, liberalism, and scientism, taking too much would mean the end of modernity as a return to premodernity. It is hardly surprising that none of the mentioned interwar thinkers completely subscribed to Gnosticism but rather adhered to it as a source of fascination and inspiration. For most postwar intellectuals, however, Gnosticism had lost this ambiguous appeal and was more univocally dismissed as horrific and dangerously irrational. The evaluation of Gnosticism thus shifted from a generally positive one before the Second World War to an explicitly negative one after the war. This evolution can also be traced in the work of the most influential Gnosticism scholar of the twentieth century, Hans Jonas. In his dissertation, written under Rudolf Bultmann and Martin Heidegger, and published in 1934 as *Gnosis und spätantiker Geist (Gnosticism and the Spirit of Late Antiquity)*, Jonas showed that studying Gnosticism could help disclose the structure of human existence itself. He even found in Gnosticism an unexpected precursor of Heidegger's existential philosophy. But Jonas became more critical of Gnosticism after the war, dismissing it as a dangerous herald of modern nihilism. To the extent that he considered this nihilism to be the very cause of the cultural, humanitarian, and environmental crises of the twentieth century, Western modernity was haunted by the specter of Gnosticism.

In radically shifting his evaluation of Gnosticism, Jonas was the figure that connected the interwar debates on Gnosticism to the postwar debates that are the main focus of the book. Not only did his changed position with regard to Gnosticism epitomize a paradigmatic shift in the debate, but his philosophical interpretation of Gnosticism also had most currency in the postwar scene. Although it was definitely Jonas's interpretation that prevailed after the war, other and earlier sources remained influential. The association of Gnosticism with crisis thinking and with the crisis of modernity certainly did not begin with Jonas's work. Before turning to Jonas's thought proper, this chapter will therefore focus on two other instances in early twentieth-century German thought where an experience of crisis was connected to a supposed return of Gnosticism. First, the chapter discusses the so-called theology of crisis, whose main representatives Karl Barth, Friedrich Gogarten, and Rudolf Bultmann, Jonas's teacher, all flirted with the theological option of Gnosticism. For them, crisis was not a historical category but designated the theological rift between God and human beings. Their conception of a radical dualism between transcendence and immanence had much in common with the kind of dualism that scholars like Reitzenstein, Harnack, and later Jonas attributed to Gnosticism. The following section explores the role of Gnosticism in Oswald Spengler's *Der Untergang des Abendlandes* (*The Decline of the West*), which is not only the single most influential example of cultural pessimism and crisis thinking of the interwar era but also a major, albeit often overlooked influence on Jonas's reading of Gnosticism. Jonas recognized important parallels between the time he was living in and the late ancient times in which Gnosticism flourished. On this point, he explicitly referred to Oswald Spengler, who considered the two periods to be contemporary.[5] For, in Spengler's speculative history of the world, the period between

---

5. Oswald Spengler, *Der Untergang des Abendlandes: Umrisse einer Morphologie der Weltgeschichte*, 2 vols. (Munich: C.H. Beck, 1922). Translations are based on the English version: Oswald Spengler, *The Decline of the West*, trans. Francis Atkinson, 2 vols. (New York: A. Knopf, 1926–28).

1800 and 2000 in Western culture and the late classical period represented analogous phases in the organic development of a culture. Both periods constitute the phase of crisis and decline of their respective cultures.

Crisis Theology and the Temptation of Gnostic Dualism

The interwar "theology of crisis" has often been considered a modern revival of Gnosticism. Adolf von Harnack, for example, dismissed Karl Barth's theology as "Gnostic occultism," arguing that crisis theology's absolute emphasis on divine transcendence implied a Gnostic denigration of the immanent world.[6] Writing his dissertation in the 1920s, Hans Jonas similarly discovered a connection between the Gnostic teachings of Marcion of Sinope and interwar theology, observing that "one could well speak of all recent theology as Marcionite through and through."[7] Although Jonas hardly developed this claim, there are indeed significant parallels between his conception of Gnosticism and the crisis theology of Karl Barth and Friedrich Gogarten.

In line with predecessors like Harnack and Reitzenstein, Jonas considered Gnosticism to be radically dualistic: "The cardinal feature of Gnostic thought is the radical dualism that governs the relation between God and world, and correspondingly that of man and world. The deity is absolutely transmundane, its nature alien to that of the universe, which it neither created nor governs and to which it is the complete antithesis: to the divine realm of light,

---

6. Adolf von Harnack, "Fünfzehn Fragen an die Verächter der wissenschaftlichen Theologie unter den Theologen," in *Aus der Werkstatt des Vollendeten* (Giessen: A. Töpelmann, 1930), 51–54; quoted in Peter Gordon, "Weimar Theology: From Historicism to Crisis," in *Weimar Theology: A Contested Legacy*, ed. Peter Gordon and John McCormick (Princeton: Princeton University Press, 2013), 160.
7. Unpublished fragment, quoted in Benjamin Lazier, *God Interrupted: Heresy and European Imagination between the World Wars* (Princeton: Princeton University Press, 2008), 33. Lazier discussed the connection between crisis theology and Jonas's interwar philosophy in detail in the second chapter of *God Interrupted*, 37–48.

self-contained and remote, the cosmos is opposed as the realm of darkness."[8] This dualism shone through every aspect of Gnostic thought, Jonas argued. A first dualism concerned the existential sense of alienation between human beings and the world. The Gnostic, as Jacob Taubes would later put it, had *no spiritual investment in the world as it is*. On a sociopolitical as well as a spiritual level, the meaningful connection between man and world was crumbling at the end of antiquity. In short, late ancient human beings could experience their existence as crisis. From this primordial existential motive, Jonas derived the other dualistic aspects of Gnostic thought—first and foremost the ontological dualism between God and the world. In Gnosticism, the historical and existential crisis of late ancient human beings was translated into an absolute ontological separation (*Krisis*) between the transcendent God and the immanent world. To use the metaphors that the Gnostics themselves applied, God is "beyond this world"; he is the "alien," the "unknown," and the "hidden."[9] This transmundane God of Gnosticism had no relation to this world whatsoever. According to Marcion, the alien God neither created the world nor governs it. Marcion even rejected the Old Testament and its creative God, opposing him with this new, truly transcendent God. In contrast to this God's infinite wisdom and benevolence, the world of Gnosticism is a sick, evil, and dark place created by an inferior deceiver-god or "demiurge." The world in the Gnostic cosmology is an "abyss."[10] In this sense, God and world are in every possible respect antithetical. In Manichaeism, this antithesis implied a dualism between the divine realm of light and the worldly realm of darkness.[11] For Jonas, this ontological crisis finally implied a radical dualism between God and human beings. Although human beings have a divine origin, they live as "strangers" in this world and

---

8. Hans Jonas, *The Gnostic Religion: The Message of the Alien God and the Beginnings of Christianity* (Boston: Beacon Press, 1958), 42.

9. Jonas, *Gnostic Religion*, 49–51.

10. Jonas, 174–205.

11. Jonas, 57–58.

are absolutely separated from the divine.[12] This separation between the human and the divine is exactly the crisis of which interwar theology spoke.

Crisis theology can largely be understood as a reaction to the liberal trend in nineteenth-century Protestant theology that tended to identify the truth of Christianity with the universal ideals and ethical values of the Enlightenment. According to crisis theologians, liberal theology thus confused divine truth with merely human values. The divine, for these theologians, transcended even the highest human possibility and went beyond ethical values or rational ideals. When the divine is reduced to such universal principles, God is wrongfully immanentized and humanized. In his groundbreaking *The Epistle to the Romans,* Karl Barth dismissed the theological fallacy at the heart of liberal theology as follows: "Transforming time into eternity, and therefore eternity into time, they stretch themselves beyond the boundary of death, rob the Unkown God of what is His, push themselves into His domain, and depress Him to their own level. Forgetting the awful gulf by which they are separated from him, they enter upon a relation with him which would be possible only if He were not God. They make him a thing in this world, and set him in the midst of other things."[13] For Barth, this liberal theological move simply negated the fact that "God is God."[14] In order to remedy this theological misconception, crisis theology paradigmatically emphasized the radical transcendence of the divine and the absolute difference between human beings and God. The relation between the divine and the human is essentially one of crisis, as the idea of transcendence questions by its very nature the legitimacy of immanent being and mere human life. But precisely by being human, one always fails to reach the divine transcendence from which one is separated by a deep "abyss."[15] In making sense of God's radical otherness, crisis

---

12. Jonas, 55.
13. Karl Barth, *The Epistle to the Romans,* trans. Edwin C. Hoskyns (Oxford: Oxford University Press, 1968), 244.
14. Barth, *Epistle,* 11.
15. Barth, 240.

theology oftentimes relied on Gnostic metaphors. In *The Epistle to the Romans,* Barth repeatedly spoke of the "unknown, hidden God"[16] and even explicitly endorsed the Gnostic conception of the divine "which Marcion admirably described as the totally alien (*Fremde*)."[17] Just like the Gnostic God, the God of crisis theology is radically absent from the immanent human world. The separation between transcendence and immanence is, moreover, not gradual but absolute. It can be conceived only as a radical break: "There is no stepping across the frontier by gradual advance or by laborious ascent, or by any human development whatsoever. The step forward involves on this side collapse and the beginning from the far side of that which is wholly Other."[18] This Gnostic issue of an absolute separation between the divine and the human spheres also surfaced in interwar Jewish theology. Relying on the same Gnostic metaphor as Barth, Gershom Scholem emphasized that "religion signifies the creation of a vast abyss, conceived as absolute, between God, the infinite and transcendental being, and Man, the finite creature."[19]

Nonetheless, it would be incorrect to interpret twentieth-century German theology, in general, and crisis theology, in particular, as mere revivals of Gnosticism. An important reason why so many of Barth's contemporaries associated his work with Gnosticism is that they wanted to dismiss his theology as heretical.[20] Calling crisis theology Gnostic was no serious scientific claim; rather, it was usually nothing more than a rhetorical statement. While the crisis theologians admittedly toyed with the idea of Gnosticism, be it consciously or unconsciously, they never completely endorsed the Gnostic possibility. Gnosticism was increasingly referred to by theologians in the interwar and postwar periods, especially after the publication of Jonas's first volume of *Gnosticism and the Spirit*

---

16. Barth, 484, 493, 505.

17. Barth, 249 (translation modified).

18. Barth, 240.

19. Gershom Scholem, *Major Trends in Jewish Mysticism* (New York: Schocken Books, 1946), 7.

20. See Barth, *Epistle*, 13.

of Late Antiquity. While this reference is significant, it has to be noted that crisis theologians explicitly distanced themselves from Gnosticism to a large extent. They were fascinated by Gnosticism, for sure, but at the same time they attempted to overcome this Gnostic temptation.

In the preface to the second edition of *The Epistle to the Romans,* Barth recognized the affinities between his own work and the Gnostic thought of Marcion. He immediately added, however, that he was hardly in complete agreement with Marcion.[21] Barth might come close to being a Gnostic, probably too close for some of his contemporaries, but on the most crucial points his theology rejected the Gnostic option. Barth made this piercingly clear in his seventh chapter, on freedom, where he addressed the meaning of religion and the law. He granted that religion, as the merely human endeavor to reach God, misapprehends the divine by its very nature. In this misapprehension religion is even potentially sinful. The same goes for the law. If the religious law concerns immanent human life, its fulfillment is ultimately a human possibility rather than a divine and could thus be perceived as sinful. Religion and the law may be the highest human possibilities for Barth, bordering closest on the abyss that separates the human from the divine, but they ultimately remain only human. From this perspective, it becomes conceivable to reject religion and the law altogether in order to discover a higher divine possibility beyond the merely human. This is the antinomian option that Marcion chose according to Barth: "Why should we not enroll ourselves as disciples of Marcion, and proclaim a new God quite distinct from the old God of the law?"[22] This option was impossible for Barth, as the negation of religion and the law inevitably remained enclosed within the realm of human possibilities too. The complete negation of the human itself is not yet the divine. For Barth, Marcion negated the

---

21. See Barth, 13: "I was puzzled . . . by the remarkable parallels between what Marcion had said and what I was actually writing. I wish to plead for a careful examination of these agreements before I be praised or blamed hastily as though I were a Marcionite. At the crucial points these agreements break down."

22. Barth, 241.

simple truth that one cannot escape the human sphere and reach for the divine:

> When men revolt, as Marcion did, and with equally good cause, against the Old Testament . . . this whole procedure makes it plain that they have not yet understood the criticism under which the law veritably stands. The veritable *Krisis* under which religion stands consists first in the impossibility of escape from it as long as a man *liveth;* and then in the stupidity of any attempt to be rid of it, since it is precisely in religion that men perceive themselves to be bounded as men of the world by that which is divine. Religion compels us to the perception that God is not to be found in religion.[23]

In spite of their radical insufficiency with regard to the divine, neither religion nor the law can be simply dismissed as sinful. Religion is merely human and can therefore only testify to the absolute distance between the human and the divine. However, this religious realization is the highest human achievement for Barth. Instead of rejecting religion and the law, he embraced them as the highest possibility in the human realm of sin.

In Barth's picture, the negative knowledge that God is not of this world and can be found only beyond the human sphere does not bring one any closer to divine grace. For the Gnostic, on the contrary, it did. In Gnosticism, the realization that God is beyond sufficed to reject this world (as well as religion and the law) as godless, unredeemed, sinful, and evil. If the divine is opposed to the world in every respect, it suffices to actively oppose the world in order to access divine grace. By detaching himself from immanent life through ascetic or libertarian practices, the Gnostic could escape this world and reach the divine. Unlike in crisis theology, the negative knowledge (gnosis) about the world and God's absence from it is already redemptive. Thus, the implications of crisis theology are much more nihilistic than in Gnosticism. Human beings are now absolutely separated from the divine, and there is no way to bridge the abyss from within this world. Rather than overcoming the temptation of Gnosticism, crisis theology radicalized it.

---

23. Barth, 242.

Nonetheless, by refusing to see the world as an evil Gnostic cosmos, crisis theology paradoxically saved the autonomy of the world and the legitimacy of human existence. It is not because God is beyond this world and because no human action can access the divine that this world or human existence is meaningless. On the contrary, because human life in this world cannot relate itself in any way to divine grace, it becomes autonomous with relation to the divine and gains an independent, albeit always finite meaning. For Friedrich Gogarten, another crisis theologian, this line of reasoning is even the theological presupposition of the secular worldview, which conceives of human autonomy and worldly reality without reference to transcendence. From a more theological point of view, Gogarten emphasized that this autonomous legitimacy of immanent existence can allow the world to appear as God's creation again. This was not possible in Gnosticism, he noted, as it considered the world to be created by an evil demiurge. In this sense, crisis theology overcame its Gnostic inclination by maintaining that the world is not evil but indifferent at worst. Although the world's meaning could only be described negatively as that which is not divine, it can still be affirmed precisely for that reason:

> Gnosticism could be content to describe these in negative terms, because it was interested in understanding and affirming God and human existence purely in opposition to the world. . . . For the Christian faith this is fundamentally different. It is true that here, too, the worldly superiority of human identity and the otherworldly God are described in negative terms. . . . However, . . . the opposition to the world, expressed in these negations, receives its meaning from a decided affirmation of the world as God's creation. For the negations are not aimed at the world in and of itself, but the world which was perverted into "this" world.[24]

What ultimately distinguished Christianity from Gnosticism, in Gogarten's view, is simply that the Christian world remains God's creation however profoundly its meaning has been corrupted by human sinfulness. In Gnosticism, "this" world is evil because it was

---

24. Friedrich Gogarten, *Despair and Hope for Our Time*, trans. Thomas Wieser (Philadelphia: Pilgrim Press, 1970), 21.

created this way; in Christianity, it is evil because human beings made it so. Rudolf Bultmann, a German theologian and contemporary of Barth and Gogarten, distinguished between Gnosticism and Christianity along the same lines: "The New Testament is in agreement with the Gnostics, for they too speak of 'this world' . . . ; and moreover they both regard man as the slave of the world and its powers. But there is one significant difference. . . . It never doubts the responsibility of man for his sin. God is always the Creator of the world, including human life in the body."[25]

A Gnosticism scholar himself, Bultmann elaborated much more than Barth and Gogarten on the historical importance of Gnosticism for early Christianity.[26] But just like these crisis theologians he also recognized the continuing significance of Gnosticism for theology without, however, losing track of the ultimate difference between gnosis and Christianity. Bultmann belonged to the tradition of German theologians that radically criticized liberal theology, although he was strictly speaking no crisis theologian. Accordingly, he assessed the stakes of the ambiguous relation between Gnosticism and Christianity somewhat differently than Barth and Gogarten. His assessment of Gnosticism has to be understood against the background of his theological project of demythologizing (*Entmythologisierung*). In his essay "New Testament and Mythology," Bultmann explained how the New Testament presented its message in a mythical language that is no longer acceptable in the modern world. Nonetheless, he was convinced that it is possible to strip the authentic message (*kerygma*) from its mythical form. Bultmann argued that the mythical worldview in which the New Testament expressed its message is essentially that of Gnostic dualism. In other words, to demythologize Christianity is to "de-gnosticize" it. In order to disclose the truth of Christianity independently of its mythical worldview, its inherent Gnosticism has to be overcome.

---

25. Rudolf Bultmann, "New Testament and Mythology," in *"New Testament and Mythology," and Other Basic Writings*, ed. and trans. Schubert M. Ogden (Minneapolis: Fortress Press, 1984), 17.

26. See Rudolf Bultmann, *Primitive Christianity in Its Contemporary Setting* (Minneapolis: Fortress Press, 1975), 162–71.

For Bultmann, the main function of myth was not so much the conception of a coherent worldview but the expression of human self-understanding. As such, demythologizing is the attempt to make explicit the understanding of human existence that is implied in specific mythical images. In other words, Bultmann wanted to interpret the New Testament existentially. Along these lines, his student Hans Jonas had already uncovered the existential motive (*Daseinshaltung*) of the Gnostic myths in *Gnosticism and the Spirit of Late Antiquity*. The most important point of reference for Bultmann's project, however, was Martin Heidegger's existential philosophy. The *kerygma* that Bultmann discovered behind the New Testament's mythical imagery essentially shared the view of human existence of Heidegger's philosophy. For both Heidegger and the New Testament, Bultmann argued, human existence is determined by anxiety, fallenness, and inauthenticity, but at the same time it strives for authentic life. In spite of this remarkable parallel, he emphasized one crucial difference between existentialist philosophy and the New Testament, which ultimately converged in the figure of Christ as the savior. In existential philosophy, on the one hand, the mere knowledge of human inauthenticity suffices to resolve on being authentic; in Christianity, on the other hand, human beings are incapable of achieving authenticity on their own and therefore need the redemptive event of Christ. Bultmann explained that, just like the existential philosopher, the Christian "knows from bitter experience that the life he actually lives is not his authentic life," but unlike the philosopher, "he is totally incapable of achieving that life by his own efforts. In short he is a totally fallen being."[27] This incapacity of human beings to redeem themselves from their inauthentic life implies that the conception of the Fall in the New Testament is much more radical than in existential philosophy. For Bultmann, this fallacy of existential philosophy was ultimately shared by Gnosticism, as the Gnostics overestimated the autonomy of human beings to reach the divine: "Glorifying the Gnostic in his wisdom [is an] illustration of the dominant attitude of man, of his independence and autonomy which lead in the end

---

27. Bultmann, "New Testament and Mythology," 30.

to frustration."[28] Both Heidegger's philosophy and Gnosticism are essential to understand what Bultmann considered the message of the New Testament, but they miss its point insofar as they make human resolve rather than the redemptive action of God the keystone of reaching authenticity. Just like Barth, Bultmann emphasized the total despair of the human condition in light of the utter impossibility of achieving grace; and, just like Barth, he criticized Gnosticism exactly for not accepting this truth of Christianity.

Although Bultmann never went as far as calling Heidegger a Gnostic, it is hardly surprising that many others have done so.[29] It was Hans Jonas, a student of both Bultmann and Heidegger, who first discovered this potential connection between Gnosticism and Heidegger's philosophy. Jonas's demythologizing of Gnosticism in *Gnosticism and the Spirit of Late Antiquity* revealed the very existential framework that he also knew from Heidegger's philosophy. In Heidegger's existentialism, Jonas had found a perspective to address Gnosticism in an entirely new and more philosophical way, just as he discovered in Gnosticism a surprising precursor to existentialism.[30] In the 1920s and early 1930s, Jonas embraced Gnosticism and Heidegger's philosophy more univocally than Bultmann did. After the Second World War, however, he took a much more critical stance. Just like Heidegger's other Jewish students, Jonas was disillusioned with his teacher's political choice of Nazism and became ever more aware of the Fascist and nihilistic implications of Heidegger's philosophy. As the philosophical value of ancient Gnosticism for Jonas primarily lay in its prefiguration of

---

28. Bultmann, 30.
29. See Susan Taubes, "The Gnostic Foundations of Heidegger's Nihilism," *Journal of Religion* 34, no. 3 (1954): 155–72; Eric Voegelin, "Science, Politics, and Gnosticism," in *The Collected Works of Eric Voegelin*, vol. 5, *Modernity without Restraint,* ed. Manfred Henningsen (Columbia: University of Missouri Press, 2000), 243–313; Micha Brumlik, *Die Gnostiker: Der Traum von der Selbstlösung des Menschen* (Frankfurt am Main: Eichborn, 1992), 312–69; Michael Pauen, *Dithyrambiker des Untergangs: Gnostizismus in Ästhetik und Philosophie der Moderne* (Berlin: Akademie, 1994), 255–336.
30. See Hans Jonas, "Gnosticism, Nihilism, and Existentialism," in *The Gnostic Religion: The Message of the Alien God and the Beginnings of Christianity* (Boston: Beacon Press, 1958), 320.

Heidegger's philosophy, through its emphasis on world alienation (*Entweltlichung*), rejecting Heidegger immediately entailed rejecting Gnosticism.[31] Interestingly, Jonas took issue with Heidegger precisely on the point where Bultmann distinguished Christianity from Gnosticism and existential philosophy, that is, with Heidegger's notion of resolve or resoluteness (*Entschlossenheit*).[32] For Jonas, the problem with Heidegger's philosophy and with existentialism was their overemphasis on a human resoluteness that disregarded any source outside of the self, be it nature or the divine. Existentialism shared this idea that human decision sufficed to reach authenticity with Gnosticism's faith in human self-salvation. For Jonas, Heidegger's concept of resoluteness entailed an empty decisionism that was susceptible to disastrous political choices.

In sum, Jonas's concept of Gnosticism increasingly became a category that diagnosed the crisis of modern philosophy. Gnosticism shifted from being an object of fascination, as it also was for his theological colleagues, to a dangerous force that had to be overcome to save modernity. In order to grasp how Gnosticism could become a metaphor for the crisis of modernity, another crucial influence on Jonas's thinking has to be discussed—namely, Oswald Spengler's philosophy of history.

Oswald Spengler: Gnosticism as a Category of Epochal Crisis

In *The Decline of the West,* Oswald Spengler famously developed a philosophy of history that attempted to uncover the

---

31. See Waldstein, "Hans Jonas' Construct 'Gnosticism'," 344: "For the early Jonas, Gnostic texts were a dim but forceful anticipation of existentialist philosophy, to be positively embraced as examples, even if ultimately unsuccessful examples, of the philosophical breakthrough achieved by existentialism, particularly Heidegger. For the later Jonas, modern existentialism was to be rejected as a symptom of nihilism, as a modern parallel of the ancient nihilism found in the Gnostics."

32. Hans Jonas, "Heidegger's Resoluteness and Resolve," in *Martin Heidegger and National Socialism,* ed. G. Neske and E. Kettering, trans. L. Harries (New York: Paragon House, 1990).

morphology and the universal laws of world history. However, he radically criticized the classic philosophies of history of the Enlightenment and German idealism for their interpretation of history as a linear and progressive development. For this reason, he also discarded the triumphalist triadic division of world history into antiquity, the Middle Ages, and modernity, and replaced it with a less Eurocentric perspective that recognized at least eight higher cultures or epochs in the history of the world—Babylonian, Egyptian, Chinese, Indian, Mexican, Classical, Arabian, and Western. Spengler conceived the internal development of each of these cultures as radically deterministic and analogous to the evolution of a living organism. Rather than a linear evolution, world history is an eternal return of cultural cycles that develop according to the biological dynamics of birth, growth, decline, and death. Spengler famously associated the development of a culture with the seasons, its different historical phases corresponding to spring, summer, autumn, and winter. As such, the evolution of a culture is determined exclusively by its internal logic, not by any external cultural influence. Accordingly, cultures form impenetrable and closed historical entities whose specific essences and worldviews are fundamentally incomparable and even inaccessible to each other. From this theoretical perspective, it seems impossible to claim that Gnosticism, which in Spengler's picture belongs to the Arabian culture, returns in the modern age. Nonetheless, Jonas's interpretation of Gnosticism and of the Gnostic return in modern existentialism and nihilism was deeply influenced by Spengler.

In Spengler's view, certain phases or events in one culture, though incomparable qua content, structurally return in specific facts or evolutions in other cultures. Because each culture shares the same iron logic of growth and decline, history necessarily repeats itself. It is possible for two completely unrelated phenomena that appear in two different cultures to have exactly the same function in the historical development of their respective cultures. Spengler even called such phenomena "contemporary": "I designate as contemporary two historical facts that occur in exactly the same—relative—positions in their respective Cultures, and therefore possess exactly equivalent importance."[33] In this regard, a structural comparison between two historically unrelated phenomena—for example, between ancient Gnosticism and modern existentialism—can be highly revealing. Indeed, the aim of Spengler's *Decline of the West* is to assess the cultural situation of the age he was living in, the period just before and after the First World War, by showing how certain evolutions in his own time correspond to developments in other cultures. This comparison allowed him to gain insight into the position of the early twentieth century within the development of Western culture, and hence into the historical fate of his culture. On this point, he recognized significant parallels between the early twentieth century and the cultural phase of late antiquity, the period in which Gnosticism flourished:

> Our narrower task, then, is primarily to determine, from such a world-survey, the state of West Europe and America as at the epoch of 1800–2000—to establish the chronological position of this period in the ensemble of Western culture-history, its significance as a chapter that is in one or other guise necessarily found in the biography of every Culture, and the organic and symbolic meaning of its political, artistic, intellectual and social expression-forms. Considered in the spirit of analogy, this period appears as chronologically parallel—"contemporary" in our special sense—with the phase of Hellenism, and its present culmination, marked by the World-War, corresponds with the transition from the Hellenistic to the Roman age.[34]

From this comparison between Hellenism and the Western culture of the nineteenth and twentieth centuries, Spengler concluded that we have reached the end of Western culture. "Long ago we might and should have seen in the 'Classical' world a development which is the complete counterpart of our own Western development, differing indeed from it in every detail of the surface but entirely similar as regards the inward power driving the great organism towards its end."[35] As the title of his book suggests, Western culture is in decline. Spengler believed he was living in a time of historical crisis.

---

33. Spengler, *Decline of the West*, 1:112.
34. Spengler, 1:26.
35. Spengler, 1:26–27.

To a large extent, Hans Jonas founded his interpretation of Gnosticism on Spengler's historical framework. He even relied on Spengler's concept of "contemporaneity" to explain the improbable connection between ancient Gnosticism and modern nihilism. Indeed, Jonas did not argue that there is an immediate historical relation between these two phenomena. The historical gap between antiquity and modernity is simply too big to make such a claim plausible. Nonetheless, he argued that Gnosticism and modern existentialism arose from fundamentally similar ("contemporary") cultural contexts. In the essay,"Gnosticism, Nihilism, and Existentialism" he stated: "The existence of an affinity or analogy across the ages, such as is here alleged, is not so surprising if we remember that in more than one respect the cultural situation of the first Christian centuries shows broad parallels with the modern situation. Spengler went so far as to declare the two ages 'contemporaneous,' in the sense of being identical phases in the life cycle of their respective cultures."[36] The two ages of which Jonas spoke represent the phase of decline of their respective cultures. Moreover, both late ancient Hellenism and twentieth-century modernity allow for a Gnostic and nihilistic mind-set to surface that radically negates the intrinsic meaning of immanent being as a result of an estrangement between human beings and the world.

For Jonas, Gnosticism appeared as a category that diagnoses epochal crisis. Nonetheless, the appeal to Spengler's analysis of cultural decline in this respect is potentially misleading. First, Jonas did not subscribe to Spengler's deterministic conception of historical evolution or to his conception of "Culture" as a closed and impenetrable historical entity. Jonas is very explicit about this: "Nonetheless, we do not share his main principle of a complete causal isolation of distinct cultural entities from the universal historical process with its manifold determinations."[37] Although Gnosticism, for Jonas, always involved crisis, there is no reason to believe that every crisis by definition implies a return of Gnosticism. He could not share Spengler's strong metaphysical conviction that the development of every culture necessarily follows the exact same pattern.

36. Jonas, "Gnosticism, Nihilism, and Existentialism," 325–26.
37. Jonas, *Gnosis*, 1:73.

Second, unlike Jonas, Spengler himself did not consider Gnosticism to be a paradigmatically late ancient phenomenon that marked the decline of classical culture. Instead, Gnosticism already represented the birth of a new culture, the Arabian or Magian (*Magische*) to be more precise. As such, Gnosticism was not, as Jonas would have it, "the spirit of late antiquity" but rather an early manifestation of the new "Magian soul."

In Spengler's view, the Arabian culture began around the first century, encompassing the rise of Christianity as well as the entire epoch in which Gnosticism flourished. The culture came to an end around the year 1000 after the rise of Islam initiated its decline. As such, the Arabian culture could be reduced neither to Hellenism and the declining classical culture nor to what we traditionally call the Middle Ages, a concept that Spengler discarded anyway. Although Jonas did not adopt Spengler's idiosyncratic periodization, he explicitly praised Spengler for recognizing how the late ancient period was structured by "a new, independent, self-determined principle" rather than by mere "phasing out of old traditions, decadence and finale."[38] For Jonas, late antiquity and Gnosticism had their own intellectual dynamic that was not reducible to the Hellenistic legacy of Greek philosophy or to mere religious syncretism. Just like Spengler, Jonas argued that this new principle, which he simply associated with the Gnostic spirit, came from the East rather than from the West. These Eastern and, more specifically, Iranian origins of Gnosticism were first discovered by scholars of the history of religions school, such as Richard Reitzenstein and Wilhelm Bousset, whose work influenced both Spengler and Jonas. Spengler showed how this new Eastern spirit was largely eclipsed by the persistence of the declining classical culture. Although Gnosticism was actually part of the springtime of the Arabian culture, it appeared historically in late antiquity, that is, in the wintertime of the classical culture. Gnosticism, in Spengler's view, could surely not be a figure of decline, but it remained closely entwined with the problem of epochal crisis because it appeared

---

38. Jonas, 1:73.

precisely at the intersection of two cultures. Rather than a diagnosis of crisis, Gnosticism, for Spengler, already appeared as its cure.

In the chapter "Problems of the Arabian Culture," Spengler tried to make sense of this strange intersection of the classical and Arabian cultures by introducing the concept of pseudomorphosis. This notion explains how a new culture's development is influenced, but especially curtailed by the legacy of an older one. As was the case with so many of his concepts, Spengler actually borrowed the notion from the natural sciences. In the context of geology, pseudomorphosis used to refer to a complex mineralogical phenomenon where crystals in a rock stratum are gradually washed out by streams of water. In this process, the crystal eventually disappears, but the mold it created in the rock remains. In this hollow mold, a new crystal can develop that necessarily takes the external shape of its predecessor. Spengler argued that a similar process could take place in world history. He defined *historical pseudomorphosis* as the case in which "an older alien Culture lies so massively over the land that a young Culture cannot get its breath and fails not only to achieve pure and specific expression-forms, but even to develop fully its own self-consciousness."[39] In short, the new Arabian culture's development was contained within the historical mold its predecessor left behind. Because the new culture had not yet developed its proper means of expression, it developed a radically new content in the older and outdated form of the classical culture. Although a different cultural dynamic was at work, the new culture took the shape (*morphe*) of the older one, and appeared as if (*pseudo*) it were still the older.

For Spengler and Jonas alike, Gnosticism was a prime example of such a pseudomorphosis, as they both understood it as a curious composite of two independent intellectual traditions. Although Gnosticism had to express itself in the form of classical mythology or Greek philosophy, its apocalyptic and dualistic connotations bore witness to a radically different content, which Spengler associated with the Arabian culture. More than just a good example

---

39. Spengler, *Decline of the West*, 2:189.

of pseudomorphosis, Gnosticism became in Spengler's and Jonas's view the intellectual principle around which all late ancient intellectual history gravitated. Spengler was never as explicit as Jonas on this point, but the Gnostic connotations of his description of the Magian soul are obvious. First of all, his chapter on Arabian culture discussed several Gnostic spiritualities in detail. He even considered the Gnostic religion of Mandaeism to be the purest expression of the early Magian soul, as it remained virtually unmarked by the classic pseudomorphosis: "All the characters of the great prophetic religions and the whole store of profound glimpses and visions later collected into apocalypses are seen here as foundations. Of Classical thought and feeling not a breath reached this Magian underworld."[40] Moreover, Spengler's description of Christ, whom he considered the central figure of the early Arabian culture, could hardly sound more Gnostic: "Jesus's utterances, which stayed in the memory of many of the devoted, even in the old age, are those of a child in the midst of an alien, aged, and sick world."[41] For Spengler, Christ was first and foremost an apocalyptic prophet solely interested in Gnostic otherworldliness; he was no moralizer, philistine, or philosopher. Finally, the alien and sick world in which Christ and the Magians lived was not just evil; it was a dark, inferior space whose extension was primarily experienced as that of a cavern (*Höhlenhaft*) or an abyss. This paradigmatically Magian experience also gave rise to a dualistic worldview, which Jonas later considered central to Gnosticism: "In the World-Cavern, . . . it elevates itself to that—'semitic'—dualism that, ever the same under its thousand forms, fills the Magian world. The light shines through the cavern and battles against the darkness (John 1, 5). Both are Magian substances. Up and down, heaven and earth become ontological powers that contend with one another. But these polarities in the most primary sensations mingle with those of the refined and critical understanding, like good and evil, God and Satan."[42] In line with these conceptions of space and dualism, Spengler considered

---

40. Spengler, 2:214.
41. Spengler, 2:212.
42. Spengler, 2:233.

anxiety (*Weltangst*) to be the foundational feeling of the Magian soul. This very anxiety necessitated a turn to an inner self, which the Gnostics called *pneuma* and which Spengler associated with the "birth of the Ego."[43] In line with Spengler, albeit relying more on Heidegger's concept of anxiety, Jonas also understood it as a fundamental existential motive of Gnosticism.[44]

Given the obvious Gnostic features of Spengler's descriptions of the Magian soul, it was hardly a coincidence that Jonas simply called it "Gnosticism." He praised Spengler's concept of the Magian soul because it uncovered an underlying unity behind the seemingly heterogeneous set of religious movements that sprang from the late ancient intellectual climate of Hellenism, but he did not associate this underlying principle with Spengler's Arabian culture. The spirit of late antiquity, for Jonas, was not the Magian soul but simply Gnosticism: "We can therefore take the latter as the most radical and uncompromising representatives of a new spirit, and may consequently call the general principle, which in less unequivocal representations extends beyond the area of Gnostic literature proper, by way of analogy the "Gnostic principle'."[45] This quote summarizes the project of Jonas's two-volume *Gnosticism and the Spirit of Late Antiquity*. Its first volume, *Die mythologische Gnosis* (*Mythological Gnosis*), published in 1934, discussed the existential ground structure of Gnosticism and the Gnostic mythology proper. In the second volume, *Von der Mythologie zur mystischen Philosophie* (*From Mythology to Mystical Philosophy*), published after the war, and in his more accessible *Gnostic Religion*, Jonas explained how its spirit extended beyond the scope of Gnosticism in the strict sense and determined all philosophical and religious formations of late antiquity, including Christianity. Along the same lines, Jonas could even claim that the Gnostic principle transcended this late ancient context and became the spirit of late modernity.

---

43. Spengler, 2:212.
44. See Jonas, *Gnosis*, 1:140–46.
45. Jonas, *Gnostic Religion*, 26.

Hans Jonas: Gnosticism and the Spirit of Late Modernity

Jonas's Gnosticism research attempted to understand the Gnostic religion by uncovering the general philosophical essence or the existential motive that underlay the specific historical instantiations of Gnosticism. If the essence of Gnosticism is to be understood independently of its historical manifestations, the Gnostic spirit can reach beyond its traditional scope. Jonas's typological understanding of Gnosticism, in principle, allowed it to determine other intellectual trends that are not associated with it historically. For this reason, Gnosticism could be applied in an analysis of modernity. This is exactly what so many of Jonas's contemporaries did. Taubes, Voegelin, Blumenberg, Marquard, and Scholem all relied explicitly on Jonas's philosophical concept of Gnosticism when they connected it to modernity. Although Jonas himself used the concept of Gnosticism to diagnose certain problems in modern culture, he primarily wanted to safeguard modernity from a return of Gnosticism. Benjamin Lazier convincingly showed in *God Interrupted* that

> Jonas hoped to defeat the Gnostic threat but could do so only by first resurrecting it. He did well to contest the Gnostic denigration of worldliness with a philosophy of organism and an environmental ethics. He did less well to contain the proliferation of the name, and in fact contributed to the expansion of its currency. Before Jonas, Gnosticism could be specified as an adaptation of Greek, Jewish, Christian, or Persian thought. After him, and against his wishes, it became shorthand for the modern condition.[46]

Jonas himself did not use Gnosticism simply as a shorthand for modernity, and he certainly never considered modernity to be entirely Gnostic, as Eric Voegelin did. However, he did discuss some Gnostic features of modern thought in detail and increasingly used the notion as a diagnosis of the crisis and nihilism of modern culture. More specifically, he was interested in the Gnostic aspects

---

46. Lazier, *God Interrupted*, 146.

of Baconian science and twentieth-century existentialism, both of
which he considered nihilistic.

Against these two instances of modern nihilism, Jonas's philosophy essentially sought to rehabilitate the Greek understanding
of nature (*physis*). He basically tried to make the belief that the
world is fundamentally alive applicable to the modern worldview.
Jonas's criticism of modern nihilism also had important ethical and
political dimensions. His theoretical criticism of modern nihilism
entailed a strong sensitivity to its practical consequences and to the
possible dangers of technical science. Rather than with Gnosticism
research, Jonas's postwar thought seemed especially concerned
with these latter issues. His most influential book, *The Imperative
of Responsibility,* for example, developed an (environmental) ethics for the technological age.[47] As Lazier argued, however, Jonas's
concern with environmental ethics, technical science, and philosophical biology was more closely intertwined with his Gnosticism
research than one might initially expect. Jonas's main discontent
with modernity clearly concerned the nihilism that reduced nature
to dead materiality. It is hardly a coincidence that he discussed the
very same problems in his writings on ancient Gnosticism. Jonas
explicitly opposed the evil, blind, and alienating world of Gnosticism to the Greek concept of a good, divinely ordered, and animate
cosmos. He suggested, furthermore, that modernity is haunted by
the same world-negation as ancient Gnosticism. In other words,
his philosophical project to rehabilitate the (Greek) dignity of the
natural world countered both Gnosticism and its return in modern
nihilism. Presupposing Hans Blumenberg's interpretation of modernity, Lazier therefore characterized Jonas's thought as an "overcoming of Gnosticism."[48]

Jonas initially recognized the acosmic features of Gnosticism in
his teacher Martin Heidegger's existential philosophy, which he
increasingly rejected as fundamentally nihilistic. In an article in
1952, "Gnosticism and Modern Nihilism," it became clear that

---

47. Hans Jonas, *The Imperative of Responsibility: In Search of an Ethics for the
Technological Age* (Chicago: University of Chicago Press, 1984).

48. Lazier, *God Interrupted,* 22.

the relation between Gnosticism and modernity went beyond the scope of Heidegger's nihilism and concerned a more general nihilistic tendency in modern thought.[49] In "Life, Death, and the Body in the Theory of Being," an essay Jonas wrote around the same time, he explained how the human conception of the world evolved from the belief that nature is fundamentally alive to the worldview that interprets nature as dead materiality. It is exactly this latter interpretation of reality that fundamentally underlay Gnosticism as well as nihilism and existentialism. Jonas obviously favored the more primordial interpretation of the world to this modern/Gnostic one: "When man first began to interpret the nature of things—and this he did when he began to be man—life was to him everywhere, and being the same as being alive. . . . Bare matter, that is, truly inanimate, 'dead' matter, was yet to be discovered—as indeed its concept, so familiar to us, is anything but obvious. That the world is alive is really the most natural view, and largely supported by prima-facie evidence."[50] This shift from life to death in ontology coincided for Jonas with the philosophical decline of the Greek conception of the cosmos as a rationally and divinely ordered universe. In Greek thought, the world was essentially akin to human beings, and could therefore be understood according to the same categories through which human beings made sense of their own existence: the world was alive, purposive, and rational. Accordingly, the primacy of the concept of death in modern materialism implied, in a more general way, the decline of anthropomorphism. Rather than being the rule for understanding reality, the very fact of its being alive makes human existence into an exception, and possibly even into a problem. One of the central issues in modern metaphysics was indeed the problem of how to account for the existence and the specificity of human life and thinking on the

---

49. Hans Jonas, "Gnosticism and Modern Nihilism," *Social Research* 19 (1952): 430–52. The extended version of this article was published as an epilogue to Jonas's *Gnostic Religion*: Jonas, "Gnosticism, Nihilism, and Existentialism," 320–40.

50. Hans Jonas, "Life, Death, and the Body in the Theory of Being," in *The Phenomenon of Life* (New York: Harper and Row, 1966), 7.

basis of purely mechanical laws of dead matter. Jonas added that
the materialization of nature and the decline of anthropomorphism
were not directed against the status of living human beings. On
the contrary, he argued that it resulted from an excessive focus
on human beings themselves. More specifically, the materialization
and devaluation of nature were caused by the late ancient spiritual
discovery of the self as being different from and opposed to external reality. This opposition and estrangement between human
beings and cosmos ontologically entailed the dualism of a material
and spiritual world. In this regard, the rise of this ontological dualism appeared as the concrete historical cause of the devaluation of
the physical world that later resulted in the materialistic monism of
modern ontology. Jonas mentioned Christianity and, not surprisingly, Gnosticism as the most significant variants of dualism in late
antiquity. These dualistic religions extracted a new reality from the
immanent world by positing transcendence that is accessible only
from within the inner depths of the human soul.

In the Gnostic dualism, an ontological shift took place where the
spiritual meaning of nature withered in favor of the inner value of
the self or the transcendent world. This shift ultimately resulted in
a complete devaluation of nature in modernity:

> The very possibility of the notion of an "inanimate universe" emerged
> as the counterpart to the increasingly exclusive stress laid on the *human*
> soul, on its inner life and its incommensurability with anything in na-
> ture. The fateful divorce, stretched to the point of a complete for-
> eignness which left nothing in common between the parted members,
> henceforth qualified them both by this mutual exclusion. As the retreat-
> ing soul drew about itself all spiritual significance and metaphysical dig-
> nity, contracting them and itself alike within its innermost being, it left
> the world divested of all such claims and, though at first decidedly de-
> monic, in the end indifferent to very question of value either way.[51]

The last sentence of this passage respectively alluded to Gnosticism and to modern nihilism. Jonas considered Gnosticism and its
demonization of immanent reality to be the early high point of

---

51. Jonas, "Life, Death, and the Body," 14.

dualism. Modern nihilism is then the radicalization of this Gnostic dualism to the point where the meaning of the immanent world is not just the negative of the value of the transcendent, but where the world even becomes altogether "indifferent to the very question of value." The world of nihilism is not evil, but it has no value at all. Nonetheless, Gnosticism and nihilism remained fundamentally intertwined for Jonas. In contrast to the Greek cosmos, the Gnostic reality was governed by blind, irrational, or evil forces that bear witness to the ignorance (*agnosia*) of the inferior creator. In this cosmological perspective, Gnosticism's conception of the natural law as blind necessity or fate (*heimarmene*) operated within modern nihilism. For both Gnostics and moderns, the material world was not a harmoniously ordered universe, but a valueless whole of indifferent forces that was not created for humanity's sake. The resemblance between Gnosticism and modern nihilism is even more explicit on the level of morality. Gnosticism nihilistically rejected the existence of any immanent moral norms or laws. If the world is governed by evil or blind lawfulness, moral and religious rules of conduct can no longer be derived from the natural order of things or from immanent rationality. In contrast to Greek cosmology, the Gnostic and nihilistic cosmos has lost its moral authority. Jonas associated this Gnostic rejection of morality explicitly with Nietzsche's proclamation of the death of God and the subsequent devaluation of the highest values. Both in ancient Gnosticism and modern nihilism, the highest moral values have lost their objective foundation.

However, this very phrase "God is dead" seems to distinguish ancient Gnostic nihilism most radically from its modern counterpart. The proclamation of God's death is ultimately the absolute negation of the transcendent beyond. In other words, modern nihilism rejects the very dualism that proved to be essential for ancient Gnosticism. Jonas granted that Gnosticism's "extreme dualism is of itself the very opposite of an abandonment of transcendence."[52] Rather than rejecting it, ancient Gnostic dualism implied the most

---

52. Jonas, "Gnosticism, Nihilism, and Existentialism," 332.

radical affirmation of transcendence. Nonetheless, Jonas argued that the difference between the Gnostic affirmation and the nihilistic rejection of transcendence was ultimately not as decisive as one might expect. Despite Gnosticism's and nihilism's opposed motivations, their implications for immanent being were exactly the same: both entailed the same radical rejection of the value of the world. Very much in the spirit of Jonas's thought, Gnosticism scholar Ioan Culianu noted that "one of the most relevant characteristics of Gnosticism . . . is its extreme and extremistic affirmation of transcendence *at the expense of* the physical world."[53] Unlike the milder forms of Christian dualism, the absolute separation between God and world in Gnostic dualism implied the impossibility of transcendence exerting any meaningful influence on immanence. This situation is structurally identical to the nihilistic rejection of transcendence. In Gnosticism and modern nihilism alike, "the supra-sensible world is without effective force."[54]

In this regard, the difference between Gnostic and modern nihilism is merely gradual. Modern thought radicalized the nihilistic implications of Gnostic dualism to such an extent that transcendence itself eventually disappeared. In a very minimal way, Gnostic transcendence was still able to give meaning to immanent life. With regard to transcendence the immanent world can be characterized anthropomorphically, albeit in a merely negative and contrastive sense, that is, as an "antagonistic, anti-divine, and therefore anti-human nature."[55] This negative characterization could give direction to human existence: human beings must renounce the world's existence and legitimacy by trying to escape or oppose it at all costs. Modern nihilism is all the more radical because it even rejects this last possibility, thus also rejecting the last portion of anthropomorphism. Clearly, Gnosticism and modern thought could no longer consider the world to be intrinsically good and divine,

---

53. Ioan Culianu, *The Tree of Gnosis: Gnostic Mythology from Early Christianity to Modern Nihilism,* trans. H. S. Wiesner (San Francisco: Harper Collins, 1992), 250 (emphasis original).

54. Jonas, "Gnosticism, Nihilism, and Existentialism," 332.

55. Jonas, 338.

but for modernity this does not entail that the world is evil in the Gnostic sense. The modern world is not simply evil, immoral, or antihuman; rather, it is absolutely indifferent to human beings, and to very question of value itself. Jonas concluded: "This makes modern nihilism infinitely more radical and more desperate than Gnostic nihilism ever could be for all its panic terror of the world and its defiant contempt of its laws. That nature does not care, one way or another, is the true abyss."[56] As indicated above, the Gnostic option had become impossible even for modern theologians like Barth and Gogarten, so that only an indifferent and nihilistic world remained.

For Jonas, this idea of an indifferent nature had extremely problematical and even dangerous implications. In line with the devaluation of the dignity of nature, which modernity shares with Gnosticism, modern nihilism also threatens the dignity of *human* nature. This is exactly what was at stake in Jonas's criticism of Heidegger's philosophy and twentieth-century existentialism. In Jonas's interpretation, existentialism paradigmatically rejected the notion of human nature as an a priori determinable set of features that determines human existence. Applying an empty conception of human nature, existentialism therefore discarded any reference to an objective set of norms that gives direction to human life. In the end, the existentialist based its motivation for action on pure self-referential resoluteness lacking any positive normative content. Moral values no longer have any ontological bearing—as Jonas formulated it, they "are not beheld in vision as being."[57] As these values solely depend upon the internal resolution of the human will, they are constituted indifferently through the formal act of deciding itself. Jonas concluded that modern human beings, as a product of the valueless world they are confronted with, in turn, become indifferent to the very question of value: "So radically has anthropomorphism been banned from the concept of nature that even man must cease to be considered anthropomorphically if he is

---

56. Jonas, 339.
57. Jonas, 338.

just an accident of that nature. As a product of the indifferent, his being, too, must be indifferent."[58]

In this respect, the notion of indifferent nature and the existentialist depreciation of objective norms and values have significant moral implications. The political implications of Heidegger's concept of resoluteness, for example, were clearly reflected in interwar German politics and in Heidegger's own choice to join the Nazi Party. In addition to his focus on Heideggerian and existentialist philosophy, Jonas's postwar thought was especially concerned with the question of technology and its implications for morality. In this regard, Jonas was highly critical of the nihilistic worldview that underlies the modern technical sciences. If nature has no intrinsic value that must be respected, human beings can use and transform the indifferent nature to their own benefit. Through the knowledge of the materialistic laws of nature, modern human beings have an unprecedented technical power over reality and over their own lives. This scientific project is famously summarized in Francis Bacon's "Knowledge is power." This "Baconian ideal," however, had an "ominous side" for Jonas.[59] He did not only condemn the Baconian depreciation of nature in a theoretical way, but he was worried about the actual dangers of this technological indifference and about the environmental crisis. If humanity does not respect nature for what it truly is, that is, a living organism, the very survival of the world is at risk. Jonas even stated that "we live in an apocalyptical situation, that is, under the threat of a universal catastrophe if we let things take their present course."[60] Rather than a solution to many human problems, today, the human power over reality has itself become problematic. In the course of the twentieth century, technology has even become a threat to the survival of the human race. The first half of the twentieth century has proven that technology is able to eradicate entire populations—Auschwitz and Hiroshima being its most horrible examples. The postwar era, in its turn, has even shown that the technological intervention in

---

58. Jonas, 339.
59. Jonas, *Imperative of Responsibility*, 140.
60. Jonas, 140.

reality threatens to eradicate the natural environment that makes human life possible in the first place.

The Crises of the Twentieth Century

Both the general fascination with Gnosticism in the interwar era and Jonas's Gnosticism research have to be understood against the background of the cultural crisis of the early twentieth century, of which crisis theology and Spengler's cultural pessimism are only two examples. Jonas perceived this crisis primarily as a crisis of modern philosophy, which he thought was increasingly decaying into nihilism. The philosophical importance of Jonas's confrontation with the political crises of the Second World War and the postwar era should not be underestimated either. The environmental crises of the end of the twentieth century confronted Jonas with the apocalyptic dangers of modern technology. Furthermore, as a German Jew, the legacy of the Holocaust left an ineradicable mark on his philosophical thought, even very explicitly in his article "The Concept of God after Auschwitz."[61] This latter crisis in particular left Jonas and his contemporaries in a much more desperate condition than the German interwar intellectuals. This situation of an aggravated crisis is exactly the context in which thinkers like Taubes, Voegelin, Blumenberg, and Marquard started referring to the category Gnosticism to make sense of the modern condition.[62] These philosophers initiated as it were a second round of the Gnostcism debates, which will be the main focus of the following five chapters. With the exception of Taubes, Gnosticism had now lost the appeal it had for the interwar philosophers and theologians, and

---

61. Hans Jonas, "The Concept of God after Auschwitz: A Jewish Voice," *Journal of Religion* 67, no. 1 (1987): 1–13.

62. Yotam Hotam also recognized the importance of the experience of crisis for the postwar German Gnosticism debates, explaining how Voegelin's, Blumenberg's and Jonas' writings developed "from a feeling of crisis to thoughts on Gnosis." Yotam Hotam, "Gnosis and Modernity: A Postwar German Intellectual Debate on Secularisation, Religion, and 'Overcoming' the Past," *Totalitarian Movements and Political Religions* 8, nos. 3–4 (2007): 594.

had a univocally negative connotation for thinkers like Voegelin, Blumenberg, Marquard, and indeed Jonas himself. Although Jonas never referred to Gnosticism in his essay on Auschwitz and never explicitly related the political crises of the twentieth century to Gnosticism, the experience of the Second World War must have influenced the shift in his evaluation of Gnosticism.

If read carefully, Jonas's "The Concept of God after Auschwitz" indeed contained a powerful, albeit tacit criticism of Gnosticism. The Holocaust can easily be made into an argument in favor of the Gnostic worldview. For Gnosticism, the world is an abysmal and evil reality from which God had turned away. This Gnostic option could explain how God was fundamentally absent from the world during the Holocaust and did not intervene. Not surprisingly, the Gnostic notion of God's absence or hiddenness often returned in Jewish Holocaust theology, notably in the notion of *Hester Panim* (the hiding face of God).[63] Jonas rejected this Gnostic option, as this hidden God would be a completely unintelligible God. If God is omnipotent and absolutely good, and if he still allowed the Holocaust to happen, he is absolutely unintelligible to human beings. However, Jonas added that this concept of an unintelligible, hidden God could not be more opposed to the Jewish religion: "The *Deus Absconditus*, the hidden God (not to speak of an absurd God) is a profoundly un-Jewish conception. Our teaching, the Torah rests on the premise and insists that we can understand God, not completely, to be sure, but something of him."[64] The only theological option that seems to be left after the Holocaust then is to give up on God entirely and to proclaim the "death of God."[65] Instead of dismissing the idea of God itself, however, Jonas claimed that the age-old notion of God's omnipotence had to be given up in face of the Holocaust: "Through the years that 'Auschwitz' raged God

---

63. See Martin Buber, *Eclipse of God: Studies in the Relation between Religion and Philosophy* (New York: Humanity Books, 1952).

64. Jonas, "Concept of God after Auschwitz," 9.

65. This is exactly what the Holocaust theologian Richard Rubenstein did; Richard Rubenstein, *After Auschwitz: Radical Theology and Contemporary Judaism* (Indianapolis: Bobbs-Merrill, 1966).

remained silent. . . . And there I say, . . . Not because he chose not to, but because he *could* not intervene did he fail to intervene."[66] Still, this silent, impotent God could be a Gnostic God whose power is limited in a dualistic theology by another, evil deity. But again, Jonas rejected this Gnostic option by claiming that God's impotence resulted from a self-limitation in the act of creation: "In order that the world might be, and be for itself, God renounced his being, divesting himself from his deity."[67] Jonas speculated that in creating the world God had lost his omnipotence to something outside of himself that he now no longer absolutely controlled.

Although the experience of the Holocaust is rarely discussed explicitly in the postwar Gnosticism debates, Auschwitz made clear what a Gnostic world could look like. After Auschwitz, Gnosticism could hardly be an object of fascination. While it could still be perceived as a mystical, esoteric cure for cultural crisis in the early twentieth century, after the Second World War, it became the diagnosis of the crisis of modernity. As the following chapters will show, however, there is one very significant exception to this general narrative: Jacob Taubes found in Gnosticism not just an object of fascination but also a conceptual tool to understand and legitimate modern thought.

---

66. Jonas, "Concept of God after Auschwitz," 10.
67. Jonas, 4.

2

ESCHATON

Gnostic Evil in History

From the late 1940s onward, the issue of modern Gnosticism was largely incorporated into the German secularization debates. In contrast to the heterogeneous contexts in which Gnosticism was referred to in the first half of the twentieth century, the reference to Gnosticism increasingly appeared in a well-defined debate about the theological roots of modern, secular thought. Although Gnosticism could be perceived as such a theological precursor of modernity, these debates initially centered on the secularization of eschatology rather than on Gnosticism. In the Judeo-Christian tradition, eschatology is the theological doctrine concerned with the end of history and the salvation of human existence. A number of postwar German philosophers debated the connection between eschatology and secular modernity—Karl Löwith's definition of modern progress as "secularized eschatology" being the classic example.[1] Along these lines, Jacob Taubes developed an eschatological interpretation of Western modernity in his *Abendländische Eschatologie* (*Occidental Eschatology*).[2] Moreover, the concept of

---

1. Karl Löwith, *Meaning in History: The Theological Implications of the Philosophy of History* (Chicago: University of Chicago Press, 1949), 2, 60.

2. See Jacob Taubes, *Abendländische Eschatologie* (Berlin: Matthes und Seitz, 1947); English translation: Jacob Taubes, *Occidental Eschatology*, trans. David Ratmoko (Stanford: Stanford University Press, 2009).

secularized eschatology was adopted by many of Löwith's contemporaries, including by Eric Voegelin and Odo Marquard.[3] However, Löwith's theory of secularization and its favorable reception were heavily criticized by Hans Blumenberg in *The Legitimacy of the Modern Age,* notably in the book's first part, "Secularization: Critique of a Category of Historical Wrong."[4] In view of the pertinence of Blumenberg's critique, the German secularization debates have often been reduced to a debate between Löwith and Blumenberg, which centered almost exclusively on the issues of progress and secularized eschatology.[5] This overemphasis on the Löwith-Blumenberg debate not only tends to misrepresent the number of people working on the issue of secularization in postwar Germany but also obscures the role of Gnosticism and the structural relation between the topics of Gnosticism and eschatology in the secularization debates.

From the outset, the eschatological interpretations of secular modernity implied the Gnostic readings of modern thought. This chapter therefore shows how Gnosticism's appeal, in postwar German thought, as an explanatory category for the modern condition cannot be understood independently of the contemporaneous

3. See Eric Voegelin, *The New Science of Politics: An Introduction* (Chicago: University of Chicago Press, 1952), 110–27; Odo Marquard, *Schwierigkeiten mit der Geschichtphilosophie* (Frankfurt am Main: Suhrkamp, 1973). Taking a very different approach, Carl Schmitt and Norman Cohn applied the concept of eschatology to modern politics: Carl Schmitt, *The Nomos of the Earth in the International Law of Jus Publicum Europaeum,* trans. G. L. Ulmen (New York: Telos Press Publishing), 59–62; Norman Cohn, *The Pursuit of the Millennium: Revolutionary Millenarians and Mystical Anarchists of the Middle Ages* (London: Pimlico, 1957).

4. Hans Blumenberg, *The Legitimacy of the Modern Age,* trans. Robert Wallace (Cambridge, MA: MIT Press, 1983), 37–52.

5. This is particularly the case for the early Anglo-American reception of the German secularization debates: Robert M. Wallace, "Progress, Secularization, and Modernity: The Löwith-Blumenberg Debate," *New German Critique* 22 (1981): 64; Martin Jay, "Review of *The Legitimacy of the Modern Age,*" *History and Theory* 24 (1985): 192; Laurens Dickey, "Blumenberg and Secularization: Self-Assertion and the Problem of Self-Realizing Teleology in History," *New German Critique* 41 (1987): 152.

debates on the secularization of eschatology.[6] It is hardly a coincidence that all the thinkers who wrote on the issue of secularized eschatology, except for Löwith himself, were also involved in the debates on the Gnostic origins of modernity. For Taubes, Voegelin, Blumenberg, and Marquard, the concepts of Gnosticism and eschatology were virtually interchangeable. As Gnosticism made salvation from an evil world the keystone of its doctrine, eschatology is evidently of paramount importance in any Gnostic speculation. In addition, these thinkers also maintained that eschatology in all variants—be it Jewish, Christian, or secular—is itself ultimately Gnostic. In a letter to Carl Schmitt, Blumenberg stated this explicitly: "It is my systematic contention that every eschatology is Gnostic by its very nature."[7] Blumenberg maintained that the more emphasis is put on the redemptive end of the world, the more this world loses its legitimacy as God's creation. The more eschatology emphasizes the hope for a utopian future or redemption beyond time, the more depraved the present and history itself appear. The eschatological notion of salvation is only conceivable assuming the existence of some form of worldly evil from which humanity has to be delivered. Thus, eschatology implies deep pessimism about the present state of the world, which, according to these German thinkers, gave rise to Gnosticism's metaphysical rejection of all immanent reality as godless, fallen, and evil.

Connecting modern thought to eschatology and Gnosticism essentially implied that secular modernity adheres to a deeply pessimistic worldview and to a theological concept of salvation. This role of pessimism and the related problem of evil remained ambiguous in Löwith's reflections on eschatology in his *Meaning in History*, which will be discussed in the first section of this chapter. To

---

6. This approach fundamentally contradicts Cyril O'Regan's Gnostic reading of modernity, as he considered the Gnostic genealogy of modernity to be not only fundamentally different from but also superior to the apocalyptic and eschatological readings of modernity: Cyril O'Regan, *Gnostic Return in Modernity* (Albany: SUNY Press, 2001), 65–76.

7. Hans Blumenberg, "Letter to Carl Schmitt of August 7, 1975," in Hans Blumenberg and Carl Schmitt, *Briefwechsel*, ed. Alexander Schmitz and Marcel Lepper (Frankfurt am Main: Suhrkamp, 2007), 132.

the extent that he recognized the importance of evil and pessimism at crucial moments, his reflections on secularized eschatology implicitly announced the Gnostic interpretations of modernity of his contemporaries, such as Taubes, Voegelin, and Marquard. Nonetheless, he was ultimately not interested in the possible continuities between eschatological pessimism and modern thought. Löwith simply wanted to point to the surprising parallels between modern philosophy of history and Christian history of salvation. Taubes's *Occidental Eschatology,* which will be discussed in the following section, is much more explicitly concerned with eschatology's pessimistic implications. In immediately connecting eschatology to Gnosticism, Taubes accounted for the pessimistic worldview that underlies every eschatological hope for or pursuit of a redemptive change in time, whether it is religious or secular. This pessimism aligns well with the Gnostic crisis-thinking that was discussed in the previous chapter. For pessimism is the prototypical response to crisis. However, pessimism should hardly be as paralyzing as the experience of crisis, Taubes observed, as eschatology implies hope for the future and incentive for change as well as radical critique of the cultural, political, and metaphysical status quo. Gnosticism's pessimism is eschatological insofar as it always points to something redemptive beyond the current evil, as Michael Pauen also noted in his book on Gnostic return in modern philosophy: "Gnosticism represents a mediated, a secondary pessimism, that has to be understood not simply as a reflection of the existing reality but as a very distinct intentional interpretation of this reality. The representatives of these visions are, as a rule, no passive victims of crises, as they frequently occur, but rather active pioneers of fundamental changes."[8] For Taubes, as for Pauen, the modern legacy of Gnosticism consisted in the secular continuation of a revolutionary eschatology. Thus, Taubes's interpretation of eschatology was more apocalyptic, heretical, and messianic than Löwith's concept of eschatology, which was decidedly orthodox and Christian. In addition to the obvious influence of Löwith and the leading Christian

---

8. Michael Pauen, *Dithyrambiker des Untergangs: Gnostizismus in Ästhetik und Philosophie der Moderne* (Berlin: Akademie, 1994), 13.

interpretations of eschatology by Rudolf Bultmann and Hans Urs von Balthasar, Taubes's work echoes the messianism of interwar Jewish thinkers like Ernst Bloch, Gershom Scholem, and Walter Benjamin.

Without knowing Benjamin's essay "On the Concept of History," Taubes and Löwith were actually continuing Benjamin's project of uncovering the tacit theological and messianic presuppositions of the modern conception of history. Benjamin hinted at this connection between theology and the modern historical consciousness at the beginning of his essay with the famous image of the puppet and the dwarf:

> There was once, we know, an automaton constructed in such a way that it could respond to every move by a chess player with a countermove that would ensure the winning of the game. A puppet wearing Turkish attire and with a hookah in its mouth sat before a chessboard placed on a large table. A system of mirrors created the illusion that this table was transparent on all sides. Actually, a hunchbacked dwarf—a master at chess—sat inside and guided the puppet's hand by means of strings. One can imagine a philosophic counterpart to this apparatus. The puppet, called "historical materialism," is to win all the time. It can easily be a match for anyone if it enlists the services of theology, which today, as we know, is small and ugly and has to keep out of sight.[9]

Karl Löwith: The Secularization of Eschatology

Eschatology is generally considered to be the theological discipline that speculates about the end of time, the final judgement, the establishment of the kingdom of God, and the salvation of humankind. The end of history (eschaton) is not just the annihilation of the present world, but, in the Christian tradition, also the fulfillment of world history by divine providence. In this regard, the

---

9. Walter Benjamin, "On the Concept of History," in *Selected Writings*, vol. 4, *1938–1940*, ed. Howard Eiland and Michael Jennings (Cambridge, MA: Harvard University Press, 2003), 389. For Benjamin and secularization, see Sigrid Weigel, *Walter Benjamin: Images, the Creaturely, and the Holy*, trans. Chadwick Truscott Smith (Stanford: Stanford University Press, 2013), 3–29.

story of time that commenced with the creation of the world will be completed by the salvation of humanity at the end of history. Both Taubes and Löwith emphasized that the eschatological theology of salvation radically broke with the classical, cyclic interpretation of time.[10] History no longer appeared as an infinite repetition of recurring patterns but rather as a linear and progressive evolution from a beginning toward an end, that is, from creation toward redemption. Both thinkers maintained that this linear structure determines, until today, our modern experience of time. By the same token, they recognized this experience as being fundamental for the modern interpretations of history and progress. In spite of this general agreement about eschatology's nature and its modern afterlife, Taubes and Löwith emphasized different aspects of eschatology.

Taubes, on the one hand, homed in on the eschatology of Apocalypticism. The apocalyptic speculations of Jewish messianism and early Christianity were probably the first manifestations of eschatological thinking. Paradigmatically, Apocalypticism does not proclaim the end of time as a fulfillment of world history in a distant future, but rather as the imminent destruction of an inferior world. As such, the Apocalypse will either be the catastrophic annihilation of immanence or the establishment of God's kingdom on earth after the destruction of the present world. In both cases, Apocalypticism has a straightforward political and revolutionary meaning that was expressed in a historical and theological framework. The proclamation of the end of time is almost always an act of political resistance of a violently suppressed minority—the Jews in Babylon, the early Christians in the Roman Empire.[11] In this sense, Apocalypticism typically implies a pessimistic view of the existing world order. While the present is sinful and depraved, the Apocalypticist

---

10. Löwith, *Meaning in History*, 1–7; Taubes, *Occidental Eschatology*, 3–9.

11. In his studies on the relation between monotheism and violence, Jan Assmann emphasized that "Apocalypticism and oppression go hand in hand. Apocalypticism is a form of religious and intellectual resistance, and . . . requires violent oppression and persecution in order to exist." Jan Assmann, *Of God and Gods: Egypt, Israel, and the Rise of Monotheism* (Madison: University of Wisconsin Press, 2008), 122.

believes that a transcendent force will settle a new and better world by destroying the immanent order.

Löwith, on the other hand, was primarily concerned with Christian eschatology. The orthodox Christian eschatology is decidedly less apocalyptic than the early Christian and Jewish eschatologies. The reason why the church rejected Apocalypticism had to do with the ambiguous ontological and eschatological nature of Christ. In Christian orthodoxy, Christ is not just considered to be a prophet proclaiming the end of history and the coming of God; rather, he is the incarnated God himself. Christ cannot just proclaim salvation, as he himself is supposed to be the savior. Paradoxically, Christian orthodoxy has situated the eschatological events in the past, that is, in Christ's incarnation and resurrection: "What really begins with the appearance of Jesus Christ," said Löwith, "is the beginning of an end."[12] Accordingly, Christian eschatology is directed to the past and present as if they were the future; that is to say, Christianity remains faithful to the temporal and future-oriented structure of eschatological hope by, at least partly, redirecting this spiritual futurity to the past and the present. Through the figure of Christ, eschatological salvation has already taken place and is now a present reality for the Christian. This conception of eschatology that Löwith subscribed to was fundamentally in tune with the leading theological interpretations of eschatology at the time. In his writings on demythologization, Rudolf Bultmann showed how the New Testament overcame the mythical expectation of an imminent cosmic apocalypse by conceiving salvation as taking place in the present: "The eschatology of Jewish apocalyptic and of Gnosticism has been emancipated from its accompanying mythology, insofar as the age of salvation has already dawned for the believer and the life of the future has become a present reality."[13]

Since God's incarnation in Christ is considered the most important eschatological event in the Christian history of the world, the

---

12. Löwith, *Meaning in History*, 197.

13. Rudolf Bultmann, "New Testament and Mythology," in *"New Testament and Mythology," and Other Basic Writings*, ed. and trans. Schubert M. Ogden (Minneapolis: Fortress Press, 1984), 20.

current state of the immanent world is the last phase of world history for the Christian. After Christ's resurrection, the world re-
tired and waits patiently for its end. No truly historical change
will or can still take place.[14] According to Löwith's interpretation,
Christian eschatology is oscillating between the past and the future. On the one hand, the eschatological expectation of salvation
is redirected to the past and present; on the other hand, Christians
still hope for salvation, as they do not yet live in the kingdom of
God. Referring to Saint Augustine, Löwith showed that the true
Christian kingdom of God is not to be realized in a future realm
coming *after* this world. The Augustinian City of God is rather
a transcendent reality *beyond* profane history—beyond the City
of Man.[15] Accordingly, the epoch that began with the incarnation
of Christ, though the last one in world history, is not the political
realization of the kingdom of God. Christian eschatology cannot
be conceived apocalyptically, for salvation is here no transcendent
intervention in political history that occurs publicly as an immanent end of time. Löwith agreed with Augustine that "the historical
destiny of Christian peoples is no possible subject of a specifically
Christian interpretation of political history."[16] Disarming the political and revolutionary dimension of Apocalypticism, Christianity
transformed the conception of salvation into a purely transcendent,
apolitical, and spiritual fulfillment or forgiveness of the individual
believer: "In Christianity the history of salvation is related to the
salvation of each single soul."[17] As such, Christian eschatology can

---

14. Hans Blumenberg added that if the eschatological events have already
taken place and the world persisted nonetheless, history regains legitimacy for the
Christian. If salvation has already happened and the world will be abolished only
in a distant future, all worldly affairs have at least temporary justification. That is
why the church could institutionalize itself within this world, in the first place. Blumenberg termed this return to worldliness "secularization *by* eschatology." Refut-
ing Löwith's main argument, he added that the "secularization *of* eschatology" in
modernity was no longer possible, as eschatology had already secularized itself in
the early Middle Ages. See Hans Blumenberg, *The Legitimacy of the Modern Age*,
trans. Robert Wallace (Cambridge, MA: MIT Press, 1983), 45.

15. Löwith, *Meaning in History*, 160–73.

16. Löwith, 195.

17. Löwith, 195.

have nothing to do with the secular. Again, Löwith subscribed here to Rudolf Bultmann's interpretation of eschatology. For Bultmann, Christian eschatology had no worldly or historical implications; he claimed that the *kerygma* "is an event whose eschatological character does not admit of secular proof."[18]

To the extent that Christian eschatology, in Löwith's perspective, broke with the apocalyptic interpretation of eschatology, it also discarded its cultural, political, and ontological pessimism. The end of history no longer appears as the destruction of an evil world, but as the providential fulfillment of the transcendent history of salvation. Therefore, the oscillation between past and present in Christian eschatology coincides with an ambiguity in the interpretation of evil. On the one hand, Christians do not believe that this world is intrinsically depraved. In Scholastic theology, evil is not even considered to be a real ontological problem. In a world created by a benevolent God, evil was just the absence of the good, the *privatio boni*.[19] The problem of evil, on the other hand, is certainly not absent in Christianity and Christian eschatology. Instead of interpreting evil gnostically as an ontological dysfunction of the world, Christianity attributed it to human sin and to God's just punishment for our evil deeds. As chapter 1 showed, this is also how the crisis theologians and Bultmann interpreted evil. In this perspective, salvation no longer appears as the historical redemption from an intrinsically evil world but as the individual and transcendent forgiveness of human sinfulness.

In the introduction to *Meaning in History*, Löwith explicitly emphasized that eschatology's linear interpretation of time assumes the experience of evil. If evil and suffering are experienced as fundamental and insurmountable, the perception of time as it were demands a progressive interpretation of history. Because the present evil seems insuperable, salvation is projected into the future. The course of history obtains meaning and direction to the extent that an evolution from an evil to a better world can take place: "The

18. Bultmann, "New Testament and Mythology," 44.
19. See Thomas Aquinas, *Summa Theologica: Volume I-Part I* (New York: Cosimo, 2007), art. 49.

outstanding element, however, out of which an interpretation of history could arise at all, is the basic experience of evil and suffering, and of man's quest for happiness. The interpretation of history is, in the last analysis, an attempt to understand the meaning of history as the meaning of suffering by historical action."[20] A radically pessimistic worldview makes it impossible to conceive time as a purposeless course of ever returning and immutable patterns. The hope for a better, and hence significantly different, future has to be imaginable one way or another. Since this projected future presupposes an ontological subversion in the course of time as the linear transition from evil to good, history has to allow for structural change. Meaning in history is thus indissolubly connected to the possibility of historical change proper.

Consequently, the interconnected problems of pessimism, hope, and salvation were, for Löwith, absent in a noneschatological conception of time. He had the Greek-Nietzschean eternal recurrence in mind.[21] Observing that "no similar hope and despair can be found in any classical writer," Löwith maintained that the classical cosmologies and Greek philosophy combined an ontological optimism with a cyclic conception of time.[22] In his perspective, the optimism of Greek cosmologies guaranteed that the experience of evil could not have had ontological bearing. These cosmological presuppositions were also reflected in the ancient experience of time. Because cosmological evil was absent, the hope for a better and different future did not exist, or was considered to be a form of hubris.[23] Since Löwith, not unlike Nietzsche, characterized the Greek experience of time as a continuous repetition of the same cycle, the past, present, and future were even structurally indistinguishable in Greek thought: "According to the Greek view of life and the world, everything moves in recurrences, like the eternal

---

20. Löwith, *Meaning in History*, 3.
21. See Karl Löwith, *Nietzsche's Philosophy of the Eternal Recurrence of the Same*, trans. Harvey Lomax (Berkeley: University of California Press, 1997).
22. Löwith, *Meaning in History*, 61.
23. See Julian Potter, "Meaning in Eternity: Karl Löwith's Critique of Hope and Hubris," *Thesis Eleven* 110 (2012): 27–45.

recurrence of sunrise and sunset, of summer and winter, of generation and corruption."[24] As such, significant events in the political or cultural history could never be conceived as real evolutions. For Löwith, structural historical changes, let alone progress, were philosophically inconceivable in ancient thought: "To the Greek thinkers a *philosophy* of history would have been a contradiction in terms." Philosophical knowledge could only be about the unchangeable: "The immutable, as visible in the fixed order of the heavenly bodies, had a higher interest and value to [the Greeks] than any progressive and radical change."[25]

According to Löwith, the ontological pessimism that gave history its eschatological meaning was absent in antiquity. Apparently, the eschatological search for meaning in history arose only when humanity could no longer conceive the world as a harmonious cosmos. When the experience of evil became so fundamental, historical change first became conceivable, and eventually even necessary. But the relation between linear time and pessimism is also valid in the opposite sense, for Löwith. Endowing history with meaning is not just an answer to pessimism, but pessimism itself is conceivable only within the eschatological perspective of the ultimate meaning of history: "It is only within a pre-established horizon of ultimate meaning, that actual history seems to be meaningless. This horizon has been established by history, for it is Hebrew and Christian thinking that brought this colossal question into existence."[26] Without the touchstone of a future that gives meaning to history as a whole, the present state of affairs cannot be experienced as meaningless. Singular historical events in their own right do not have any meaning at all—as such, they are neither good nor bad.

Löwith's discovery of the structural connection between eschatology and the pessimistic experience of meaninglessness also shows that the comparison between the modern philosophies of history and Christian eschatology assumed an interpretation of the role of pessimism in modern thought. Because pessimism and the

---

24. Löwith, *Meaning in History*, 4.
25. Löwith, 4 (emphasis original).
26. Löwith, 4.

problem of evil are the driving forces of eschatology, they must have played a crucial role in the genesis of modern progress, in Löwith's perspective. Without a pessimistic attitude to the present world or to humanity, there would be no need for future salvation and progress: "The starting point of the modern religions of progress is an eschatological anticipation of the future salvation and consequently a vision of the present state of mankind as one of depravity."[27] For Löwith, the secularization of eschatology progress is not to be understood as a mere transfer of theological contents from one age to the other. In defining progress as secularized eschatology, he discovered, rather, a substantial continuity of ontological problems between premodernity and modernity. Both the eschatological problem of evil and the possibility of salvation appear fundamental for modern thought.

Nonetheless, Löwith argued that modern thought rejected the Christian interpretation of salvation, and tried to solve the problem of evil by new—now secular—means. The modern overcoming of evil was no spiritual salvation of the individual believer; rather, it became a historical and controllable progress toward an immanently perfect world. Rather than simply adopting Christian eschatology, modernity modified the traditional answer to the problem of eschatology. Interpreted in this way, Löwith's position seems to dodge Hans Blumenberg's most fundamental criticism of the theory of secularization. Blumenberg argued, explicitly targeting Löwith, that "the continuity of history across the epochal threshold lies not in the permanence of ideal substances but rather in the inheritance of problems."[28] As such, Blumenberg's criticism missed the point. Löwith's conception of secularization implied not only mere transfer of the "ideal substance" of eschatology but also a continuity of the underlying problems. Nonetheless, the point of Blumenberg's criticism was more subtle. He argued that progress cannot be understood as a mere immanent answer to the age-old theological question of eschatology. Progress, in Blumenberg's view, arose quite independently from this question and was rather the product

---

27. Löwith, 61.
28. Blumenberg, *Legitimacy*, 48.

of human self-assertion in history. Progress is an originally modern answer to a legitimately modern question. It did not arise as an answer to the theological question of the meaning of world history or to the question of salvation. Rather, progress had a more narrow scope that concerned the possibility of transgenerational progress in science. But even as a genuinely novel interpretation of historical evolution, Blumenberg maintained, progress had to conform itself to the dominant theological interpretations of history. The modest interpretation of progress was therefore generalized and totalized in order to answer a theological and eschatological question about the meaning of history that could not yet be dismissed. For this reason, Blumenberg rejected Löwith's category of secularization, as it obscured the real historical dialectic between medieval and modern intellectual history: "What mainly occurred in the process that is interpreted as secularization . . . should be described not as the *transposition* of authentically theological contents into secularized alienation from their origin but rather as the *reoccupation* answer positions that had become vacant and whose corresponding questions could not be eliminated."[29] In this quote, Blumenberg not only rejected Löwith's descriptive account of secularization but also dismissed its normative implications. Secularization not only designated the transfer of contents from one epoch to another, for Löwith, but also implied the alienation of that content from its origin. While Blumenberg sought to defend the "legitimacy of the modern age," such alienation delegitimized modern thought.

Löwith indeed radically criticized modernity and modern progress. He argued that the modern secularization of Christian eschatology corrupted the transcendent and individual meaning of Christian salvation. The modern notion of progress is therefore an illegitimate heir of Christian theology: progress is eschatology's bastard. The modern philosophers of history, such as Voltaire, Condorcet, Hegel, and Marx, borrowed the theological framework of the history of salvation but applied it to the immanent course of profane history. These modern thinkers attributed meaning and

---

29. Blumenberg, 65 (emphasis original).

direction to history by transforming the spiritual faith in the transcendent fulfillment of history into the rational belief in a historical progress toward a perfect world. This immanent, and hence politico-historical eschatology is inconceivable in Christianity, Löwith argued. By definition, Christian eschatology and providence are not concerned with the immanent course of history (*Weltgeschichte*) but with the structure of the transcendent history of salvation and the possibility of a spiritual redemption (*Heilsgeschehen*).[30] Therefore, Christianity does not allow for a real philosophy of (world) history. Because Christian eschatology is essentially transcendent, an immanent Christian eschatology is a contradiction in terms. The modern confusion between world history and the history of salvation, however, was not just an innocent category-mistake. For Löwith, it was a potentially dangerous illusion. In illegitimately applying the eschatological structure of *Heilsgeschehen* to *Weltgeschichte*, modernity generated the illusion that the meaning of world history and the possibility of salvation are immanent and therefore essentially controllable. Although Löwith was not as explicit on this point as some of his contemporaries, such as Eric Voegelin, he assumed that this modern illusion is actualized most radically in the totalitarian movements—the secular religions—of the twentieth century.[31]

For Löwith, the modern philosophies of history were not so much misguided because of their unconscious continuity with the premodern framework of Christianity, whose influence the moderns categorically tried to renounce. If this were the only problem, modernity would have just misunderstood itself: it emphasized discontinuity between modernity and theology where there was actually continuity. However, Löwith considered this continuity preeminently a corruption, and a dangerous deformation of the

---

30. See the German translation of *Meaning in History*: Karl Löwith, *Weltgeschichte und Heilsgeschehen: Die theologischen Voraussetzungen der Geschichtphilosophie* (Stuttgart: W. Kohlhammer, 1953).

31. See Jeffrey A. Barash, "The Sense of History: On the Political Implications of Karl Löwith's Concept of Secularization," *History and Theory* 37 (1998): 69–82.

original Christian message. By secularizing eschatology, modernity negated Christianity's most essential feature: its transcendent God. For Löwith, modernity's rejection of transcendence ultimately led to radical nihilism and groundlessness.[32] In *Heidegger's Children,* Richard Wolin perfectly summarized Löwith's criticism of modern nihilism: "For the Greeks, the structure of the world was eternal; for Christianity, it was created by God. Modernity, as an ideology of radical immanence, brusquely dismisses both standpoints and finds itself, unsurprisingly, destitute and disoriented, lacking a permanent ground."[33] Although Löwith saw his former teacher Martin Heidegger as a prime example of such nihilism, Wolin also emphasized how his critique of the history of Western thought as degeneracy and decline was fundamentally influenced by Heidegger's history of being.[34] Metaphors of decline are indeed omnipresent in *Meaning in History.* For Löwith, modernity copied Christian theology, but also distorted its original meaning: "The modern world is as Christian as it is un-Christian. . . . The whole moral and intellectual, social and political, history of the West is to some extent Christian, and yet it dissolves Christianity by the very application of Christian principles to secular matters."[35]

For Löwith, a secularized eschatology could no longer be a Christian eschatology. However, what he described in *Meaning in History* as the modern application of Christian eschatology to secular affairs could just as well be considered a return to the early or pre-Christian eschatology of Apocalypticism. Since Apocalypticism conceived redemption not as individual salvation but as the revolutionary break within history that appears publicly, it can perfectly pass for political and even secular eschatology. This, we will see, was Taubes's position. Unlike the Christian providential interpretation of history, apocalyptic eschatology shares a revolutionary

32. Karl Löwith, *Heidegger and European Nihilism,* ed. Richard Wolin and trans. Gary Steiner (New York: Columbia University Press, 1995).

33. Richard Wolin, *Heidegger's Children: Hannah Arendt, Karl Löwith, Hans Jonas, and Herbert Marcuse* (Princeton: Princeton University Press, 2001), 78.

34. Wolin, *Heidegger's Children,* 97.

35. Löwith, *Meaning in History,* 201–2.

vigor with modern political movements such as Marxism and social utopianism. However, this apocalyptic interpretation of eschatology hardly suited Löwith's project, as it could not account for
modern progress. Although redemption can appear within history
according to the apocalyptic speculations, it is never the result of
historical evolution, let alone of progress. Salvation rather opposes
historical immanence. In this sense, progress could hardly be secularized eschatology, although it could be secularized providence.
Löwith indeed often made such claims: "The belief in an immanent
and indefinite progress replaces more and more the belief in God's
transcendent providence."[36]

Blumenberg rightly observed that Löwith remained ambiguous on this point. He failed to opt for either eschatology or providence: "In regard to progress, the advocates of secularization
theory should have decided early on whether they were going to
make the Last Judgment or Providence the *Terminus a quo*. . . .
The eschatological God of the end of history cannot at the same
time be the God who makes himself known and credible in history as its caretaker."[37] Blumenberg argued that if Löwith wanted
to appeal to Christian providence in his analysis of modern historical thought, he could not at the same time have maintained
that "the starting point of the modern religions of progress is an
eschatological anticipation of a future salvation."[38] Löwith's ambiguity also obscured his interpretation of modern pessimism. The
eschatological, apocalyptic interpretation of history is pessimistic;
redemption implies here a revolutionary break with a depraved
history. The providential, progressive interpretation of history is
optimistic; progress even implied human self-assertion and the self-
justification of the present, for Blumenberg. On this point, Taubes
was more coherent. In connecting modern thought to eschatology,
he opted more univocally for an apocalyptic and revolutionary

---

36. Löwith, 60.
37. Blumenberg, *Legitimacy,* 32. For a similar criticism, see Amos Funkenstein, *Heilsplan und natürliche Entwicklung: Formen der Gegenwartsbestimmung
im Geschichtsdenken des hohen Mittelalters* (Munich: Nymphenburg, 1965).
38. Löwith, *Meaning in History*, 61.

interpretation of eschatology and hence for a pessimistic understanding of history that ultimately implied the Gnostic rejection of all historical immanence.

Jacob Taubes: Apocalypticism, Gnosis, and Modernity

In 1949, Hans Jonas received an invitation from Jacob Taubes to discuss the latter's recently published book, *Occidental Eschatology*. In his book, Taubes referred repeatedly to Jonas's *Gnosticism and the Spirit of Late Antiquity*.[39] Not unlike Jonas, Taubes's eschatological analysis of the history of Western thought recognized Gnostic features in modern philosophy. Jonas, however, knew neither Taubes nor the book in question, and asked his colleague Karl Löwith whether he was familiar with Taubes's work:

> Before the meeting I asked Karl Löwith, "Do you happen to know a Jacob Taubes?" "Of course I know him," he replied. "Well could you tell me something about him? He's sent me a letter. I've never heard of him, but he refers to a book he's written and asks to meet me. Do you know the book?" "Oh, yes," he said, "I know the book." "Well, is it any good?" At that he said, laughing, "Oh, it's a very good book. And that's no accident—half of it's by you and the other half's by me."[40]

The thematic scope of Taubes's *Occidental Eschatology* was strikingly similar to that of Löwith's *Meaning in History*: both developed a genealogy of the modern historical consciousness by uncovering its eschatological roots, both argued that the secularization of eschatology originated in Joachim of Fiore's medieval philosophy of history, and both agreed that it culminated in the nineteenth-century philosophies of Hegel and Marx. However, since Löwith's *Meaning in History* (1949) was published two years later than Taubes's *Occidental Eschatology* (1947), one would expect that

---

39. Hans Jonas, *Gnosis und spätantiker Geist* (Göttingen: Vandenhoeck und Ruprecht, 1934–54).

40. Hans Jonas, *Memoirs*, trans. Krishna Winston (Lebanon, NH: University Press of New England, 2008), 168.

Löwith was influenced by Taubes rather than vice versa, as Jonas recounted. As a matter of fact, the influence of Taubes's conception of eschatology on Löwith's book was minimal. Löwith referred only twice to *Occidental Eschatology*,[41] as he had already developed his basic thesis on the secularization of eschatology in several texts from the early 1940s, that is, before the publication of *Occidental Eschatology*.[42] In this regard, the line of influence has to be reversed. The numerous references to Löwith's *Von Hegel zu Nietzsche* (*From Hegel to Nietzsche*) in Taubes's *Occidental Eschatology* clearly prove the former's profound influence on Taubes's early thought. In the autobiographical introduction to *Ad Carl Schmitt*, Taubes even explicitly praised this very same book: "It was like the scales falling from my eyes as I grasped the line that Löwith traced from Hegel via Marx and Kierkegaard to Nietzsche."[43]

Löwith and Jonas suggested that Taubes's analysis, though interesting, largely plagiarized their own work. Taubes indeed heavily relied on both Jonas's conception of Gnosticism and Löwith's interpretation of the secularization of eschatology. Although Taubes had a dubious reputation as an intellectual, has often been accused of plagiarism, and can hardly be called an original thinker, his *Occidental Eschatology* is highly relevant if one wants to gain insight into the German Gnosticism debates. Taubes's main strength as an intellectual was his ability to recognize the potential for debate and comparison in existing scholarship rather than conceiving of innovative theories himself. Thus, Taubes can be considered the originator and mediator of the postwar debates on modern Gnosticism. The originality of *Occidental Eschatology* precisely consisted in bringing the two perspectives of modern Gnosticism and secularized eschatology together.

---

41. Löwith, *Meaning in History*, 248n19 and 255–56n4.

42. Karl Löwith, *Von Hegel zu Nietzsche: Der revolutionaire Bruch im Denken des neunzehnten Jahrhunderts* (Zurich: Europa, 1941), pt. 1, chaps. 1, 5; Karl Löwith, "Nietzsche's Doctrine of Eternal Recurrence," *Journal of the History of Ideas* 6, no. 3 (1945): 274.

43. Jacob Taubes, *To Carl Schmitt: Letters and Reflections*, trans. Keith Tribe (New York: Columbia University Press, 2013), 2.

In reading Löwith's reflections on eschatology in the light of Gnosticism, Taubes emphasized the apocalyptic and pessimistic aspects of eschatology. Unlike Christian eschatology, which was central in Löwith, the ancient heresy of Gnosticism explicitly emphasized the fundamental depravity of the immanent world, and the absolute necessity of eschatological salvation from this evil world.[44] In light of this, Taubes's conception of eschatology was apocalyptic rather than Christian. He even argued that the orthodox Christianity of the Middle Ages did not have eschatology. Because of its focus on a purely transcendent and individual salvation, traditional Christian eschatology lost its fundamentally historical nature. For Taubes, the imminent and revolutionary threat of the Apocalypse is discarded in the Christian providential interpretation of history. Since the imminence and the historicity of the end of time are essential in Taubes's concept of eschatology, he primarily referred to Apocalypticism and Gnosticism, which behold "the turning point not in some indeterminate future but entirely proximate."[45]

This emphasis on Apocalypticism aligned Taubes's thought with Jewish messianism and with the revival of this tradition in early twentieth-century German-Jewish thought. Thinkers like Gershom Scholem, Walter Benjamin, and Ernst Bloch all found in Jewish messianism a theological tool both to make sense of and to remedy secular modernity.[46] Unlike Christian eschatology, messianism is by definition apocalyptic. For Scholem, this meant that in Judaism redemption appears as a public and visible event, taking place in or at the end of history. He opposed this to the Christian concept

44. For Taubes's notion of Gnosticism, see Carsten Colpe, "Das eschatologische Wiederlager der Politik: Zu Jacob Taubes' Gnosisbild," in *Abendländische Eschatologie: Ad Jacob Taubes,* ed. Richard Faber, Eveline Goodman-Thau, and Thomas Macho (Würzberg: Königshausen und Neumann, 2001), 105–29.

45. Taubes, *Occidental Eschatology,* 10.

46. See Anson Rabinbach, "Between Enlightenment and Apocalypse: Benjamin, Bloch, and Modern German Jewish Messianism," *New German Critique* 34 (1984): 78–124; Paul Mendes-Flohr, "'To Brush History against the Grain': The Eschatology of the Frankfurt School and Ernst Bloch," *Journal of the American Academy of Religion* 51, no. 4 (1983): 631–50.

of redemption that takes place personally and spiritually.[47] The apocalyptic nature of messianic redemption also shows itself in its radical opposition to historical immanence. Unlike Christian providence and modern progress, messianism never posits redemption as the result of historical evolutions but rather as the repudiation of history itself. Benjamin stated in his "Theological-Political Fragment" that "nothing that is historical can relate itself, from its own ground, to anything messianic. Therefore, the Kingdom of God is not the telos of the historical dynamic; it cannot be established as a goal."[48] This messianic-apocalyptic opposition against the world and history culminated in Bloch's *Spirit of Utopia*. "This book," he said, "will never make peace with the world."[49] Bloch's concept of utopia implied an overcoming of history and a radical critique of all exiting reality. Utopianism is premised on a cultural pessimism characteristic of all apocalyptic thinking: "The task and problem here is to make our acknowledged permanence triumph over empirical adversity, over our own insufficiency, that is: to overcome, . . . through the Apocalypse, as the absolute work of the Son of Man, the history that cannot be experienced in its entirety."[50] This apocalyptic dynamic that Bloch ascribed to modern revolution and utopia was both secular and theological. Although he emphasized that modern utopia can be man-made, rejecting its theological aspects would inevitably compromise the utopian pursuit of that which is radically other than this world.

This modern Jewish messianism clearly suited Taubes's conception of eschatology, in particular, and his philosophical thinking, in general. His Gnostic-apocalyptic motto *No spiritual investment in the world as it is* indeed repeated the messianic critique of all

---

47. Gershom Scholem, "Toward an Understanding of the Messianic Idea in Judaism," in *The Messianic Idea in Judaism* (New York: Schocken, 1971), 1. See also chapter 3 in this book.

48. Walter Benjamin, "Theological-Political Fragment," in *Selected Writings*, vol. 3, *1935–1938*, ed. Howard Eiland and Michael Jennings (Cambridge, MA: Harvard University Press, 2006), 305.

49. Ernst Bloch, *The Spirit of Utopia*, trans. Anthony A. Nassar (Stanford: Stanford University Press, 2000), 247.

50. Bloch, *Spirit of Utopia*, 255.

historical immanence. In spite of being a German-Jewish thinker himself, however, Taubes never mentioned the messianic tradition in *Occidental Eschatology*. Instead, he focused almost exclusively on the apocalyptic heresies in Christianity, thus implicitly challenging the radical distinction that Scholem made between the apocalyptic messianism of Judaism and the nonapocalyptic eschatology of Christianity.[51] Again, the originality of Taubes's position consisted in bringing together two radically divergent perspectives, applying as it were the insights of the modern Jewish messianists to Christian eschatology. For *Occidental Eschatology* primarily discussed figures like Jesus and Paul, and was interested in the apocalyptic features of the ancient Christian heresy of Gnosticism or of modern revolutionary heretics like Thomas Müntzer or the Anabaptists. On this point, Taubes's position probably came closest to Bloch's, which recognized the same revolutionary potential in early Christianity and in the revolutionary Christian heresies as in Jewish messianism. Bloch even wrote an entire book on Thomas Müntzer's "theology of revolution," which Taubes frequently referenced.[52] More importantly, Bloch was also fascinated by Jewish messianism's "latent Gnosticism."[53] The worldview that underlay Bloch's apocalyptic concept of utopia had obvious Gnostic overtones.[54] This is especially true of the section in *The Spirit of Utopia* entitled "Forms of Universal Self-Encounter, or, Eschatology."

---

51. Taubes later criticized Scholem more explicitly on this point: Jacob Taubes, "The Price of Messianism," in *From Cult to Culture: Fragments toward a Critique of Historical Reason*, ed. Charlotte Elisheva Fonrobert and Amir Engel (Stanford: Stanford University Press, 2010), 3–9. See also chapter 3 in this book.

52. Ernst Bloch, *Thomas Münzer als Theologe der Revolution* (Munich: Kurt Wolff, 1921).

53. Ernst Bloch, *Geist der Utopie* (Munich: Verlag von Duncker und Humblot, 1918), 330.

54. For Bloch's modern Gnosticism, see Pauen, *Dithyrambiker des Untergangs*, 199–254; Richard Faber, *Politische Dämonologie: Über modernen Marcionismus* (Würzburg: Königshausen und Neumann, 2007), 45–92. Not unlike his colleagues from the Frankfurt school Benjamin and Bloch, Theodor W. Adorno also recognized the connection between utopian hope and Gnostic pessimism in his lectures from 1964–65: "Without the hope that things might improve with time, the heinous aspects of the world and its ways really would become immortalized in thought and creation itself would be turned into the work of a gnostic demon."

Here, he wrote about "the God of this world, ever more clearly becoming Satan," and associated this notion with "the demiurgic principle," finally adding, "So maliciously random is the world's causal nexus."[55] For Bloch, Apocalypticism, messianism, and modern utopianism all shared this Gnostic pessimism. In its turn, this pessimism and the experience of worldly evil immediately entailed the possibility of radical critique, revolution, and redemption. Bloch concluded his book accordingly: "What was specific to *The Spirit of Utopia* became especially definite, something entrusted peculiarly to evil, as to its remedy: revolutionary gnosis."[56]

In *Occidental Eschatology*, Taubes also used the notions of eschatology, Apocalypticism, and Gnosticism interchangeably, albeit for different reasons than Bloch. These religious movements, he argued, introduced together a new experience of history that radically broke with the classic Greek conceptions of being and time. Despite their widely divergent modes of expression, the Gnostic and the apocalyptic speculations ultimately shared a sense of existential alienation: "In their narration of the history of the world the apocalyptic myths introduce self-estrangement as a dramatic leitmotif, and it is on this very theme that the more theoretical, ontological speculations of gnosis are founded. The boundaries between Apocalypticism and gnosis are, of course, fluid."[57] Taubes actually repeated Jonas's interpretation of the existential role of alienation in Gnosticism and applied it to Apocalypticism. In Gnosticism, human beings are estranged from themselves because they are ontologically separated from their divine origins. The Gnostics saw themselves as prisoners in a godless world. This alienation gave rise to a radically dualistic ontology, for Jonas and Taubes. God himself is alienated and estranged from the world to the extent that he is radically separated from it. On this point, Taubes almost literally copied Jonas: "God and the world are not distant

---

Theodor W. Adorno, *History and Freedom: Lectures, 1964–1965*, ed. Rolf Tiedemann and trans. Rodney Livingstone (Cambridge: Polity Press, 2006), 148.

55. Bloch, *Spirit of Utopia*, 274, 270.

56. Bloch, 279.

57. Taubes, *Occidental Eschatology*, 36.

but estranged and divided, and therefore hold each other in mutual tension. Just as there is nothing of God in the cosmos, so God is the nothing of the world."[58] This radical separation between God and world entailed, in Gnosticism and Apocalytpicism alike, an extremely pessimistic ontology that simply reversed the optimism of Greek cosmology and rejected the Christian notion of creation. "Even if in the earliest statements of Apocalypticism the world is still within the sphere of God's omnipotence, then God's alienation from the World progresses until the World is identified with the fullness of evil, which God opposes as the fullness of good. The equation cosmos=skotos, world=darkness, expresses the concept of life to be found in Gnosis."[59] Emphasizing again the continuity between Gnosticism and Apocalypticism, Taubes argued how the problem of evil, which was only implicitly operative in medieval Christian eschatology, became more explicit in Apocalypticism, and was the very cornerstone of the Gnostic ontology.

Taubes then showed how Gnosticism cast the historical content of Apocalypticism in an ontological mold. The historical separation between the present world and the future kingdom of God was transformed into an ontological antithesis between transcendence and immanence, between good and evil. The ontological perspective of Gnosticism, however, did not abolish the historical and eschatological features of Apocalypticsm. On the contrary, the ontological evil of Gnostic cosmology is conceivable only as historical evil, according to Taubes's interpretation. Just like Löwith, but more explicitly so, Taubes argued that the problem of evil is fundamentally intertwined with historicity and with the linear direction of time. In Gnosticism, immanence is depraved insofar as it is finite and historical. The world is finite because its being is temporary and because it has a history with a beginning and an end. The world's essential temporality is the antithesis of God's eternity. For Taubes, history is by definition the absence of the divine, hence sinful and depraved: "History is identical with the aeon of sin, which

---

58. Taubes, 39. See Hans Jonas, *Gnosis und spätantiker Geist* (Göttingen: Vandenhoeck und Ruprecht, 1934), 1:151: "God—the nothing of the world."

59. Taubes, *Occidental Eschatology,* 28.

is embedded between creation and redemption."[60] Therefore, the end of time is conceivable only as salvation. The end of history is indeed the transition from temporality to eternity, that is, from godlessness to God, and from evil to good.

Taubes's *Occidental Eschatology* now tried to make the case that these Gnostic and apocalyptic dynamics returned in modern thought: "Apocalypticism and Gnosis inaugurate a new form of thinking which, though submerged by Aristotelian and Scholastic logic, has been preserved into the present and was taken up and further developed by Hegel and Marx."[61] For Taubes, the early modern age and German idealism were eschatological to the extent that Apocalypticism and Gnosticism resurged in modern culture; not because Christian theology was secularized. In this respect, Taubes was less concerned than Löwith with the question of secularization, and with the ways it distorted eschatology. Rather, he wanted to fathom, in a more substantial way, what it means for modernity to be eschatological. For Taubes, the pessimistic cosmology of Gnosticism and Apocalypticism as well as their historical structure returned in what he called the "apocalyptic waves of the modern age."[62] The discovery of the genealogical connection between modernity and eschatology is also the discovery of the epochal role of pessimism in modern thought and German idealism: "It is vitally important for the history of German idealism that the eschatology of early Christianity, even if clandestine and apocryphal, continue . . . alongside the Enlightenment, so that knowledge of the radical nature of evil is preserved."[63]

Taubes suggested that the historical and pessimistic dynamics of eschatology were suppressed, marginalized, and hereticized at two different moments in the history of the West—first, in the medieval church and the Scholastic tradition; second, during the Enlightenment. Instead of secularizing medieval Christian eschatology, modernity radically broke with traditional Christianity and revived the

---

60. Taubes, 28.
61. Taubes, 35.
62. Taubes, 85.
63. Taubes, 130.

revolutionary Gnostic and apocalyptic spirit of early Christianity. This Gnostic and apocalyptic modernity rejected Scholasticism's static and ahistorical rationality. In the same vein, Taubes's interpretation of modernity was also highly critical of the rationalism and optimism of the Enlightenment. Referring to the earthquake of Lisbon, he claims that modern human beings are confronted with experiences of evil and irrationality "which the system of reason is unable to fathom."[64] Thus rejecting the Enlightenment as well as Scholasticism, Taubes maintained that modern thinkers could interpret the world neither as a reflection of a transcendent reality nor as a good and rationally ordered universe. Thus, the modern world is cut off from transcendence, and becomes a de-divinized, meaningless, and possibly evil facticity that is not created for the sake of human beings. In this nihilistic worldview, Taubes recognized, not unlike Jonas, the modern return of Gnosticism.[65]

Because of this disappearance of transcendence, not only did the modern world lose its goodness and rationality, but the traditional Christian hope for a transcendent salvation also became insignificant. For this reason, Taubes argued, modernity reintroduced history: "The Copernican world is an earth deprived of the heaven, which used to be an archetype to the earth. . . . Because the space between heaven and earth has become meaningless, Copernican man seeks to revolutionize the world according to an ideal that can become reality in the course of time."[66] Instead of seeking personal and spiritual salvation in Christian transcendence, modern humanity redirected its gaze toward fulfillment in the future. To the extent that the future is the touchstone of modern thought, modernity recovered Apocalypticism's eschatology. Consequently, the meaning of the modern world is no longer determined a priori but depends solely upon its historical development. The historical realization of this meaning is not gradual, but it is a revolutionary, apocalyptic

---

64. Taubes, 86.

65. Hans Jonas, "Gnosticism and Modern Nihilism." *Social Research* 19 (1952): 430–52.

66. Taubes, *Occidental Eschatology*, 137.

rupture at the end of history as the eschatological transition from evil to goodness.

In line with Scholem, Benjamin, and Bloch, Taubes evaluated the role of eschatology in modern thought very positively. Unlike these interwar Jewish thinkers, he did not associate eschatology with Jewish messianism but with Christianity. Thus, he zeroed in on an existing debate within Christian theology on the nature of eschatology and secularization rather than on a Jewish debate.[67] Taubes obviously relied on Löwith's theory of the secularization of Christian eschatology, but he also took up Christian theological sources like Hans Urs von Balthasar's *Apokalypse der deutschen Seele (Apocalypse of the German Soul)*.[68] These Christian writings on eschatology as well as Löwith's theory were typically critical of the secularization of eschatology in modernity. Taubes applied the positive evaluation of modern messianism to these more negative Christian interpretations of secularized eschatology. Unlike Löwith and the Christian theologians, he did not criticize modernity on account of its eschatological nature. On the contrary, he recognized in these apocalyptic waves of modernity the fundamental dynamics of Western thought. The modern renaissance of eschatology is not a corruption of theology, as Löwith and many Christian thinkers believed, but merely its legitimate transformation.

In his personal life as well as in his philosophical writings, Taubes was fascinated with the antinomian, revolutionary, and nihilistic nature of Apocalyptcism, which he recognized in secular as well as religious phenomena. In an article on Taubes's early thought, Joshua Robert Gold argued that the scope of Taubes's account of Apocalypticism went beyond the domain of theology: "Taubes transforms the theological concept of Apocalypse into a critical category, and he does so by thinking through the

---

67. See Rudolf Bultmann, *Geschichte und Eschatologie* (Tübingen: J.C.B. Mohr, 1958). For Albert Schweitzer's notion of consistent eschatology, see Albert Schweitzer, *Das Messianitäts- und Leidensgeheimnis: Eine Skizze des Lebens Jesu* (Tübingen: J.C.B. Mohr, 1956).

68. Hans Urs von Balthasar, *Apokalypse der deutschen Seele: Studien zu einer Lehre von letzten Haltungen*, 3 vols. (Salzburg: Anton Pustet, 1937).

political and ethical implications of the claim that there is an end to time."[69] In this regard, Taubes's notion of eschatology did not have the function of a general definition of the nature of modernity, which the concepts of secularization and secularized eschatology definitely had. Taubes was interested in the different continuities between the theological concept of theology and secular politics, thus affiliating himself more with Carl Schmitt's project of political theology than with Löwith's theory of secularization. From a Schmittian perspective, Taubes could have seen the Apocalypse as the ultimate state of exception that overcomes liberal normativity's static lawfulness. Taubes was typically sympathetic toward political revolution, whether it was on the Far Left or Right. In addition to this political-theological interest, however, he was just as much concerned with the ways in which the structure of apocalyptic theology returned in modern aesthetics, and in the artistic avant-garde.[70]

Although Taubes was decidedly less critical of modernity than Löwith, he was highly dismissive of any ahistorical or static modes of thinking. The church and the Enlightenment epitomized, for Taubes, these moments where the eschatological and apocalyptic dynamics of Western thought were absent or artificially fixated. Western eschatology can be brought to a halt, argued Taubes, only by the illegitimate historical proclamation of the kingdom of God. The claim that salvation is realized in the present makes a relative and merely historical perspective absolute and inviolable by history: "Medievalism and the Enlightenment are two static spheres of life in Europe. The Medieval Church and the church of the Enlightenment establish themselves as absolute and are based on the equation the church *is* the Kingdom of God."[71] For Taubes, the strength of Western eschatology was precisely the impossibility of any historical position to claim absoluteness. In the light of redemption, everything that is historical can be reversed, overthrown, and

---

69. Joshua R. Gold, "Jacob Taubes: Apocalypse from Below," *Telos* 134 (2006): 142.

70. See Jacob Taubes, "Notes on Surrealism," in *From Cult to Culture*, 98–123.

71. Taubes, *Occidental Eschatology*, 86 (emphasis original).

annihilated. Thus, Taubes warned, not unlike Löwith, "Beware of
the illusion that redemption happens on the stage of history."[72] In
Occidental Eschatology, Taubes never mentioned a third moment
after the Middle Ages and the Enlightenment when the illusion of
a historical salvation was created. Nonetheless, it is not hard to
imagine what Taubes might have had in mind when he was writing his dissertation, which would later be published as *Occidental
Eschatology*, in Switzerland during the Second World War. Could
he not have written just as much that "Nazism established itself
as absolute and was based on the equation: the *Third Reich* is the
Kingdom of God"? For this is exactly what some of Taubes's contemporaries later argued, associating the notion of a Third Reich
with Joachim of Fiore's Trinitarian philosophy of history or showing how fascism presented itself as an "immanent eschaton."[73]

Criticism versus Apologetics of Political Eschatology

Given the particular historical context of Löwith's and Taubes's
discussions of eschatology—two Jewish thinkers, writing only a
few years after the end of the Second World War—it is hardly a coincidence that their concern with the problem of evil is so central.
Unlike Hannah Arendt's more conceptual analyses, Taubes's and
Löwith's historical outlook kept them from confronting the evils
of totalitarianism and the Holocaust head-on.[74] Nonetheless, these
events must have been in the back of their minds when they tried
to make sense of the history of Western thought. Although neither thinker developed an explicit interpretation of totalitarianism,
their respective positions can be thought through in such a way
that they do allow for an implied evaluation of it. Eric Voegelin did

72. Jacob Taubes, "Price of Messianism," 9.
73. Voegelin, *New Science of Politics*, 110–17. See also Cohn, *Pursuit of the Millennium*, 288.
74. See Hannah Arendt, *The Origins of Totalitarianism* (New York: Harcourt Brace, 1951); Hannah Arendt, *Eichmann in Jerusalem: A Report on the Banality of Evil* (New York: Penguin Books, 1977).

exactly that. Heavily relying on Taubes and Löwith, Voegelin used the concepts of secularized eschatology and modern Gnosticism to develop an analysis of totalitarian politics.[75]

Strikingly, neither Taubes's nor Löwith's philosophical framework allowed for any real consolation, or even hope to overcome the evils of the Second World War. For Löwith, hope is no longer an option today. On the contrary, it was the modern eschatological structure of hope itself that had made the horrible events of the Second World War possible in the first place. In this regard, totalitarianism appeared as the ultimate human attempt to create a historical eschaton as the immanent overcoming of evil. For Löwith, this was the most explosive and dangerous feature of modern hubris, as it paradoxically generated new and even greater forms of evil: "There are in history not only 'flowers of evil' but also evils which are the fruit of too much good will and of a mistaken Christianity that confounds the fundamental distinction between redemptive events and profane happenings, between *Heilsgeschehen* and *Weltgeschichte*."[76] Because the fundamentalist faith—"too much good will"—in a final solution for the problem of evil has proven to be fraught with dangers, Löwith proposed to abandon the eschatological principle of hope altogether. In view of its modern and totalitarian excesses, every form of eschatology had become suspect. He thereby rejected any simple return to Christianity or, for that matter, Judaism as a solution to the modern crisis. In contrast to many of his Jewish contemporaries, including Gershom Scholem, Walter Benjamin, Ernst Bloch, and Taubes himself, Löwith wondered "whether the future is really the proper horizon of a truly human existence."[77] The Judeo-Christian perspective of future-oriented hope had been perverted to such an extent that it had become impossible to return to its transcendent origins. In line with another Jewish thinker, Leo Strauss, Löwith rather suggested that human beings had to recover their place within the ahistorical cosmos of Greek philosophy by interpreting existence

---

75. Voegelin, *New Science of Politics*, 110–27.
76. Löwith, *Meaning in History*, 203.
77. Löwith, 204.

as constituted in relation to an eternal and immutable order. He proposed to abandon the linear conception of time, and revalue pagan, Greek-Nietzschean eternal recurrence.

Taubes, in his turn, rejected such a naïve return to Greek philosophy. In an often-quoted interview he stated: "There is no eternal return, time does not enable nonchalance; rather it is distress."[78] In this respect, he equally dismissed any naïve abstract hope for the future. Quoting the same line in an article on Taubes's time in Jerusalem, Nitzan Lebovic adds: "Two short years after the end of the most horrible destruction the Jewish people had ever known, Taubes offered no comforting words. Against the passive hope of those confronting the end of the world, Taubes emphasized in 1947 the need for an immediate decision . . . Taubes had in mind a Schmittian operation from within the destructive situation: it involved using and abusing destruction as a tool, acknowledging its inevitability."[79] In this respect, the evil of the Holocaust would be the ultimate confirmation of the Gnostic-apocalyptic worldview for Taubes. Paradigmatically, it is in the most intense moments of violent oppression and radical evil that the end of time is nearest. The Holocaust itself could appear for Taubes as the apocalyptic catastrophe par excellence, as Martin Treml maintained.[80] The force of the Apocalypse is always primarily destructive, nihilistic, and negative. Moreover, it is only from within this negation itself that an absent God, who is in every respect opposite to the world, can manifest himself. God's fundamental absence is the condition of possibility of apocalyptic redemption. Thus, the case of Taubes is an interesting exception to Anson Rabinbach's observation that "unlike after World War I, neither intellectuals nor politicians were inclined to adopt a redemptive vision, . . . World War II might therefore be called 'the

---

78. "Jacob Taubes," in *Denken, das an der Zeit ist,* ed. Florian Rötzer (Frankfurt am Main: Suhrkamp, 1987), 317.

79. Nitzan Lebovic, "The Jerusalem School: The Theopolitical Hour," *New German Critique* 35 (2008): 106.

80. See Martin Treml, "Nachwort," in Jacob Taubes, *Abendländische Eschatologie* (Munich: Matthes und Seitz, 2007), 287.

nonredemptive apocalypse'."[81] Unlike any of his contemporaries, Taubes strangely upheld the notion of a redemptive Apocalypse, which Rabinbach ascribed to interwar thinkers like Benjamin and Bloch, even after the Second World War.

Taubes would have emphasized the fundamental importance of eschatology and Apocalypticism as the only possible response to totalitarian politics. Western modernity could therefore retain its legitimacy, even after the horrors of the Second World War, but only to the extent that it continued the legacy of occidental eschatology. Contrary to Löwith, eschatology did not appear as the cause of the modern crisis, but rather as its solution. By the same token, it was not the presence of (secularized) eschatology, but its absence that made totalitarianism dangerous for Taubes. Totalitarianism entailed a return to paganism, and was therefore a reaction against Apocalypticism and its survival in modern times: "If Fascism is a reaction against the Jewish or Christian apocalyptic, which in many respects attracts something apocalyptic itself, it is still a pagan reactionary form and opposes itself against the philosophy of history."[82]

In view of these opposed political evaluations of eschatology, the main difference between Löwith and Taubes can be highlighted again. As Peter Gordon sharply put it, "Taubes embraced the eschatological tradition Löwith reviled."[83] The real problem for Löwith was not so much eschatology's illegitimate secularization, but eschatology as such, and by extension even history in general. This

---

81. Anson Rabinbach, *In the Shadow of Catastrophe: German Intellectuals between Apocalypse and Enlightenment* (Berkeley: University of California Press, 1997), 11.

82. "Jacob Taubes," in *Denken, das an der Zeit ist,* 319.

83. Peter Gordon, "Jacob Taubes, Karl Löwith, and the Interpretation of Jewish History," in *German-Jewish Thought between Religion and Politics,* ed. Christian Wiese and Martina Urban (Boston: De Gruyter, 2012), 351. It is also on this point that most other comparisons between Löwith and Taubes have focused: Jürgen Moltmann, *The Coming of God: Christian Eschatology,* trans. Margaret Kohl (London: SCM Press, 1996), 41–44; Mark Jaeger, "Jacob Taubes und Karl Löwith: Apologie und Kritik des Heilsgeschichtlichen Denkens," in *Abendländische Eschatologie: Ad Jacob Taubes,* ed. Richard Faber, Eveline Goodman-Thau, and Thomas Macho (Würzberg: Königshausen und Neumann, 2001), 485–508.

is where Blumenberg's interpretation of Löwith tends to miss the point. Löwith's theory of modernity did not just revolve around the concept of secularization, and the way in which it deprived Christianity of its transcendent eschatology. Rather, it revolved around the meaning and illegitimacy of eschatology itself, and the way in which it constituted modernity. As Odo Marquard cryptically summarized in his own writings on eschatology and the philosophy of history, "For Löwith, the philosophy of history is the legitimate continuation of the illegitimacy of biblical salvation, for Taubes it is the legitimate continuation of its legitimacy: for Löwith the theology of history as such was already bad; for Taubes the philosophy of history is still, and even a fortiori, good: for both the category of secularization does not, as it does for Blumenberg, function as category of distinction."[84] While heavily relying on Löwith's conceptual framework, Taubes reversed its valuation.[85] Despite the former's undeniable influence, Taubes's thought is much closer to the messianic legacy of Gershom Scholem and Walter Benjamin than to Löwith, as chapters 3 and 4 will show in detail. Taubes's later *Die politische Theologie des Paulus* (*The Political Theology of Paul*) showed more clearly that he continued to be fascinated with those phenomena Löwith radically mistrusted—not only with eschatology and the philosophy of history, but just as much with heresy and nihilism.

---

84. Odo Marquard, *Schwierigkeiten mit der Geschichtsphilosophie: Aufsätze* (Frankfurt am Main: Suhrkamp, 1973), 15.

85. See Jerry Z. Muller, "Reisender in Ideeen: Jacob Taubes zwischen New York, Jerusalem, Berlin und Paris," in *"Ich staune, dass Sei in dieser Luft atmen können": Deutsch-jüdische Intellektuelle in Deutschland nach 1945*, ed. Monika Boll and Raphael Gross (Frankfurt am Main: Fischer Taschenbuch, 2013), 48.

3

Subversion

Heresy and Its Modern Afterlives

However difficult it is to give an accurate historical account of Gnosticism, nothing seems more evident than that it is a heresy. If all substantial definitions are ultimately bound to fail, one could at least characterize Gnosticism negatively as the opposite of Christian or Jewish orthodoxy. Gnosticism has indeed often been presented as being a mere subversion of established religious norms and traditions. Approached from the perspective of heresy, Gnosticism is first and foremost associated with a countercultural drive that has no substantial doctrine of its own except for the active negation of all existing conventions. This subversive attitude that is often ascribed to Gnosticism was an important practical implication of Taubes's *No spiritual investment in the world as it is.* The world-negation that this motto implied should not necessarily be understood in an exclusively metaphysical sense, but it can just as much entail a rule of negative political or moral conduct. If one has no attachment to the world as it is, and hence to its political, cultural, and moral status quo, the most reasonable thing to do is to subvert its current order and recreate it from scratch. From a political perspective, this Gnostic attitude is the complete opposite of any conservative impulse to justify the world and society as they currently are. In this regard, Gnosticism appeared as the first genuinely revolutionary movement in history, and accordingly as the historical precursor of the avant-gardist, anarchist, reformatory, and revolutionary subversions of the modern age.

In antiquity, Gnosticism's revolutionary attitude primarily took shape in the rejection of religious tradition and in the antinomian rejection of religious law. This Gnostic antinomianism could entail both a passive negation and an active transgression of the law. Instead of acting in accordance with the traditional religious norms and virtues, the Gnostic could decide either not to act at all or to act in opposition to the law. The former attitude led to asceticism, the latter to libertinism. The libertine attitude was obviously the more subversive of the two, and ranged from a general nonconformist attitude that caricaturizes biblical stories and practices to more explicit forms of immoral action such as sexual transgression and violence. These antinomian rejections of the law always had an explicitly religious motivation. The Gnostic did not reject religious and moral standards from a secular point of view; rather, he discovered a completely different religious truth beyond these immanent conventions that radically delegitimized their religious and moral authority.

In modernity, the antinomian criticism of religious tradition has led to the possibility of secularism and atheism. The modern legacy of antinomianism, however, goes beyond the secular criticism of religion. The concept of revolution, for example, can be read as the modern counterpart of Gnosticism's heretical subversions. This was indeed an important aspect of Eric Voegelin's and Jacob Taubes's analyses of Gnosticism and modernity. Taking the modern scientific innovations, religious reformations, political revolutions (French, American, Communist, anarchist, Fascist, etc.), and aesthetic avant-gardes into account, revolution was omnipresent in the modern age. If modernity is the age of revolutions and if the concept of revolution goes back to ancient Gnostic heresy, modernity can just as well be called the Gnostic age. Calling modernity Gnostic thus suggests the modern afterlife of religious subversion. In line with Carl Schmitt's general claim that "all significant concepts of the modern theory of the state are secularized theological concepts,"[1] one could specify that modern revolution is secularized Gnostic heresy. Just like the ancient Gnostic, the

---

1. Carl Schmitt, *Political Theology: Four Chapters on the Concept of Sovereignty*, trans. George Schwab (Chicago: University of Chicago Press, 1985), 36.

modern revolutionary is not attached to the current sociopolitical, aesthetic, or religious reality; he rather wants to oppose it as radically as possible by negating, abolishing, and changing its order. Along these lines, it has been argued that ancient Gnosticism and modern thought ultimately shared a revolutionary "critique of all existence."[2]

The Gnostic subversions and their revolutionary afterlives have often been evaluated very negatively. Almost by definition, the concepts of Gnosticism and heresy have a negative connotation. This connotation is developed in the first section of this chapter. From the point of view of orthodoxy, heresy is an inauthentic and dangerous deformation of an original religious doctrine. Heresy refuses to conform to a religious tradition, and in the case of Gnostic heresy it even explicitly wants to abolish tradition. For a conservative thinker like Eric Voegelin this already sufficed to radically condemn Gnosticism and its return in modernity. Such a condemnation of Gnostic heresy seems evident in view of the subversive potential for violence, transgression, and immoral behavior, which are also the dangers of the modern revolution. However, a fascination with the subversive and destructive aspects of heresy is also conceivable. The remaining sections of the chapter focus on two Jewish intellectuals who studied the phenomenon of heresy extensively, often focusing on the heresy of Gnosticism: Gershom Scholem and his disloyal student Jacob Taubes. Instead of taking the conservative or orthodox position that Voegelin represented, Scholem and Taubes chose the less usual option of identifying with the subversive and revolutionary impulse of (Gnostic) heresy. Accordingly, they were also more favorably disposed to the secularization of heresy.

Gnosticism as a Metaphor for Heresy

In view of recent research into the history of early Christianity, Gnosticism has become an extremely problematical concept,

---

2. Michael Pauen, *Dithyrambiker des Untergangs: Gnostizismus in Ästhetik und Philosophie der Moderne* (Berlin: Akademie, 1994), 15.

especially as a historical category. In *What Is Gnosticism?* Karen King even argued that "there was and is no such thing as Gnosticism, if we mean by that some kind of ancient religious entity with a single origin and distinct set of characteristics." Rather, she maintained that Gnosticism is "a term invented in the early modern period to aid in defining the boundaries of normative Christianity."[3] This observation that Gnosticism is a modern construction rather than a historical reality seems to invalidate, right from the start, the entire project of connecting Gnosticism to modernity. Indeed, what sense does it make to define the modern age in terms of this allegedly ancient religion of Gnosticism if the concept of Gnosticism is itself a modern invention (King traces it back to Henry Moore, who coined the term in 1669[4])? Moreover, what can Gnosticism tell us about the modern condition if it is not even clear what Gnosticism itself is?

Although it is impossible to uphold the historical validity of Eric Voegelin's and Jacob Taubes's theories in the light of King's claim, her observations do teach us a lot about the implied motivations behind their respective philosophical projects. Rather than just invalidating the notion of Gnosticism and its possible relation to modernity, King actually offered us the conceptual tools to understand the idiosyncratic attempts to trace modernity back to ancient Gnosticism. If Gnosticism is a rhetorical tool, constructed by Christian orthodoxy to help determine the "normative identity of Christianity," inevitably the concept has certain—mainly negative—connotations that simply cannot be dismissed. In King's view, Gnosticism is essentially a metaphor for heresy: "Gnosticism has been constructed largely as a heretical other in relation to diverse and fluctuating understandings of orthodox Christianity. This means that modern historical constructions of Gnosticism reflect many of the characteristics and strategies used by early Christian polemicists like Irenaeus and Tertullian to construct heresy."[5]

---

3. Karen L. King, *What Is Gnosticism?* (Cambridge, MA: Harvard University Press, 2003), 2.

4. King, *What Is Gnosticism?* 7.

5. King, 3.

King argued that the metaphorical connotations of heresy will return, either implicitly or explicitly, in any discourse on Gnosticism. Accordingly, this metaphorical background will also be present in the Gnostic genealogies of modernity. These interpretations of modernity actually dealt with the complex of heresy: what is true Christianity, and what is merely derivative?

This question is exactly what was at stake for Eric Voegelin when he called Gnosticism "the nature of modernity" in *The New Science of Politics*.[6] Strictly speaking, Voegelin was not interested in the historical relation between an illustrious ancient religion and modern philosophy or politics—even though he emphasized the historical validity of his claim as well.[7] What was really at issue is the relation between modernity and Christianity. Voegelin was actually making a normative claim about the inherent value of Christianity and the derivative nature of modern culture: from the perspective of Christianity, modernity equals heresy. Voegelin characterized modern thought as the illicit secularization of Christian theological concepts. In this regard, he subscribed to the classic secularization theorem that was developed most explicitly by his contemporaries Karl Löwith and Carl Schmitt. Especially in Löwith's case, secularization appeared as a historical process in which an original, theological content was degraded into an inauthentic, secular one. For Voegelin, this was heresy pure and simple. He did not so much claim that a heretical rather than an orthodox theological content was secularized, but that the process of secularization itself was heretical. Secular modernity is an inauthentic— hence heretical—derivation and immanentization of Christianity's

---

6. Eric Voegelin, *The New Science of Politics: An Introduction* (Chicago: University of Chicago Press, 1952), 107.

7. "On the historical continuity of Gnosticism from antiquity to modern times, let it be said here only that the connections in the development of Gnostic sects from those of the eastern Mediterranean in antiquity through the movements of the high Middle Ages up to those of Western Renaissance and Reformation have been sufficiently clarified to permit us to speak of a continuity." Eric Voegelin, "Science, Politics, and Gnosticism," in *The Collected Works of Eric Voegelin*, vol. 5, *Modernity without Restraint*, ed. Manfred Henningsen (Columbia: University of Missouri Press, 2000), 297.

transcendent message. Applied to Gnosticism, it is not the case that gnosis is secularized in modernity, but that secularization *is* Gnostic. Gnosticism, Voegelin argued, made Christianity's transcendent message of salvation immanent so as to have certain knowledge and control over it. This Gnostic immanentization, which was not only inauthentic but ultimately illusory and dangerous, then returned in a more radical guise in modernity: "Secularism could be defined as a radicalization of the earlier forms [i.e., ancient Gnosticism] of paracletic immanentism."[8] In other words, Voegelin recuperated the concept of (Gnostic) heresy, not to engage in a polemic with ancient competitors of Christian orthodoxy, but to develop a critique of secular culture. As King argued, no discourse on heresy is actually interested in the heretical phenomenon as such. What is at stake is an indirect treatment of orthodoxy—in the case of Voegelin, a treatment of Christian orthodoxy and its relation to secular culture. Voegelin's interpretation, therefore, presupposed the discourse of heresy that constituted the ineradicable metaphorical background of the notion of Gnosticism. As such, Gnosticism is an extremely negative concept that functions as a category of illegitimacy. Indeed, Voegelin radically questioned modernity's legitimacy on the basis of its Gnostic nature.

The notion of heresy is absolutely crucial to make sense of the twentieth-century reflections on Gnosticism. By definition, heresy has a negative connotation: it is an inauthentic, dangerous, derivative creed that is in every way inferior to the original message of orthodoxy. From a rhetorical perspective, heresy is "the other" of religion's doctrinal core, in the sense that it serves as its limit concept. The negative concept of heresy is necessary to delimit the positive identity of orthodoxy itself. In the case of Gnostic heresy as well, this negative connotation is almost ineradicable. On this point, King recognized a clear continuity between the ancient Christian heresiologists (Irenaeus and Tertullian) and modern and twentieth-century Gnosticism research. Voegelin's use of this notion is one example of such a carryover of Gnosticism's essentially negative

---

8. Voegelin, *New Science of Politics*, 125.

connotation; Hans Jonas's concept of Gnosticism is another. Even as one of the most profound Gnosticism scholars of the twentieth century, Jonas was not able to escape entirely the strength of Gnosticism's implied rhetoric. Especially in his postwar philosophical writings, he was extremely critical of Gnostic dualism and associated it with the dangerous nihilistic trends of modern thought.[9] But even in his historical studies on ancient gnosis Jonas's implied evaluation of Gnosticism was unambiguously negative. In the seemingly neutral essay "Delimitation of the Gnostic Phenomenon," Jonas described Gnosticism's lack of authenticity as one of its main characteristics: "It is, in short, secondary and derivative mythology, its artificiality somehow belonging to its character."[10] Although Jonas interpreted Gnosticism as an inauthentic derivation from mythical thought rather than from Christianity, he unconsciously adopted the typical vocabulary of the theological discourse on heresy.[11] In a similar vein, Jonas denounced Gnosticism's impiety and its rejection of religious traditions. Finally, he also recognized in Gnosticism a dangerous tendency toward fundamentalism: "Its rejection of the world, far from the serenity or resignation of other non-worldly creeds, is of peculiar, sometimes vituperative violence, and we generally note a tendency to extremism, to excess in fantasy and feeling."[12]

If one is fascinated by this Gnostic potential for the extreme, however, heresy can become a more valuable cultural and religious resource than heresiologists and Gnosticism scholars have traditionally wanted to admit. The thought of Gershom Scholem and Jacob Taubes is a perfect example of this more positive approach

---

9. See Hans Jonas, "Gnosticism and Modern Nihilism," *Social Research* 19 (1952): 430–52; Hans Jonas, "Life, Death, and the Body in the Theory of Being," in *The Phenomenon of Life* (New York: Harper and Row, 1966), 7–37.

10. Hans Jonas, "Delimitation of the Gnostic Phenomenon: Typological and Historical," in *Le origini dello Gnosticismo: Colloquio di Messina 13–18 Aprile 1966*, ed. Ugo Bianchi (Leiden: Brill, 1967), 100.

11. "His evaluation of Gnosticism reproduced many of the elements of the polemicists' discourse of heresy, and he constructed it as the deficient 'other' of true religion." King, *What Is Gnosticism?* 135.

12. Jonas, "Delimitation," 100.

to the phenomenon of heresy. Instead of interpreting heresy as a mere derivation of an original religious creed, these two Jewish intellectuals wanted to study heresy for its own sake. Accordingly, they had an entirely different and much more positive take on the phenomenon of heresy and its possible afterlife in modernity. This different approach can partly be explained by their Jewish background, as the influence of the Christian heresiology is less decisive for Taubes and Scholem than for Voegelin. Their different approach, however, also attested to an incompatible philosophical agenda: some thinkers, like Voegelin and Jonas, have a more conservative disposition toward emphasizing the value of established norms and of a religious and philosophical canon; others, like Taubes and Scholem, are simply more attracted to the subversive potentials of a (religious) avant-garde. With regard to Gnosticism, these latter two thinkers were genuinely interested in exactly those phenomena that Jonas and Voegelin radically denounced, that is, in Gnosticism's nihilistic, fundamentalist, impious, or world-negating dynamics.

Since the concepts of heresy and Gnosticism are constructions of established religion to clearly define the boundaries of orthodoxy, the research into the nature of heresy has almost always presupposed the biased point of view of orthodoxy. If, however, heretical movements are studied for their own sake, the constructed nature of the concepts of heresy and orthodoxy could be unmasked. Rather than an inauthentic derivation of original religiosity, heresy could now appear as a sincere manifestation of the same religious message that underlies orthodoxy. Such research would show that the boundaries between heresy and orthodoxy are not always as straightforward as often presented. The distinction between both would be blurred: if orthodoxy can no longer found its legitimacy in its alleged authenticity, heresy could become as genuine an expression of a religious creed as orthodoxy itself. This project can be termed *the deconstruction of orthodoxy*, and it will be shown how the thought of Gershom Scholem and Jacob Taubes can be characterized as such. This deconstruction of orthodoxy is essentially the unmasking of the theological construct of heresy on which the legitimacy of orthodox religion is negatively grounded. As the concept of orthodoxy makes sense only in opposition to the concept of heresy, the deconstruction of the distinction between heresy and orthodoxy essentially involves the delegitimization of orthodoxy itself.

Karen King pursued this project from a Christian perspective. She argued that the distinction between heretical Gnosticism and genuine Christianity is simply incorrect from a historical point of view: "Early Christian literature does not divide neatly into orthodox and heretical camps; there are unexpected overlaps and surprising similarities, and crucial points of difference are not always where we expect them to be."[13] This argument can equally be applied to the distinction between orthodoxy and heresy in the Jewish tradition. A deconstruction of Jewish orthodoxy will obviously not only take Gnosticism into account, which can be just as much a Jewish heresy as a Christian one, but will also involve a whole range of specifically Jewish heresies. Scholem's and Taubes's deconstructions of orthodoxy, however, went beyond the merely historical observation that King made with regard to early Christian orthodoxy. What was at stake for them is ultimately a more fundamental theological issue. Scholem and Taubes deconstructed the notion of orthodoxy by claiming that the subversive and countercultural dynamics of heresy actually do more justice to the messianic core of the Jewish religion than does rabbinic orthodoxy. In this regard, they reversed the traditional theological rhetoric on heresy: orthodoxy no longer appears as the authentic and original doctrine from which heresy is derived, but is itself an inauthentic and ossified derivative of a religious dynamism that precedes the distinction between heresy and orthodoxy.

Taubes's and, to a lesser extent, Scholem's deconstructions of orthodoxy allowed for a reflection on the secularization of heresy. If Voegelin considered secular modernity as a heretical derivation of a more authentic religious doctrine, the deconstruction of the distinction between heresy and orthodoxy also entails a deconstruction of the distinction between secular modernity and religion. This was a key aspect of Taubes's intellectual project. Just like Löwith's

---

13. King, *What Is Gnosticism?* 152.

and Voegelin's theories of secularization, Taubes emphasized the continuities between religion and modernity. In line with his own ideas on heresy, however, he did not consider secularization as an inauthentic derivation of a more original religious doctrine. Rather, secularization was, just like heresy, one of the many possible and legitimate transformations of an inherently dynamical religious force. Taubes recognized this secular continuation of heresy and religion primarily in subversive phenomena as diverse as modern political revolt and modernist avant-garde.

The Scholem-Taubes Soap

The story of Gershom Scholem and his disloyal student Jacob Taubes was one of continuing intellectual quarrel and even personal enmity. Scholem was probably the most enigmatic modern scholar of Judaism, Taubes the *enfant terrible* of postwar Jewish philosophy and one of Scholem's most talented students. Nevertheless, their story was also one of a deep intellectual affinity that both were stubbornly unwilling to face.

Jacob Taubes studied at the Hebrew University in Jerusalem under Scholem's supervision from 1949 to 1952, but their professional and personal relationship went irreparably wrong around the fall of 1951. The immediate cause of their break was Taubes's lack of discretion after Scholem had confided in him. Scholem had told Taubes that he had found indications of mental illness in the last parts of his student Joseph Weiss's dissertation, and Taubes had shared this information with Weiss himself. Scholem first raised this issue in a letter dated October 7, 1951, and asked Taubes, "How [can] you think to combine such a grave breach of trust at all with our continuing collaboration?"[14] Their discord seemed initially only personal and took shape in petty and childish ways in the years to come. The list of anecdotes is endless—Scholem hiding in Jean Bollack's bathroom when Taubes paid him a surprise visit

---

14. Gershom Scholem, "Letter to Jacob Taubes of October 7, 1951," in *Briefe: 1948–1970*, ed. Thomas Sparr (Munich: C.H. Beck, 1995), 26–27.

in Paris; Taubes's wife, Susan, calling Scholem an "SS man"; Jacob
Taubes mocking Scholem's enmity in the last letter he ever wrote
to him: "First with Taubes you met radical evil in person, . . . a
Kabbalist of your standing should not have to turn fifty before
getting to know radical evil."[15] The suicides of both Joseph Weiss
and Susan Taubes would later give this personal enmity a bitter
aftertaste.

Scholem blocked any attempt at reconciliation by emphasizing time and again that their quarrel was personal and not merely
academic.[16] Nonetheless, these personal issues coincided from the
outset with a profound intellectual disagreement centered on Jewish messianism. The point where these intellectual and personal
motives intersected most clearly was Taubes's lecture "Messianism
and Its Price," delivered at the World Jewish Congress in Jerusalem
in 1979. Later published as "The Price of Messianism,"[17] this lecture was a frontal attack on Scholem's conception of Jewish messianism; Jan Assmann even suggested it was "perhaps the most
radical critique that Scholem encountered in his lifetime."[18] Such
a claim might sound a little exaggerated, especially because Scholem's thought had been radically challenged before, for example,

---

15. See, respectively, Jacob Taubes, *Der Preis der Messianismus: Briefe von
Jacob Taubes an Gershom Scholem und andere Materialen,* ed. Elletra Stimilli
(Würzburg: Könighausen und Neumann, 2006), 115; Christina Pareigis, "The
Connecting Paths of Nomads, Wanderers, Exiles: Stationen einer Korrespondenz;
Nachwort," in Susan Taubes, *Die Korrespondenz mit Jacob Taubes 1950–51*
(Munich: Wilhelm Fink, 2011), 288; Jacob Taubes, "Letter to Gershom Scholem
of December 5, 1979," in *Der Preis der Messianismus,* 123.

16. In a reply to a rather tactless attempt at reconciliation from Taubes, Scholem made this very clear: "What has separated us irreparably for 25 years does not
belong in any way to the vanities of academic life, but are existential judgments
of my life (not academic, but moral, if I may use this word)." Gershom Scholem,
"Letter to Jacob Taubes of March 24, 1977," in *Briefe: 1971–1982,* ed. I. Shedletzky (Munich: C.H. Beck, 2000), 154; Gershom Scholem, *A Life in Letters,* ed.
and trans. Anthony David Skinner (Cambridge, MA: Harvard University Press,
2002), 467–68.

17. Jacob Taubes, "The Price of Messianism," in *From Cult to Culture: Fragments toward a Critique of Historical Reason,* ed. Charlotte E. Fonrobert and
Amir Engel (Stanford: Stanford University Press, 2010), 1–9.

18. Wolf-Daniel Hartwich, Aleida Assmann, and Jan Assmann, "Introduction," in Fonrobert and Engel, *From Cult to Culture,* xxiv.

by Baruch Kurzweil's and Isaiah Tishby's critiques.[19] Nonetheless, Assmann's claim does bear witness to the impact of Taubes's lecture. Since Taubes had not been welcome in Jerusalem for over twenty-five years, the choice of topic for this lecture was hardly coincidental. Combining a complete lack of tact and a hint of revenge, he could not possibly have chosen a more controversial topic for his lecture. In his talk, Taubes developed a radical critique of Scholem's rigid distinction between Christian and Jewish concepts of salvation. In his essay "Zum Verständnis der messianischen Idee im Judentum" (Toward an Understanding of the Messianic Idea in Judaism), Scholem had opposed the Jewish, messianic concept of public and historical redemption to the Christian concept of inner and spiritual redemption.[20] Taubes argued that this distinction is artificial and negates the historical dynamism of messianism: rather than a mere abstract theological concept, messianism is a real historical force that can take very different forms when confronted with concrete historical contexts, hopes, and disappointments. One such essential transformation according to Taubes is the Christian interiorization of salvation. Contrary to Scholem, he considered interiorization as a perfectly legitimate form of messianism, even as the inevitable outcome of its historical logic. By showing how the Christian concept of inner salvation belongs to the messianic tradition, Taubes actually deconstructed Scholem's rigid distinction between Christianity and Judaism.

In view of their intellectual irreconcilability and personal enmity, one could ask whether it makes sense at all to study Taubes and Scholem together. Except if there were a common ground that

---

19. For the debate between Scholem and Kurzweil, see David Myers, "The Scholem-Kurzweil Debate and Modern Jewish Historiography," *Modern Judaism* 6, no. 3 (1986): 261–86. For Tishby's criticism of Scholem, see Isaiah Tishby, "The Messianic Idea and Messianic Trends in the Growth of Hasidism," *Zion* 32 (1967): 1–45.

20. Gershom Scholem, "Zum Verständnis der messianischen Idee im Judentum," in *Judaica 1* (Frankfurt am Main: Suhrkamp, 1963), 7–74; English translation: Gershom Scholem, "Toward an Understanding of the Messianic Idea in Judaism," in *The Messianic Idea in Judaism and Other Essays on Jewish Spirituality* (New York: Schocken, 1971), 1.

both failed to recognize, such an endeavor would simply result in an enumeration of their unbridgeable differences. Their radical differences notwithstanding, there is indeed a shared intellectual project that unites these two thinkers and makes a promising dialogue between them possible. Since a sincere intellectual dialogue was never possible in real life, it might be interesting to stage such a dialogue and reassess their differences from the perspective of a common intellectual vantage point.[21] Taubes and Scholem clearly disagreed about the *scope* of messianism; for Scholem, messianism was an inner-Jewish phenomenon, whereas for Taubes it was a dynamic phenomenon that structures Judaism, Christianity, and secularism alike. They had, however, a surprisingly similar concept of the *nature* of messianism. Taubes, arguably, adopted Scholem's interpretation of messianism as a subversive, paradoxical, anarchic, apocalyptic, and revolutionary phenomenon that is best understood from the perspective of heresy.

A crucial theological presupposition of Taubes's and Scholem's thought was exactly this subversive fascination with the phenomenon of heresy and their discontent with both rabbinic and liberal Judaism.[22] The rabbinic tradition is characterized by a strong emphasis on law and Torah, and could be called "orthodox" or traditional Judaism; liberal Judaism is characterized by an enlightened, rationalist approach to religion that aims at the assimilation of Judaism into modern Western culture. Both strands typically suppress Judaism's messianic or revolutionary impulses. Scholem's and Taubes's research, by contrast, focused precisely on these messianic, mystic, and heretical phenomena that were negated by orthodox and modern Judaism. Instead of understanding these phenomena from the perspective of rabbinic orthodoxy as inauthentic and corrupted modes of Jewish religiosity, Scholem and Taubes wanted to

---

21. Howard Caygill applies a similar strategy in a recent article, but focuses exclusively on the role of Jewish heretic Sabbatai Zevi: Howard Caygill, "The Apostate Messiah: Scholem, Taubes, and the Occlusions of Sabbatai Zevi," *Journal of Cultural Research* 13, nos. 3–4 (2009): 191–205.

22. For a more exhaustive overview of the young Scholem's engagement with heresy, see Benjamin Lazier, *God Interrupted: Heresy and the European Imagination between the World Wars* (Princeton: Princeton University Press, 2008).

study them for their own sake—Scholem from a historical perspective, Taubes from a more interdisciplinary and philosophical perspective. In this respect, they both considered heresy as an equally legitmate or even more legitimate expression of Judaism than traditional orthodoxy. Their common theologico-philosophical project can thus be called a *deconstruction of orthodoxy*—or, more precisely, a deconstruction of the classic dividing line between heresy and orthodoxy on which the legitimacy of established, orthodox religion is negatively grounded.[23]

This shared background, however, does not negate the differences between Scholem and Taubes. On the contrary, their fundamental disagreements now become all the more obvious. Again, these differences do not so much concern the nature but the scope of their intellectual project. For Scholem, the deconstruction of orthodoxy remained within the boundaries of Judaism and concerned the distinction between Jewish heresy and orthodoxy, whereas Taubes applied his former teacher's deconstructive project to the distinction between Judaism and Christianity, as well as to the distinction between religion and secularism. In Taubes's perspective, the deconstruction of orthodoxy entailed a reflection on the secularization of heresy.

Heresy and the Deconstruction of Orthodoxy

In Gershom Scholem's work, the mystical heresy of Sabbatianism and its self-proclaimed messiah, Sabbatai Zevi (1626–1676),

---

23. Taubes's and Scholem's criticism of orthodoxy was obviously based on a very biased and caricatured conception of traditional rabbinic Judaism that bears little relation to recent scholarship on Jewish orthodoxy. See Michael Silber, "The Emergence of Ultra-Orthodoxy: The Invention of a Tradition," in *The Uses of Tradition: Jewish Continuity in the Modern Era*, ed. Jack Wertheimer (New York: Jewish Theological Seminary of America, 1992), 23–84; Jacob Katz, *A House Divided: Orthodoxy and Schism in Nineteenth-Century Central European Jewry*, trans. Ziporah Brody (Lebanon, NH: University Press of New England, 2005). It is generally recognized that Scholem's understanding of traditional Judaism is to a certain extent a caricature: Elisheva Carlebach, *The Pursuit of Heresy* (New York: Columbia University Press, 1990).

were without doubt the most important examples of Jewish heresy. The study of Sabbatianism indeed occupied him throughout
his career. In his renowned essay on Sabbatianism from 1936, "Redemption through Sin," Scholem showed how Zevi and his followers "form an integral part of Jewish history and deserve to be
studied objectively."[24] From a methodological perspective, this aim
for objectivity and the attempt to avoid the normative perspective of orthodox Judaism obviously make sense in studying Jewish heresy. From a religious perspective, Scholem's project was an
extreme provocation, as Sabbatian heresy negated almost everything that Judaism has ever stood for. From the perspective of rabbinic Judaism, Sabbatai Zevi was indeed much more than a simple
pseudo-Messiah. Although such pseudo-Messiahs are omnipresent
in Jewish history, they have never seriously challenged the legitimacy of rabbinic Judaism as such. For different reasons, the Sabbatian messiah did.

After claiming to be the Jewish messiah and gathering an enormous following, Sabbatai Zevi incomprehensibly converted to
Islam. This apostasy was probably the most decisive reason why
Zevi posed such a serious threat to traditional Judaism. The Turk-
ish sultan, who had captured the dissident Zevi, offered him a
choice between death and conversion. Although death as a martyr
would have been the more appropriate choice for a Jew, his conversion as such is not yet problematic.[25] One would expect that

---

24. Gershom Scholem, "Redemption through Sin," in *The Messianic Idea in
Judaism and Other Essays on Jewish Spirituality* (New York: Schocken, 1971),
78. See also Gershom Scholem, *Major Trends in Jewish Mysticism* (New York:
Schocken Books, 1946), 287–324; Gershom Scholem, *Sabbatai Zevi: The Mystical
Messiah, 1626–1676* (Princeton: Princeton University Press, 1973).

25. Jacob Taubes caricaturizes this beautifully: "Now, I know that death is a
hard thing, but nothing is more ingrained in the Jewish soul and in the Jewish body
than to die for the sanctification of the name of God. For that you don't need to
be a Messiah, you don't need to be a Rabbi, for this the communities in Worms
slaughtered their Children, so that they wouldn't fall into the hands of the Crusad-
ers. And in Speyer. So it really isn't a problem. Yet the astonishing thing occurs:
he converts to Islam and gets a position at court with an annual salary." Jacob
Taubes, *The Political Theology of Paul,* trans. Dana Hollander (Stanford: Stanford
University Press, 2004), 8–9.

Zevi's apostasy had just proven to his followers that he had been a false Messiah all along, and that they had recognized his deception. Zevi's followers did nothing of the kind. Instead of admitting that their inner messianic belief had been falsified by history, the Sabbatians paradoxically wanted to maintain their faith in this apostate Messiah. This paradox was for Scholem the crux of Sabbatian heresy: " 'Heretical' Sabbatianism was born at the moment of Sabbatai Zevi's totally unexpected conversion, when for the first time a contradiction appeared between the two levels of the drama of redemption, that of the subjective experience of the individual on the one hand, and that of the objective historical facts on the other. . . . 'Heretical' Sabbatianism was the result of the refusal of large sections of the Jewish people to submit to the sentence of history by admitting that their own personal experience had been false and untrustworthy."[26] The central concern for Sabbatian theology was the resolution of this paradox, which consisted in the tension between subjective experience and historical facts. The Sabbatians had to explain how Zevi could be both the Jewish messiah and Muslim at the same time. The question was how Zevi could abandon Judaism and transgress Jewish law without ceasing to be the Jewish messiah. In an attempt to justify their messianic belief against a seemingly obvious historical refutation, the Sabbatians claimed that Zevi's conversion was an intrinsic part of his messianic vocation: "The apostasy of the messiah was itself a religious mystery of the most crucial importance!"[27] In order to complete the process of redemption, the Messiah had to eradicate evil root and branch, but he could do so only by descending into the realm of evil itself. If Islam and the sultan represented the oppressive forces of evil most explicitly in Zevi's time, his conversion to Islam would allow him to destroy evil from within.

Scholem argued that it is difficult to turn more radical consequences aside once this kind of reasoning is called upon. If the Messiah could transgress Jewish law and if this transgression intrinsically belonged to his mission, the validity of the law and even

---

26. Scholem, "Redemption through Sin," 88.
27. Scholem, 94.

of traditional Judaism itself was fundamentally at risk. Radical Sabbatians considered themselves Jews by negating everything that traditional Judaism had stood for. On a more concrete level, these radicals started to believe that the sinful transgression of the law would ultimately bring salvation. If the legitimacy of the law were negated by the acts of the Messiah, a sinful rather than a moral life would lead to redemption. This attitude obviously led straight into antinomianism, anarchism, and even moral and religious nihilism. Not unlike Gnosticism, radical Sabbatianism entails a complete rejection of any immanent standard or law for morality. Everything this-worldly had to be rejected and opposed, even the law itself. In messianic times, what is good or evil can no longer be determined by the religious and moral standards of olden days.

Discussing these radical consequences of Sabbatian heresy, Scholem now made his fascinating point: "And yet in spite of all this, one can hardly deny that a great deal that is authentically Jewish was embodied in these paradoxical individuals too."[28] Such a bold claim entailed a deconstruction of orthodox Judaism. Instead of rejecting the Sabbatian provocations against traditional Judaism as heretical, Scholem considered them to be a genuine expression of Jewish religiosity. He rendered the distinction between heresy and orthodoxy obsolete because the very concept of orthodoxy is based on the alleged authenticity of its religious message as opposed to the derivative nature of heresy. But Scholem's deconstruction of orthodoxy was more than just a fundamental equivalence of heresy and orthodoxy. Indeed, he claimed that Sabbatianism's anarchic, nihilistic, or antinomian impulses imply a purer form of Jewish messianism that he deemed completely absent in traditional Judaism. Ultimately, the dynamics of heresy and their disruptive powers do more justice to the nature of Jewish messianism than the orthodoxy of rabbinic Judaism. More is at stake here than a mere historiography of Jewish heresy. Scholem was using heresy to determine the normative identity of Judaism and, as the next section will show, its role in modern culture. Focusing on the heresies

---

28. Scholem, 106.

of Gnosticism and pantheism in Scholem's work, Benjamin Lazier drew the same conclusion: "The program is clear: heresy in the service of Jewish self-assertion."[29]

If we look at the picture Scholem drew in his renowned essay "The Messianic Idea in Judaism," messianism coincides to a large extent with the religious impulse of heresy itself, and in particular with that of Sabbatian heresy. By definition, heresy rejects the established religious norms and traditions. Messianism, too, wants to overcome the established system of values, as the coming of the Messiah will transform the moral and metaphysical constitution of the old world itself. Scholem therefore ascribed a strong anarchic force to messianism. In view of the new messianic realm of freedom, the old laws and constraints lose their validity, and even the legitimacy of lawfulness itself is undermined. Although this anarchism, which Scholem clearly recognized in Sabbatianism, is an essential force in Judaism, it is completely overlooked in the conservatism of rabbinic Judaism.[30] In this regard, Scholem recognized an irresolvable tension in Judaism between messianic and conservative forces. The messianic anarchically breaks the old order, whereas the conservative systematically defends the legitimacy of the order of law (*Halakhah*) by projecting the messianic hope into a distant future. In this regard, Scholem radically criticized rabbinic Judaism's negation of the essentially apocalyptic nature of messianism in favor of the coherence and stability of its creed: "From the point of view of *Halakhah*, to be sure, Judaism appears as a well-ordered house, and it is a profound truth that a well-ordered house is a dangerous thing. Something of messianic apocalypticism penetrates into this house; perhaps I can best describe it as a kind of anarchic breeze."[31]

Scholem's anarchism entailed an apocalyptic interpretation of Jewish messianism.[32] In his view, messianism is neither an abstract

---

29. Lazier, *God Interrupted*, 143.

30. For an overview of the role of anarchism in Scholem's (early) thought, see Eric Jacobson, *Metaphysics of the Profane: The Political Theology of Walter Benjamin and Gershom Scholem* (New York: Columbia University Press, 2003), 52–81.

31. Scholem, "Messianic Idea," 21.

32. For a critical reflection on Scholem's apocalyptic interpretation of messianism, see Moshe Idel, "Messianic Scholars: On the Early Israeli Scholarship, Politics, and Messianism," *Modern Judaism* 32 (2012): 34–36.

hope for change in the distant future nor a gradual and immanent development, which is also characteristic of the secular idea of
progress. The coming of the Messiah could both entail a restorative
return to a primeval state of perfection and a utopian creation of
something completely new, but the messianic shift itself always has
to be sudden, catastrophic and without relation to previous history
or to immanence: "Redemption is not the product of immanent
developments such as we find in modern Western reinterpretations
of Messianism since the enlightenment where, secularized as the
belief in progress, Messianism still displayed unbroken and immense vigor. It is rather transcendence breaking in upon history, an
intrusion in which history itself perishes, transformed in its ruin because it is struck by a beam of light shining into it from an outside
source."[33] The messianic force introduces something completely
foreign to immanence but can do so only by catastrophically destroying the immanent order of history and anarchically uprooting
political lawfulness. This apocalyptic dualism implies the complete
incommensurability of the before and after. In a way it relegates
the ontological dualism between transcendence and immanence,
which is characteristic of Gnosticism, to the sphere of history. The
redemptive meeting point of two opposite poles—historical versus
messianic, immanent versus transcendent—is therefore essentially
paradoxical. This paradox is initially manifested in Apocalypticism's catastrophic nature. In order to attain the positive of redemption, the negative of catastrophe is necessary, as redemption
is not possible without the nihilistic, anarchic revolution against
immanence. This catastrophe can take shape along the lines of the
traditional apocalyptic imaginaries—war, famine, killing, natural
disasters, and so on—but it can just as much become a conscious
religious practice to enact the catastrophe in immoral and antinomian behavior—"in apostasy and the desecration of God's name,
in forgetting of the Torah and the upsetting of all moral order to
the point of dissolving the laws of nature."[34] Scholem implicitly
referred here to the paradoxes of Sabbatianism. The paradoxical nature of Sabbatian faith, even more so than its anarchic and

33. Scholem, "Messianic Idea," 10.
34. Scholem, 12.

antinomian forces, expressed the true nature of Jewish messianism. In a discussion of Scholem's work on Sabbatianism, Jacob Taubes made this claim even more explicit: "The concentration on the paradoxical," said Taubes, belongs to "the inner logic of the messianic."[35]

More fundamentally, the paradox of messianism consists in the necessary discrepancy between the messianic faith and the historical facts that always seem to contradict it. As was the case in Sabbatianism, every historical faith in a concrete messiah is confronted with the fact that reality actually remains unchanged after the coming of the messiah. Every messianic movement, by definition, leads to such untenably paradoxical situations in which the most absurd, dangerous, or nihilistic arguments are applied to resolve this tension. As the faith in concrete salvation, messianism seems untenable, but when reduced to a mere abstract hope in the future it always remains unfulfilled. This ambiguity is what Scholem called *the price of messianism*: "The messianic idea is not only consolation and hope. Every attempt to realize it tears open abysses which lead each of its manifestations ad absurdum. There is something grand about living in hope, but at the same time there is something profoundly unreal about it."[36] A genuinely Jewish life thus consists in this messianic tension: it cannot reject messianism, as rabbinic and liberal Judaism tended to do, but neither can it go all the way and expect a concrete historical moment as the messianic age. For Scholem, and even more so for Taubes, the latter option would have been the danger of Sabbatianism. The messianic is essentially a transhistorical force that breaks into history. Only from this transcendent perspective can the Messiah create something truly other and redemptive. If, however, the messianic lacks this transhistorical force, its revolution against world history is merely negative and will end up in nihilism. Already deviating significantly from Scholem's point of view, Taubes concluded as follows: "If one is to enter irrevocably into history, it is imperative to beware of the

35. Taubes, *Political Theology of Paul*, 10.
36. Scholem, "Messianic Idea," 35.

illusion that redemption . . . happens on the stage of history. For every attempt to bring about redemption on the level of history without a transfiguration of the messianic idea leads straight into the abyss."[37]

In order to avoid these dangers, Taubes argued that the messianic idea must be interiorized. In his essay "The Price of Messianism," which develops a direct critique of Scholem's conception of messianism, Taubes recognized this transformation of messianism first and foremost in (early) Christianity, where salvation is no longer considered as a public, political, or historical force but rather as spiritual fulfillment. As we will see, Taubes considered it the great merit of Paul and his Gnostic successor Marcion to respond to the paradox of a crucified Messiah by interiorizing redemption. On this point, Taubes radically criticized Scholem's position. For Scholem, Christianity and the Christian conception of an inner redemption had nothing to do with Jewish messianism whatsoever. On the very first page of "The Messianic Idea in Judaism," he introduced a rigid distinction between Judaism and Christianity, which was based precisely on the interiorization of redemption: "Judaism, in all its forms and manifestations, has always maintained a concept of redemption as an event which takes place publicly, on the stage of history and within the community. . . . In contrast, Christianity conceives redemption as an event in the spiritual and unseen realm, an event which is reflected in the soul, in the private world of each individual."[38] While the interiorization of redemption was for Scholem the dividing line between Jewish messianism and Christianity, and hence foreign to Judaism as such, the process of interiorization was for Taubes the true fulfillment of the logic of Jewish messianism. Early Christianity is therefore the prime example of Jewish messianism. Taubes argued that "redemption is bound to be conceived as an event in the spiritual realm, reflected in the human soul." Radically criticizing Scholem's distinction between Christian and Jewish redemption, he added that "interiorization is not

---

37. Taubes, "Price of Messianism," 9.
38. Scholem, "Messianic Idea," 1.

a dividing line between 'Judaism' and 'Christianity'; it signifies a crisis within Jewish eschatology [messianism]."[39]

Just like Sabbatianism, early Christianity was faced with a crisis of its messianic faith, with the paradoxical failure of its Messiah. Christ had died on the cross, but the world had not changed, at least not in any political or apocalyptic sense. In spite of this ostensible failure, the early Christians paradoxically wanted to persevere in their messianic faith. Unlike Sabbatianism, Christianity solved this paradox by interiorizing redemption, according to Taubes. Salvation failed to take place publicly and historically, but it actually happened spiritually. Redemption has nothing to do with any change or action in the external world, but it is only by turning inward that we can discover a redemptive transcendence. If messianic redemption indeed presupposes an antinomian revolution against everything this-worldly, one cannot judge whether redemption has taken place on the basis of immanent and historical criteria. The immanent and historical sphere is by definition unredeemed, and the attempt to realize the messianic within history is a dangerous illusion for Taubes. In this regard, interiorization is the *necessary* outcome of messianism. In Christianity, the interiorization concretely took shape in Gnosticism's conception of an inner mystical knowledge (gnosis) or in Paul's emphasis on "faith" rather than on "works" ("For we hold that one is justified by faith apart from works of the law," Romans 3:28). In Paul's perspective, redemption could be achieved only through faith, rather than through a pious life in accordance with Jewish law. It is important to note that, for Taubes, this dynamic had nothing to do with the Lutheran *sola fide* but only with the inherently paradoxical nature of the messianic. The rejection of works was the outcome of the necessary interiorization of the messianic into the paradoxical faith in a crucified Messiah. Precisely because this messianic faith had been explicitly contradicted by historical facts, it transcended the works of the law: "Here something is demanded at such a high price to the human soul that all works are nothing

---

39. Taubes, "Price of Messianism," 4.

by comparison."[40] The interiorization of the messianic into "faith" ultimately also safeguarded Christianity's antinomianism from the nihilistic action within the external world that is characteristic of the "work" on redemption through sin. When confronted with a paradoxical crisis in messianic faith—the crucifixion of the Messiah in Christianity or his apostasy in Sabbatianism—interiorization is the only legitimate response. Any other response would lead to absurd and untenable aberrations.

In view of Taubes's reflections on the interiorization of messianism, the substantial distinction between Judaism and (early) Christianity crumbles. For Taubes, Pauline Christianity was a genuine expression of Jewish messianism. Taubes thus unmasked the opposition between Judaism and Christianity as a theological construct—as a rhetorical invention of the church fathers or as a "hangover from the classic Jewish-Christian controversy of the Middle Ages."[41] From the historical perspective of early Christianity (before AD 70), it did not make sense for Taubes to differentiate between Judaism and Christianity. He claimed that "the word 'Christian' . . . doesn't yet exist for Paul."[42] Taubes was actually deconstructing Scholem's rigid distinction between Judaism and Christianity. The distinction, on which Scholem insisted, is ultimately just a theological construct that cannot be maintained in view of the consequences of Scholem's own criticism of orthodoxy and his conception of messianism. If the distinction between Jewish heresy and orthodoxy became problematical for Scholem in the perspective of the messianic idea, so did the distinction between Judaism and Christianity for Taubes. Just like Scholem, Taubes was actually just "gathering the heretic back into the fold,"[43] but he was not interested in an enigmatic Jewish mystic like Sabbatai Zevi, who is only a marginal figure from the point of view of world history. Rather, Taubes applied Scholem's strategy to an infinitely more influential Jewish heretic—namely, the founder of

---

40. Taubes, *Political Theology of Paul*, 10.
41. Taubes, "Price of Messianism," 4.
42. Taubes, *Political Theology of Paul*, 21.
43. Taubes, 11.

Christianity, Paul of Tarsus. In spite of Taubes's radical criticism of Scholem, he was actually just taking Scholem's deconstruction of orthodoxy one logical step further. Taubes did not just deconstruct the traditional distinction between heresy and orthodoxy by claiming that heresy is a purer representation of Jewish religiosity; he radicalized Scholem's project by applying it to the very distinction between Judaism and the Jewish heresy of Christianity.

For Taubes, Pauline Christianity represented the messianic idea in its purest and hence most paradoxical form: "Paul comes and says: here is the Messiah. People have got to know that he died on the cross. . . . This is a death by defamation. Here is the son of David hanging on the Cross! . . . This is a total and monstrous inversion of the values of Roman and Jewish thought." In spite of all this, Taubes claimed that Paul is "more Jewish than any re-form rabbi, or any liberal rabbi."[44] In other words, Paul was a Jew precisely in his rejection of Judaism. Taubes literally applied Scholem's strategy for interpreting Sabbatai Zevi to Paul. All the elements of Scholem's analysis of Zevi are present in Taubes's reading of Paul: the heretic as the more genuine representative of the religious message, the antinomian rejection of Jewish tradition, and most importantly the inherently paradoxical nature of messianism. Taubes discovered the same paradoxes in Pauline Christianity as those Scholem had recognized in Sabbatianism but hesitated to apply to Christianity. Scholem did recognize the paradoxical nature of Christian messianism in the crucifixion of the Messiah, but immediately denounced it as far less radical than the paradoxes of Sabbatai Zevi's apostasy: "What now took place in Sabbatianism was similar to what happened in Christianity at the time of the apostles, the chief difference being the shifting of the tragic moment in the Messiah's destiny from his crucifixion to his apostasy, a change which rendered the paradox in question even more severe."[45] Taubes did not seem to be convinced by Scholem's distinction between the death and apostasy, and applied the latter's framework for analyzing Sabbatianism to Pauline Christianity.

---

44. Taubes, 10.
45. Scholem, "Redemption through Sin," 96.

Ultimately, everything that Taubes wrote about Paul is already present in Scholem, but Taubes faced up to the ultimate consequences of this line of thought. In his very first letter to Scholem, he already announced this project of reading Paul through Sabbatai Zevi, and immediately admitted Scholem's profound influence: "It was through M. tr. [*Major Trends in Jewish Mysticism*] that I conceived of the problem of a comparison between Paulinian and Sabbatian theology."[46] Although Scholem already hinted at such a comparison in his chapter on Sabbatianism in *Major Trends in Jewish Mysticism*, he expressed his doubts about such a project in his reply to Taubes.[47] For Scholem, the comparison between Paul and Zevi would not succeed without a sufficient historical background in Pauline Christianity and Sabbatianism, which Taubes clearly lacked: "A comparison between Paulinian and Sabbatian theology would be interesting and fruitful, if you can approach it from both sides."[48]

Finally, Taubes also adopted Scholem's reflections on antinomianism in his reading of Paul. Criticism of the law is indeed omnipresent in Paul's writings, especially in his Letter to the Romans. Taubes, however, did not interpret the concept of law in a strictly Jewish way. He claimed that the Pauline concept of law not only designates religious law, but also refers to the metaphysical concept of lawfulness in Hellenistic philosophy and to the political concept of Roman law. This latter connotation in particular charged Paul's theological writings with an intense political message. On this point, Taubes appealed to Carl Schmitt's concept of political theology and subscribed to the inevitable intertwinement of

---

46. Jacob Taubes, "Letter to Gershom Scholem of October 27, 1947," in Taubes, *Der Preis der Messianismus*, 94.

47. "Inevitably there is a far-reaching and highly illuminating similarity between the religious characteristics and the development of Sabbatianism on the one hand, and of Christianity on the other." Scholem, *Major Trends*, 307.

48. "Ein Vergleich der paulinischen mit sabbatianischen theologie wäre interessant und fruchtbar, wenn Sie an die beiden Seiten herankönnen." Gershom Scholem, "Letter to Jacob Taubes of December 30, 1947," Jacob Taubes Archiv, ZfL-Berlin. This unpublished letter will appear in the complete correspondence between Jacob Taubes and Gershom Scholem: Jacob Taubes, *Taubes in Jerusalem*, ed. Nitzan Lebovic and Martin Treml (Berlin: Wilhelm Fink, 2019).

theological and political motives in Paul's thought. In this regard, Paul's theological rejection of the law was actually a political rebellion against the legitimacy of the Roman Empire. This idea is an important leitmotif in Taubes's posthumously published intellectual testament *Die politische Theologie des Paulus* (*The Political Theology of Paul*).

With regard to its content, Taubes's political theology deviated from Schmitt's project. While Schmitt wanted to legitimize political power by showing how it mirrors divine sovereignty, Taubes emphasized that Paul's political theology uproots the foundations of Roman power, and for that matter of political legitimacy as such. In this regard, Taubes was a political theologian of the apocalyptic revolution, whereas he considered Schmitt to be an "apocalyptic prophet of counterrevolution."[49] Taubes summarized their difference as follows: "The jurist has to legitimate the world as it is. . . . Schmitt's interest was in only one thing: that the party, that the chaos not rise to the top, that the state remain. That isn't my worldview, that isn't my experience. I can imagine as an apocalyptic: let it all go down. I have no spiritual investment in the world as it is."[50] In the same vein, Taubes read Paul as an apocalyptic prophet who is ultimately interested in the end of the world as the transcendent destruction of immanent lawfulness. Taubes's and Paul's apocalyptic perspective did not allow for any legitimate political order. Taubes's position has often been called a "negative political theology."[51] Scholem's interpretation of messianic anarchism also resurfaces here. Anarchism is indeed the conviction that political order is wrong as such. Consequently, messianism does not coincide with any gradual change within the immanent realm of politics; rather, it implies total revolution. Such a revolution aims at the anarchic and apocalyptic destruction of politics,

49. Jacob Taubes, *To Carl Schmitt: Letters and Reflections,* trans. Keith Tribe (New York: Columbia University Press, 2013), 1.

50. Jacob Taubes, "Appendix A: The Jacob Taubes-Carl Schmitt Story," in Taubes, *Political Theology of Paul,* 103.

51. Wolf-Daniel Hartwich, Aleida Assmann, and Jan Assmann, "Afterword," in Taubes, *Political Theology of Paul,* 139.

but its antinomianism is just as much directed against metaphysical, moral, and religious law. For Taubes, only Pauline Christianity actually ventured such a complete revolution. It was therefore not just the only significant example of genuine messianism; it was also the single most important revolution in world history. Taubes adds: "It isn't *nomos* but the one who was nailed to the cross by *nomos* who is the imperator! This is incredible, and compared to this all the little revolutionaries are *nothing*. This transvaluation turns Jewish-Roman-Hellenistic upper-class theology on its head."[52]

The Secularization of Heresy

Up to this point, Taubes's project entailed a dual deconstruction of orthodoxy. In line with Scholem, he first deconstructed the distinction between Jewish orthodoxy and heresy. Deviating from Scholem's project, he then radicalized this criticism of the concept of orthodoxy to the very distinction between Judaism and Christianity. If Christianity is just a very successful Jewish heresy, the distinction between both can never be absolute. In the spirit of this dual deconstruction, Taubes introduced a third deconstruction that concerns the distinction between Judeo-Christian religion and secular modernity.[53] Taubes not only believed that heretical messianism structured Judaism and Christianity but also maintained that its legacy continues in the entire tradition of Western modernity. Moreover, he was not only interested in uncovering the religious

---

52. Taubes, *Political Theology of Paul*, 24 (emphasis original).
53. Although the characterization of Taubes's and Scholem's thought as a deconstruction of orthodoxy does not intend to suggest any relation to the French philosophy of deconstruction, there are certain parallels between Taubes's project and Jean-Luc Nancy's "deconstruction of monotheism." Not unlike Taubes, Nancy criticized the radical opposition between monotheistic religion and modernity. For Nancy, modernity is not opposed to Christianity but is itself a modification of it. The deconstruction of monotheism is an analysis of monotheistic religion, and of Christianity in particular, that shows how religion reaches beyond its traditional scope and into modernity. See Jean-Luc Nancy, *Dis-enclosure: The Deconstruction of Christianity,* trans. Bettina Bergo, Gabriel Malenfant, and Michael B. Smith (New York: Fordham University Press, 2008), 29–41.

origins of modernity but also wanted to show how the history of
the West is actually a manifestation of a single, albeit very dynamical, force—namely, messianic eschatology.

As the previous chapter has shown, Taubes's reflections on modernity and religion have to be understood in the context of the
postwar German secularization debates. Not unlike Karl Löwith
and Carl Schmitt in their theories of secularization, Taubes was
interested in unmasking the distinction between religion and secularity as a construction of modern self-understanding. By uncovering the religious roots of modern thought, Taubes showed how
modernity is less secular than it thinks it is. The role of political
theology in his thought was crucial on this point. Taubes's appeal
to Schmitt's notion, for example, reflected the significant continuities between the concepts of theology and secular politics. Going
beyond the traditional scope of political theology, Taubes was also
interested in the ramifications of theological forces in a wider range
of modern cultural manifestations. For example, he applied the
strategy of political theology to the domain of modern aesthetics in
a remarkable essay on surrealism.[54] For Taubes, surrealism's revolutionary impulse to create a surreal world—literally, a world beyond
(*sur*) the reality we know—repeated the world-negating nihilism of
Gnosticism and the revolutionary vigor of Apocalypticism in the
modern age.

Unlike Schmitt and Löwith, however, Taubes was ultimately
interested in the relation between secularization and heresy, and
more specifically in the transposition of heretical contents into
secular modernity. Taubes thereby gave his own twist to Voegelin's
interpretation of modernity as a heretical immanentization of orthodox Christianity.[55] If modernity is just a (Christian) heresy, then
Taubes's deconstruction of orthodoxy also implied a deconstruction of the distinction between religion and modern secularism.

Unlike Voegelin, Taubes did not want to discredit secular modernity on this account. On the contrary, he wanted to show that

---

54. See Jacob Taubes, "Notes on Surrealism," in Fonrobert and Engel, *From
Cult to Culture*, 98–123.
55. See Voegelin, *New Science of Politics*, 107–32.

the entire dynamic of Western culture is actually a legitimate manifestation of a single force that he calls *Abendländische Eschatologie (Occidental Eschatology)*—also the title of his doctoral dissertation and the only book he published during his lifetime.[56] Although he associated these eschatological dynamics explicitly with the apocalyptic heresy of Gnosticism, they can ultimately be secular as well as religious, Jewish as well as Christian, orthodox as well as heretical. In this regard, the belief in the end of time (eschaton) structures the entire history of the West. Sometimes these eschatological forces are very strong, while at other times they can be largely dormant. *Occidental Eschatology* basically attempted to trace the vicissitudes of eschatology in the history of the Western thought. Also on this point, Taubes's project differs significantly from Voegelin's. For Voegelin, the process of secularization itself was already heretical—secularism equals Gnosticism. What is at stake for Taubes is not this *heresy of secularization,* but the *secularization of heresy.* In his thinking, the theological contents of heretical Gnosticism and Apocalypticism are secularized in the modern age. Almost forty years after the publication of *Occidental Eschatology,* Taubes pursued a similar project in *The Political Theology of Paul.* The eschatological dynamics were obviously exceptionally active in Paul's thought. When Taubes described the relation between Paul and modern illiberals like Carl Schmitt, Walter Benjamin, and Karl Barth, he was actually interested in the modern transformations and secularizations of Paul's messianic eschatology.

Eschatology, Taubes argued, is manifested first in Judeo-Christian Apocalypticism and Gnosticism. As such, these movements radically broke with the pagan understanding of time and reality, and returned in different, sometimes even secular guises in Western history. Taubes essentially associated the dynamics of Apocalypticism and Gnosticism with the revolutionary movements in Western history, not just with the religious revolutions of Pauline Christianity or Sabbatianism, but just as much with twentieth-century

---

56. Jacob Taubes, *Occidental Eschatology,* trans. David Ratmoko (Stanford: Stanford University Press, 2009).

avant-garde or with revolutionary politics and the Marxist phi-losophy of history. It is important to emphasize that Taubes's con-ception of apocalyptic revolution was fundamentally in line with Scholem's understanding of messianism. Revolution had nothing to do with social change or progress in Taubes's perspective, but only with the historical destruction of reality in order to establish something completely other:

> Apocalypticism is at first not concerned with changing the structure of society, but directs its gaze away from this world. If revolution were to mean only replacing an existing society with a better one, then the con-nection between apocalypticism and revolution is not evident. But if revolution means opposing the totality of this world with a new totality that comprehensively founds anew in the way that it negates, namely in terms of the basic foundations, then apocalypticism is by nature revolu-tionary. Apocalypticism negates this world in its fullness.[57]

It is not clear to what extent Taubes was already influenced by Scholem's work when he was writing this several years before he visited Scholem in Jerusalem in 1949.[58] The obvious resemblance between both thinkers notwithstanding, Taubes also deviates from Scholem's interpretation of messianism by applying it to non-Jewish phenomena. For Taubes, messianism and Apocalypticism are not just Jewish theological concepts; they are historical forces that precede the distinction between Judaism and Christianity and even between religion and secularism. These theological concepts gain their full significance only when also carried over into a histor-ical analysis of modern, secular phenomena, such as revolutionary

---

57. Taubes, *Occidental Eschatology*, 9.

58. In *Occidental Eschatology*, published in 1947, Taubes never refers to Scho-lem. Unlike Scholem's work, this book is indeed not so much concerned with the history of Judaism, but with Christian eschatology. Taubes's first letter to Scho-lem from October 1947, however, indicates that he was familiar with Scholem's thought. He discussed some of Scholem's writings with fellow emigré Margerete Susman in Switzerland and probably read *Major Trends in Jewish Mysticism* when he moved in 1947 from Switzerland to New York. See Taubes, "Letter to Scholem of October 27, 1947," in Taubes, *Der Preis der Messianismus*, 93–97.

politics and aesthetics.[59] The legacy of Walter Benjamin, in fact a close friend of Scholem, can hardly be overestimated in Taubes's thinking. Benjamin's essays, time and again, used religious categories and Jewish messianism in particular to make sense of modern cultural phenomena as diverse as revolutionary violence, the philosophy of history, and the surrealistic experience.[60] Not surprisingly, Taubes often referred in his later works to Benjamin as a modern Paul or a modern Marcion, and criticized Scholem's strictly theological and Jewish reading of Benjamin's work.[61]

Scholem's concept of messianism or heresy did not allow for this elaborate theory of secularization. For Scholem, messianism is fundamentally an intra-Jewish phenomenon; it has nothing to do with Christianity and even less with the secular concepts of progress or revolution. Nonetheless, Scholem did reflect on the problem of secularization. Not unlike Taubes's thinking, these reflections on secularization were often related to his discussions of heresy. At the end of his essay "Redemption through Sin," for example, Scholem showed how Sabbatian heresy in particular paved the way for Jewish Enlightenment (Haskalah). He claimed that Sabbatianism's religious dynamics paradoxically made secularism possible, as its heretical criticism of established religion prefigured the

---

59. "I don't think theologically. I work with theological materials, but I think in terms of Intellectual history, of actual history." Taubes, *Political Theology of Paul,* 69. See also Joshua R. Gold, "Jacob Taubes: Apocalyps from Below," *Telos* 134 (2006): 142.

60. See, respectively, Walter Benjamin, "Critique of Violence," in *Selected Writings,* vol. 1, *1913–1926,* ed. Marcus Bullock and Michael Jennings (Cambridge, MA: Harvard University Press, 2004), 236–52; Walter Benjamin, "On the Concept of History," in *Selected Writings,* vol. 4, *1938–1940,* ed. Howard Eiland and Michael Jennings (Cambridge, MA: Harvard University Press, 2003), 389–400; Walter Benjamin, "Surrealism," in *Selected Writings,* vol. 2, pt. 1, *1927–1930,* ed. Michael Jennings, Howard Eiland, and Gary Smith (Cambridge, MA: Harvard University Press, 2005), 207–21.

61. See Taubes, *Political Theology of Paul,* 70–76; Jacob Taubes, "Walter Benjamin—ein moderner Marcionit? Scholems Benjamin-Interpretation religionsgeschichtlich überprüft," in *Apokalypse und Politik: Aufsätze, Kritiken und kleinere Schriften,* ed. Herbert Kopp-Oberstebrink and Martin Treml (Munich: Wilhelm Fink, 2017) 286–98.

atheist possibility of rejecting religion altogether. The radical forms of Sabbatian messianism had challenged Jewish religion to such an extent, argued Scholem, that "the world of traditional Judaism was shattered beyond repair."[62] Only a strong and negative messianic faith remained in Sabbatianism, which ultimately proved to be unbearable in view of its inherently paradoxical nature. When this messianic faith itself eventually crumbled away, every form of Jewish religious authority had lost its legitimacy, leaving only enlightened secularism in its wake. The relation between Sabbatianism and Jewish Enlightenment was for Scholem not just a structural one, it was also historical: "They [the Sabbatians] had been drawing closer to the spirit of the Haskalah all along, so that when the flame of their faith finally flickered out they soon reappeared as leaders of Reform Judaism, secular intellectuals, or simply complete and indifferent skeptics."[63]

In order to grasp Scholem's implied theory of secularization, it is essential to understand the religious thought of Sabbatianism's most radical and nihilistic representative, Jacob Frank. Frank was an eighteenth-century Sabbatian nihilist who claimed to be the reincarnation of Zevi.[64] The Frankist rejection of established laws and traditions entailed "the annihilation of every religion and positive system of belief."[65] Everything that had a mere hint of immanence had to be rejected as unredeemed and godless; any positive religious expression was impossible. In this sense, the Frankist creed was empty; it became pure negativity. In Frankism, this negativity did not entail spiritual retreat from this world but rather destructive action within it. Moreover, this negativity not only concerned established religion; it wanted to nihilistically abolish all political, moral, and even metaphysical laws and conventions. Only through the sinful rejection and destruction of everything this-worldly

---

62. Scholem, "Redemption through Sin," 126.
63. Scholem, 140.
64. For Jacob Frank and the Frankists, see Pawel Maciejko, *The Mixed Multitude: Jacob Frank and The Frankist Movement, 1755–1816* (Philadelphia: University of Pennsylvania Press, 2011).
65. Scholem, "Redemption through Sin,"130.

could a redemptive transcendence open up. From the point of view of the messianic, immanence has indeed no relation to the divine whatsoever. In this regard, the Torah as well as creation itself is falsely attributed to God. Just as Marcion and the ancient Gnostics had already claimed, neither scripture nor the immanent world had divine origins for the Frankists.

For the Frankists, the nihilistic degradation of nature (*physis*) was ultimately secondary to the nihilistic rejection of religious or moral norms (*nomos*), although both are obviously intertwined. As a scholar of religion, Scholem too was concerned more with the nihilistic rejection of *nomos* that concretely took shape in the withering of the divine origins of the Torah, the law and religious authority itself. In view of Frankist nihilism, there is virtually no difference between secular criticism of religion and heretical rejection of established religion. As Sabbatianism and secularism abolish the legitimacy of every religious authority, both entail a form of anarchism for Scholem. Because both question the divine origins of religious writings, laws, and institutions, there can be no immanent standard for the authority on religious truth. Every religious claim and any system of authority are ultimately human constructions that lack divine legitimation. This observation can be made from both secular and religious points of view. The divine origins of the Bible, for example, can be rejected either by an enlightened philosopher like Spinoza, who wants to develop a scientific and historical interpretation of the Bible as a man-made document, or by a religious heretic, who wants to emphasize the absolute transcendence and otherness of God by rejecting the presence of the divine in any immanent position, even in the Bible itself. Their different motivations notwithstanding, both positions are functionally equivalent: they anarchically uproot the immanent possibility of religious authority.

The secularist and Sabbatian criticism of religion had thus rendered every form of religious authority suspect. Scholem claimed that everyone is an anarchist in modernity: "Thus as far as religion is concerned, we are all . . . , to some extent, anarchists today, and this should be plainly stated. Some know it and admit it fully; others . . . twist deviously to avoid facing the essential fact that in our time a continuity of Jewish religious awareness is beyond the principle of the 'Law from on High.' Such a conclusion inevitably leads to anarchic forms of religion."[66] In other words, not only is the secularist an anarchist with regard to religion, but every religious position is anarchic too, in the sense that religious positions by definition lack divine or transcendent origins as their legitimation. As religious claims have no ontological ground, they are literally "an-archic" (groundless). This modern condition of religion is paradoxically also the fulfillment of genuine messianic thinking. Remember that Scholem considered anarchism to be central to Jewish messianism. In view of the messianic, no immanent religious position can claim absolute knowledge about the divine. In this regard, messianic and modern religiosities share the instability, relativity, and preliminary nature of their creed. The modern anarchic criticism of established religion then continues the legacy of Jewish messianism within secular modernity and even realizes its religious potential better than any previous epoch in the history of religion.

If religious and secular positions are equally anarchic with regard to religion in modernity, the distinction between religion and secularism becomes blurred. By appealing to the notion of anarchism to characterize modern religiosity, rather than to secularism or unbelief, Scholem emphasized the fundamental equivalence of the religious and the nonreligious. In this sense, the unbeliever himself is religious, albeit in an anarchistic manner. Scholem paradoxically called him the "pious atheist."[67] Not unlike Taubes's thinking, Scholem's reflections on secularization also entailed a deconstruction of the traditional distinction between religion and secularity, thus allowing for significant continuities between the modern and the premodern. As David Biale also argued in an article on Scholem and anarchism, "What is often assumed to be characteristically modern . . . becomes in his hands the key to understanding

---

66. Gershom Scholem, "Reflections of the Possibility of Jewish Mysticism," *Ariel* 26 (1970): 50; quoted in Jacobson, *Metaphysics of the Profane*, 78.

67. Gershom Scholem, "Reflections on Jewish Theology," in *On Jews and Judaism in Crisis* (Philadelphia: Paul Dry Books, 2012), 283.

the pre-modern or, more precisely, that which in the pre-modern incubates modernity. Modernist terms illuminate the religious tradition just as the religious tradition casts a long shadow over the modern."[68]

In a letter of 1926 addressed to Franz Rosenzweig, the young Scholem had already elaborated on such continuities between the modern and the premodern, focusing especially on the ineradicable religious traces that are imperceptibly present in the modern Hebrew language:[69] "They think they have secularized the Hebrew Language, have done away with its apocalyptic point. . . . But if we transmit the language to our children as it was transmitted to us, if we, a generation of transition, revive the language of the ancient books for them, that it may reveal itself anew through them, shall not the religious power of that language explode one day?"[70] This letter is one of the few places in Scholem's substantial oeuvre where he explicitly discussed the problem of secularization. His account of secularization was initially very pessimistic: modern Jewish culture has forgotten the religious meaning of its language and has completely ignored its mystical and messianic connotations in favor of its secular communicative function. In spite of this very pessimistic account of secularization, Scholem still allowed for a possible return of religion. He suggested that the religious substratum of the Hebrew language is ultimately ineradicable and unconsciously continues to inform the meaning of the language Jews use in their everyday communication. Using the words but forgetting their original meaning, they unwittingly use religious formulas that

---

68. David Biale, "Gershom Scholem on Nihilism and Anarchism," *Rethinking History* 19, no. 1 (2015): 63.

69. The letter was first published by Stéphane Mosès (in French) as Gershom Scholem, "Une lettre inédite de Gerschom Scholem à Franz Rosenzweig: À propos de nôtre langue, une confession," *Archives des Sciences Sociales des Religions* 60, no. 1 (1985): 83–84; English translation: Gershom Scholem, "Language and Secularization," in Stéphane Mosès, *The Angel of History: Rosenzweig, Benjamin, Scholem*, trans. Barbara Harshav (Stanford: Stanford University Press, 2009), 168. This letter has received much academic attention: Mosès, *Angel of History*, 168–82; Jacques Derrida, "The Eyes of Language: The Abyss and the Volcano," in *Acts of Religion*, ed. Gil Anidjar (New York: Routledge, 2002), 189–22.

70. Scholem, "Language and Secularization," 168.

function as it were as magic spells from which the religious or messianic force can suddenly explode.

Scholem's pessimism about secularization would be nuanced in his later writings, but he would remain very critical of the secularization of Judaism and its assimilation to modern culture throughout his career. Scholem's criticism of the secularization of messianism into the idea of modern progress would be an important example of his continuing discontent with secularized or modern versions of Judaism.[71] Although Scholem's account of the unnoticed presence of religious traces in secular culture seemed to be in tune with the more explicit theories of secularization of thinkers like Schmitt, Taubes, and Löwith, he would certainly have rejected Löwith's interpretation of modern progress as secularized eschatology. Also in "Redemption through Sin," Scholem hesitated to defend such an immediate transposition of theological contents into secular modernity. Scholem deployed a much more nuanced and historically complex picture of the relation between religion and secularism than either Taubes or his own earlier reflections in his letter to Rosenzweig could account for. Unlike Taubes, Scholem did not believe that messianism is transposed into modernity; rather, he believed that its internal religious logic, in parallel with certain historical evolutions, made (Jewish) modernity possible.[72] The revolutionary climate of the eighteenth and nineteenth centuries was the concrete historical context in which the logic of messianism, more specifically heretical Frankist messianism, intersected with Jewish Enlightnement. In other words, Frankism or Sabbatianism as such did not make the genesis of Jewish Enlightenment possible, but rather the contingent meeting of their religious dynamic with a cultural-political context that seemed to be in tune with Sabbatianism's revolutionary potential. Sabbatianism's religious desire

---

71. Scholem, "Messianic Idea," 10, 26.

72. For much the same reasons, Scholem also opposed Jacob Talmon's concept of "political messianism." See Jacob Talmon, *Political Messianism: The Romantic Phase* (London: Secker and Warburg, 1960); David Ohana, "J. L. Talmon, Gershom Scholem, and the Price of Messianism," *History of European Ideas* 34, no. 2 (2008): 171.

for revolution found its correlate in real political revolutions at the
end of the eighteenth century, argued Scholem: "Toward the end
of Frank's life the hopes he had entertained of abolishing all laws
and conventions took on a very real historical significance. As a
result of the French revolution the Sabbatian and Frankist subversion of the old morality and religion was suddenly placed in a new
and relevant context."[73] The French Revolution was the concrete
locus where the Sabbatian potential for secularization was realized.
The inner logic of Sabbatian religiosity allowed for an important
secularization of Jewish culture once it had been paired with the
revolutionary dynamics of eighteenth-century Western history.

In contrast to the thoughts expressed in his letter to Rosenzweig,
Scholem seemed to recognize on this point the inevitability of the
process of secularization. The entwinement of Sabbatianism and
Enlightenment is a dialectical process that is historically irrevers-
ible. In this sense, the secularization of Judaism and Jewish concepts was a necessary and inevitable result of historical evolutions
that were related to the dynamics of Judaism and Jewish heresy.
Scholem's theory of secularization, which was implied in the last
pages of "Redemption through Sin," seemed less univocally critical
of secular modernity than his older writings and showed important
parallels with Taubes's thought. Nonetheless, it certainly did not
open the door to the complete secularization of Jewish messianism that we find in Taubes's reflections on occidental eschatology,
where messianism and heresy were extricated from their Jewish
context and became categories for understanding Christianity and
the modern condition.

The Scope of Judaism and Jewish Dissidence

In view of the problem of secularization, the main difference between Taubes and Scholem is highlighted again. Although both
agreed on the constitutive role of messianism and heretical

---

73. Scholem, "Redemption through Sin," 137.

dissidence for modernity, it is clear that for Scholem messianism remained a strictly Jewish phenomenon, whereas for Taubes it did not. In the latter's perspective, it was not even a strictly religious category. Messianism and eschatology are forces that precede the distinction between religion and secularism as much as they make the separation between Judaism and Christianity problematical. Nevertheless, these differences between Scholem and Taubes make sense only in view of a shared intellectual background, which this chapter has tried to uncover. This shared perspective was, more-over, not just academic or intellectual but also psychological. It did not just consist in a similar interpretation of Jewish messian-ism as a nihilistic, antinomian, and paradoxical phenomenon, nor even in their theological preoccupation with heresy, but particu-larly in their idiosyncratic fascination with revolt and dissidence. In an attempt to explain the role of Gnosticism and messianism in Scholem's work, Moshe Idel confirmed the importance of Scho-lem's preoccupation with subversion: "Another implication may be that the nonconformist nature of these catalysts [Gnosticism and messianism] is obvious and very striking. It is precisely that subver-sive facet, the aspect that does not fit within the rabbinic conser-vative mindset, that changed the course of Jewish history. Scholem always presented these elements as positive and vitalizing while treating the conservative mindset as inert and hypertrophic."[74] In-terestingly, Scholem's and Taubes's preoccupation with subversion was also reflected in their polemical literary style. The literary me-dium Taubes and Scholem preferred was not the academic mono-graph but the shorter and more dialogical mediums of the letter or the (review) essay.[75] These literary forms are essentially polem-ical and potentially subversive, as they allow for real discussion,

---

74. Moshe Idel, "Subversive Catalysts: Gnosticism and Messianism in Scho-lem's View of Jewish Mysticism," in *Old Worlds, New Mirrors: On Jewish Mys-ticism and Twentieth-Century Thought* (Philadelphia: University of Pennsylvania Press, 2010), 150.

75. For interesting reflections on the role of letters in Taubes's oeuvre, see Her-bert Kopp-Oberstebrink, "Die Subversion der Reformation der Revolution: Jacob Taubes' Bermerkungen zur Kleinschreibung," *Trajekte* 23 (2011): 27–32: Her-bert Kopp-Oberstebrink, "Affinitäten, Dissonanzen: Die Korrespondenz zwischen Hans Blumenberg und Jacob Taubes," in Hans Blumenberg and Jacob Taubes,

disagreement, and in the case of their own correspondence even dissidence.

It is only in view of this shared fascination with subversion and revolt that their differences can be assessed. As Thomas Macho sharply summarized it, their disagreement basically concerned the scope of dissidence and revolt:

> Scholem interpreted the question of Jewish revolt as an inner-Jewish problem—for example, the tension between messianic break and rabbinical orthodoxy. . . . Taubes, on the other hand, understood the same question always as an expression of a Jewish account of the limits of Judaism, including its experimental transgression—in the direction of the foundation of a new religion (in the case of Paul and his student Marcion), in the direction of the conversion to another religion (in the case of the Marranos, but also of Sabbatai Zevi), in the direction of enlightenment and a secularization of messianism in the philosophy of history (from Maimonides to Spinoza or to the mystical Marxists Bloch and Benjamin).[76]

On a less explicit level, there also seemed to be a more fundamental question at stake in this personal disagreement about the scope of Jewish revolt, a question that has been absolutely central in the history of modern Judaism: What is Judaism's relation to Western modernity? Does the Jew intrinsically belong to the West, or is he an outsider—a "pariah," to use Hannah Arendt's words? Taubes chose the first option but without relapsing into liberal Judaism's plea for complete assimilation to modern culture. Judaism does not belong or should not be assimilated to modern Western culture. On the contrary, this tradition was from the outset itself entirely Jewish.[77] These were the ultimate stakes of Taubes's concept

---

Briefwechsel 1961–1981, ed. Herbert Kopp-Oberstebrink and Martin Treml (Berlin: Suhrkamp, 2013), 305. For Scholem's letters, see Anthony Grafton, "The Magician," *New Republic*, March 3, 2003.

76. Thomas Macho, "Der intellektuele Bruch zwischen Gershom Scholem und Jacob Taubes: Zur Frage nach dem *Preis der Messianismus*," in *Abendländische Eschatologie: Ad Jacob Taubes*, ed. Richard Faber, Eveline Goodman-Thau, and Thomas Macho (Würzberg: Königshausen und Neumann, 2001), 540.

77. "In Taubes' experimental account, modernity as such is Jewish—while all modern thinkers, with Hegel as their paradigmatic centre, remain modern only insofar as they can be reclaimed by Jewish messianism." Agata Bielik-Robson, "Modernity: The Jewish Perspective," *New Blackfriars* 94 (2013): 204.

of occidental eschatology: it is the dynamic force of Jewish eschatology that unifies the multiplicity of cultural manifestations in the
West. Scholem, by contrast, emphasized the exceptional nature of
Judaism and Jewish messianism. Judaism is nothing like Christianity or Enlightenment, and with regard to the Western tradition it
is a complete outsider. In this exceptional nature of Judaism, Scholem also found legitimation for his Zionism, which Taubes rejected
ever more radically.[78]

This different commitment to the project of Zionism highlights
a final, but decisive difference between Scholem's and Taubes's fascination with heresy. Scholem's account of heresy in "Redemption
through Sin" has been understood both as a critique and as an
endorsement of Zionism. On the one hand, Scholem's fascination
with Sabbatianism can be viewed as an indirect legitimation of Zionism, which according to the standards of Orthodox Judaism can
itself be considered a heresy. Sabbatianism could thus be a kind of
historical precursor of Zionism, a premodern heresy announcing
Jewish modernity.[79] On the other hand, it has been argued that
Scholem's discussion of Sabbatianism should actually be read in
light of his disappointment with the way Zionism was put into
practice. The connection Scholem saw between Sabbatianism and
Zionism can therefore also be read as a warning that Zionism is
susceptible to the same messianic radicalism as Sabbatianism.[80] In
any case, the connection between Scholem's views on heresy and
his views on Zionism is undeniable. This Zionist motivation explains why, for Scholem, the messianic heresies of Sabbatianism and
Gnosticism had no relevance beyond Judaism.[81] It is no coincidence

---

78. For a comparison between Scholem's and Taubes's views on Zionism, see
Macho, "Der intellektuele Bruch," 537–40; Benjamin Lazier, "On the Origins of
Political Theology: Judaism and Heresy between the World Wars," *New German
Critique* 35 (2008): 143–64.

79. See David Biale, *Gershom Scholem: Kabbalah and Counter-History*
(Cambridge, MA: Harvard University Press, 1982); Lazier, *God Interrupted.*

80. See Amir Engel, *Gershom Scholem: An Intellectual Biography* (Chicago:
University of Chicago Press, 2017), 94–167.

81. For the relation between Gnosticism and Zionism, in particular, see Yotam
Hotam, *Modern Gnosis and Zionism: The Crisis of Culture, Life Philosophy, and
Jewish National Thought* (London: Routledge, 2009).

that "Redemption through Sin" is one of the few essays that Scholem wrote in Hebrew. His fascination with heresy, dissidence, and revolt was ultimately concerned with an internal Jewish problem. This Zionist context was largely absent in Taubes's discussions of heresy, messianism, and Gnosticism. Rather than being a Zionist, Taubes as it were embodied the Diaspora, traveling his entire life between Berlin, Paris, New York, and Jerusalem, never staying too long in one place and never being at home in any of these cities.

These political and existential differences, which are neither merely academic nor purely personal, separated Scholem and Taubes from the early 1950s until Scholem's death in 1982. It was not until 1987 that Taubes credited the relevance of Scholem's paradoxical interpretation of the messianic logic for his own project in the lecture series that was later published as *The Political Theology of Paul*. Too late an attempt at intellectual rapprochement, the recognition of this common ground marked the end of a failed dialogue.

4

Nothingness

Dialectics of Religious Nihilism

A recurring topic in the debates on modern Gnosticism is the alleged nihilistic nature of the Gnostic teachings. What ultimately connected Gnosticism to modern thought, in this perspective, is a shared sense of meaninglessness and nothingness. Nonetheless, nihilism is usually considered to be a secular and atheistic phenomenon, while Gnosticism is obviously a religious phenomenon. In line with Nietzsche's famous proclamation of the death of God, nihilism is traditionally thought to entail a rejection of a transcendent beyond (*Hinterwelt*) that structures immanence.[1] Accordingly, the nihilistic negation of the supernatural implies that the meaning and order of this world are no longer guaranteed by it. This is also the gist of Martin Heidegger's interpretation of Nietzsche's

---

1. Although this interpretation of Nietzsche's nihilism has been all pervasive in twentieth-century thought, it is to a large extent misguided. See James Chappel, "Nihilism and the Cold War: The Catholic Reception of Nihilism between Nietzsche and Adenhauer," *Rethinking History* 19 (2015): 95–110. For Nietzsche, not only did the end of the old religious and moral frameworks led to nihilism, but Christianity itself was a nihilistic construct to the extent that it wanted to conceal the primordial meaninglessness of reality: Friedrich Nietzsche, *On the Genealogy of Morality* (Cambridge: Cambridge University Press, 2007).

nihilism: " 'God is dead' means: the supersensory world has no effective force."[2] As a consequence of this negation of transcendence, the nihilistic worldview typically denies the intrinsic value of the natural world as well as the objective justification of morality. Nietzsche famously associated this latter point in particular with the nihilistic devaluation of the highest values.

Although nihilism initially appears as an atheistic and even explicitly antireligious philosophy, this chapter argues that it is conceivable to be nihilistic for religious reasons as well, however paradoxical this might sound. It will be shown that thinkers as diverse as Hans Jonas, Gershom Scholem, Walter Benjamin, and Jacob Taubes conceived of what will be called here *religious nihilism*. This notion, which Scholem used in passing but never developed systematically, refers in this chapter to related religious constellations. On the one hand, religious nihilism designates a tendency in twentieth-century theology that paradoxically tried to take modern nihilism and atheism into account. On the other hand, the concept can be used to identify a range of premodern religious practices and ideas that have been called nihilistic in retrospect— ancient Gnosticism being the obvious example. These latter religious nihilisms are sometimes even considered to be a necessary historical condition for the genesis of secular nihilism in modernity. It does not come as a surprise that such nihilistic tendencies were not tolerated by the orthodox traditions but typically arose as Jewish or Christian heresies.

This chapter will combine the two aspects of religious nihilism by focusing on the nihilistic implications of Gnostic heresy and their role in twentieth-century Jewish and messianic thought. Gnosticism increasingly appeared here as a model for a modern religiosity after the death of God. Taking Hans Jonas's and especially Gershom Scholem's reflections on the subject as a point of departure, the chapter explores how similar problems surface in the writings of Walter Benjamin and Jacob Taubes. In all these

---

2. Martin Heidegger, "Nietzsche's Word: God Is dead," in *Off the Beaten Track,* ed. and trans. Julian Young and Kenneth Haynes (Cambridge, Cambridge University Press, 2002), 162 (translation modified).

thinkers, a dialectical relation is manifested between an initial religious rejection of the meaning of the world (passive nihilism) and an antinomian investment in this world that subverts its immanent logic (active nihilism). Thus, the chapter can be read as a further elucidation of a specific feature of Scholem's and Taubes's more general fascination with heresy, developed in the previous chapter.

Gershom Scholem: Nothingness, Gnosticism, and Redemption through Sin

Just like modern nihilism, Gnosticism is often thought to reject the intrinsic value of the natural world and the justification of the moral law. Gnosticism's nihilistic rejection of immanent lawfulness, however, was based on a religious affirmation of transcendence rather than on the secular negation of transcendence. Gnosticism dissociated transcendence and immanence in favor of an extreme emphasis on the radical otherness of God. Although Gnosticism's point of departure was thus opposed to the modern nihilistic rejection of transcendence, its outcome was exactly the same. In his essay "Gnosticism, Nihilism, and Existentialism," Hans Jonas argued that Gnosticism and modern nihilism equally reject the structuring role of transcendence for immanence. Appealing to Heidegger's interpretation of nihilism, he argued that "a transcendence withdrawn from any normative relation to the world is equal to a transcendence which has lost its effective force."[3] In other words, both Gnosticism and nihilism reject the Platonic-Christian metaphysics of participation and deny that there is an ontological connection between transcendence and immanence, where the former gives meaning and structure to the latter. In spite of these similarities between Gnostic and modern nihilism, Jonas eventually also emphasized their differences. He showed that the existential consequences

---

3. Hans Jonas, "Gnosticism, Nihilism, and Existentialism," in *The Gnostic Religion: The Message of the Alien God and the Beginnings of Christianity* (Boston: Beacon Press, 1958), 332. For Jonas's interpretation of Gnosticism and nihilism, see chapter 1.

of modern nihilism are much more radical than those of ancient Gnosticism. Although both result in a rejection of the intrinsic value of immanence, the complete modern negation of transcendence leaves humanity in a more desperate condition than the radical dissociation of God and world. In the Gnostic perspective, there was at least a meaningful point to which human hopes could be directed and to which an escape from a nihilistic immanence was conceivable. This option is completely absent in modern nihilism.

Although Gershom Scholem and Jacob Taubes relied heavily on Jonas's understanding of Gnosticism, they did not attach great importance to his emphasis on the difference between Gnostic and modern nihilism. The main reason was that their respective understanding of Gnostic transcendence was itself nihilistic. Transcendence, in their perspective, appeared as nothingness rather than as a positive and substantial point of reference toward which hope can be directed. As a matter of fact, Jonas himself also granted elsewhere that the Gnostic understanding of God did not differ all that much from the nihilistic rejection of transcendence: "The Gnostic concept of God is first and foremost . . . a nihilistic one: God—the nothing of the world (*das Nichts der Welt*)."[4] For the modern nihilist and Gnostic alike, transcendence is empty. For the former, it literally does not exist, as it is a figment of the imagination, but the latter too would characterize the supernatural as empty, nihilistic, and in this sense even nonexistent. For the Gnostic, however, the notion of God's nothingness essentially designated that God's being consists in the denial of everything that is immanent. If God is not just absent from the world but opposed to all things earthly, any immanent category falls short in accounting for the true nature of transcendence. If this world is understood through the category of being, the Gnostic transcendence can be characterized only as "nothingness." In this regard, Taubes maintained that Gnostic transcendence can be described only negatively: "The negative statements about God—unrecognizable, unnamable, unrepeatable, incomprehensible, without form, without bounds, and

---

4. Hans Jonas, *Gnosis und spätantiker Geist* (Göttingen: Vandenhoeck und Ruprecht, 1934), 1:151.

even nonexistent—all orchestrate the . . . Gnostic proposition that God is essentially contrary to the world."[5] From the point of view of immanence, transcendence is literally nothing. Alluding to Jonas's historical account of Gnosticism, Taubes claimed: "Just as there is nothing of God in the cosmos, so God is the nothing of the world."[6] For Taubes, as for Scholem, there was no real distinction between secular and religious nihilism. More than that, Taubes and Scholem themselves were actually both nihilist and Gnostic at the same time: as modern intellectuals they took the death of God absolutely seriously but paradoxically attributed a religious meaning to it.[7] God's otherness is so radical that he is actually closer to nothing than to being—closer to death than to life.

This connection between religion and nihilism was for Scholem reflected most intensely in the writings of Franz Kafka: "For, like no one else before, he expressed the limit between religion and nihilism."[8] He argued that Kafka bore witness to the modern experience of a meaningless world where God is completely absent and where revelation and salvation are unrealizable. Kafka's nihilistic experience, paradigmatic for modernity in general, was not the atheistic realization that there is nothing beyond this world; it

---

5. Jacob Taubes, *Occidental Eschatology*, trans. David Ratmoko (Stanford: Stanford University Press, 2009), 40.

6. Taubes, *Occidental Eschatology*, 39.

7. Similar reflections on the religious meaning of the death of God, albeit in a Christian context, can already be found in Hegel: G. W. F. Hegel, *Faith and Knowledge*, trans. Walter Cerf and H. S. Harris (Albany: SUNY Press, 1977), 190. In the postwar era, the topic of God's death even developed into a central issue in Christian and Jewish theology— respectively in death of god theology and Holocaust theology. See, respectively, Thomas Altizer, *Living the Death of God: A Theological Memoir* (Albany: SUNY Press, 2006); Richard Rubenstein, *After Auschwitz: Radical Theology and Contemporary Judaism* (Indianapolis: Bobbs-Merrill, 1966). Finally, the Christian meaning of nihilism has also been discussed in contemporary Continental philosophy: Gianni Vattimo, *Belief* (Stanford: Stanford University Press, 1999).

8. Gershom Scholem, "Zehn unhistorische Sätze über Kabbalah," in *Judaica 3* (Frankfurt am Main: Suhrkamp, 1973), 10. Scholem treats the relation between religion and nihilism in a more historical way in Gershom Scholem, "Der Nihilismus als religiöses Phänomen," in *Judaica 4* (Frankfurt am Main: Suhrkamp, 1984), 129–88.

was ultimately a religious experience of divine nothingness: "This is the experience of modern man, surpassingly well depicted in all its desolation by Kafka, for whom nothing has remained of God but the void, in Kafka's sense, to be sure, the void of God."⁹ This divine nothingness is manifested first and foremost in the meaninglessness of revelation. Again, this modern meaninglessness does not mark the end of religion but uncovers the true nihilistic nature of revelation itself. For Scholem, the significance of God's revelation is by definition inexhaustible, infinite, and as such incomprehensible and meaningless to human understanding. God's word is overdetermined and gains its concrete meaning only in its mediation by tradition and interpretation. Although God's word is essentially void of meaning, this meaninglessness is initially masked by religious traditions—in Scholem's case, the rabbinic tradition—that establish certain interpretations of revelation as absolute. However, when religious traditions start to lose their authority in secular modernity the "nothingness of revelation" (*das Nichts der Offenbarung*) becomes apparent.¹⁰ Kafka's writings represented this condition where the crumbling legitimacy of Jewish law and tradition problematized revelation. The concept of the law was absolutely central in his stories and novels but always appeared as fundamentally inaccessible and incomprehensible. According to Scholem's interpretation of Kafka, revelation therefore does take place in Kafka's universe and in the modern world but is absolutely void of meaning. Similarly, the law absolutely determines Kafka's main character K., but it is impossible for him to know its meaning or its lawgiver. In a letter to his friend Walter Benjamin, Scholem characterized this as "a state in which revelation appears to be without meaning, in which it still asserts itself, in which it

9. Gershom Scholem, "Reflections on Jewish Theology," in *On Jews and Judaism in Crisis* (Philadelphia: Paul Dry Books, 2012), 283.

10. Gershom Scholem, "Letter to Walter Benjamin of September 20, 1934," in Walter Benjamin and Gershom Scholem, *Briefwechsel 1933–1940* (Frankfurt am Main: Suhrkamp, 1997), 173; English translation: Walter Benjamin and Gershom Scholem, *The Correspondence of Walter Benjamin and Gershom Scholem, 1932–1940*, trans. Gary Smith and Andre Lefevere (Cambridge, MA: Harvard University Press, 1992), 141.

has validity but no significance."[11] This empty and meaningless revelation reveals literally nothing, but is a manifestation of divine nothingness.

In view of Scholem's theological reflections on revelation, the parallel between Gnosticism's religious nihilism and modern nihilism is much more fundamental than the mere formal resemblance that Jonas emphasized. For Scholem, Gnosticism could even offer a model for a modern religiosity in a world without God. However, he was not seeking to smuggle a premodern religiosity into the secular world as an attempt to save religion by making it compatible with the modern worldview. On the contrary, he was wary of every attempt to modernize religion or to adjust it to the demands of enlightened rationality. Rather, Scholem showed how the secular condition itself coincides with a specific religious condition, albeit a very unusual, heretical, and nihilistic one. More than that, secularism paradoxically appears as a fully religious phenomenon. Modernity, in this respect, is neither opposed to religion nor is it the result of religious transformations; rather, it *is* religion. Modernity is just another episode, probably even the most interesting, in the long history of religious evolutions. What was ultimately at stake in Scholem's fascination with Gnosticism was therefore not just the possibility of a modern religiosity but a precept for modernity as such. If the modern worldview is characterized by an absolute absence of the divine and accordingly by a nihilistic conception of the world as devoid of any meaning, the crucial question is what our comportment with this world is. In other words, how do we make sense of the world and our lives if meaning is no longer given?

It is unusual, to say the least, to expect an answer to the question of meaning from Gnosticism, the most world-negating trend in the history of Western thought. As Jonas had always maintained, Gnosticism is about *Entweltlichung*, about rejecting and escaping the world at all costs. So why would it be able to tell us how to live in this world at all? Given its radical world-negation, how can Gnosticism serve as a precept for our relation to the profane realm of politics and history? As a radically dualistic and world-negating

---

11. Scholem, "Letter to Walter Benjamin of September 20, 1934," 173; Benjamin and Scholem, *Correspondence*, 141.

movement, Gnosticism could not answer these questions. According to this line of thought, the Gnostic was directed exclusively toward transcendence, and his attitude toward immanence was one of pure negativity. Thus, Gnosticism's return in the modern world would be potentially destructive. This why Eric Voegelin and Hans Jonas fiercely criticized the Gnostic aspects of modern thought and why Hans Blumenberg wanted to safeguard modernity from this Gnostic legacy at all costs. If, however, this Gnostic negation is approached dialectically, it could nevertheless serve as a guideline for action within the immanent world. This was Scholem's approach. As a metaphysical system, Gnosticism was of course dualistic: it rejected immanence as depraved, inferior, evil, and so on, and it promoted an escape to a transcendent world of salvation. From a practical point of view, things are more complicated. Someone who rejects the immanent world as meaningless in favor of an exclusive focus on transcendence still has to live in this world. A mere passive resignation might be speculatively attractive, but it is practically impossible. However hard the Gnostic hoped for salvation, he still lived in an unredeemed world and inevitably had to decide how exactly he wanted to do this in a meaningful way that squared with his Gnostic convictions. Paradoxically, even the most extreme negation of the world requires us to take a position within this world. In spite of its exclusive emphasis on transcendence, the Gnostic speculations necessarily had implications for the way one had to live in the immanent world. In other words, the dual schema of rejection and escape requires a third move: a return to immanence. This return can obviously not involve a simple acceptance of the profane, but it will be a dialectical return mediated by the initial rejection.

Although this all sounds very speculative, the course of action that derives from a Gnosticism conceived dialectically is simple: "Try to be as contrary as possible!" In this regard, the Gnostic did not stop short at mere passive resignation and escapism; he also turned this negativity into an active principle of subversion, revolt, and antinomianism.[12] On this point, Gnostic dualism's passive

---

12. As Jonas emphasized, Gnosticism's "rejection of the world, far from the serenity or resignation of other nonworldly creeds, is of peculiar, sometimes

nihilism turned dialectically into an active nihilism. This nihilistic revolt could then take many different shapes, going from religious apostasy to immoral behavior and sexual transgression. This kind of revolt was also paradigmatic for Scholem's concept of redemption through sin, developed in his discussion of the Jewish heresy of Sabbatianism. The only course of action that could be derived from a Gnostic or Sabbatian rejection of the world was a negative one. Since nothing positive could be achieved in this world, the only option was saying no to it. In Scholem's view, Sabbatians refused to go along with immanence by living this world in the opposite direction. If the messianic and the transcendent are in every respect opposite to history and immanence, the only meaningful comportment to this world is to invert every current moral, political, historical, and religious standard. In the case of radical Sabbatianism, this took shape in an active nihilism that implied first and foremost an inversion of the religious norms of traditional Judaism: "Through a revolution of values, what was formerly sacred has now become profane and what was formerly profane has become sacred. . . . The violation of the Torah is now its true fulfillment."[13] The sinful transgression of moral and religious laws paradoxically became the epitome of holiness and a precondition for salvation— hence redemption through sin. Not surprisingly, Scholem explicitly associated these Frankist and Sabbatian impulses with ancient Gnosticism:

> Indeed, to anyone familiar with the history of religion it might seem far more likely that he [Jacob Frank] was dealing here with an antinomian myth from the second century composed by such nihilistic Gnostics as Carpocrates and his followers than that all this was actually taught and believed by Polish Jews living on the eve of the French revolution, among whom neither the master nor his disciples had the slightest inkling that they were engaged in resuscitating an ancient tradition! Not only the

---

vituperative violence, and we generally note a tendency to extremism, to excess in fantasy and feeling." Hans Jonas, "Delimitation of the Gnostic Phenomenon: Typological and Historical," in *Le origini dello Gnosticismo: Colloquio di Messina 13–18 Aprile 1966,* ed. Ugo Bianchi (Leiden: Brill, 1967), 100.

13. Gershom Scholem, "Redemption through Sin," in *The Messianic Idea in Judaism and Other Essays on Jewish Spirituality* (New York: Schocken, 1971), 110.

general train of thought, but even some of the symbols and terms are the
same! And yet, none of this seems as surprising as it may appear to be at
first glance when we reflect that no less than the Frankists, the Gnostics
of antiquity developed their thought within a biblical framework, for all
that they completely inverted the biblical values.[14]

For Scholem, the legacy of Gnosticism in the Jewish tradition was
not confined to Sabbatian heresy alone. Rather, he considered it
to be a structural, albeit always subversive and antinomian force
in the entire tradition of Jewish mysticism, spanning from the ancient Merkabah and the Bahir to the modern mystical heresies of
Kabbalah and Sabbatianism.[15] Rather than understanding Gnosticism, like Jonas did, as a specific historical constellation, Scholem
interpreted it as a theological option that could be recognized in a
wide range of religious phenomena—both Christian or Jewish—
and be relied on in different times—both ancient and modern.
Scholem made this explicit in a letter to Jonas: "Your definition
of Gnosticism is not mine, and to make this an object of discussion would be completely pointless. For me gnosis is a constantly
self-repeating structure within religious thinking, for you it is a
unique historical-philosophical phenomenon."[16] In view of Gnosticism's mythical caricatures of the Old Testament and its rejection
of the Jewish God of creation, it seemed paradoxical to emphasize the Gnostic legacy in the Jewish tradition. Scholem himself
even called Gnosticism, with Jonas's consent, "the greatest case of

---

14. Scholem, "Redemption through Sin," 132–33.

15. See Gershom Scholem, *Major Trends in Jewish Mysticism* (Jerusalem:
Schocken, 1941), 40–49; Gershom Scholem, *Jewish Gnosticism, Merkabah Mys-
ticism, and Talmudic Tradition* (New York: The Jewish Theological Seminary
Press,1960); Moshe Idel, "Subversive Catalysts: Gnosticism and Messianism in
Scholem's View of Jewish Mysticism," in *Old Worlds, New Mirrors: On Jewish
Mysticism and Twentieth-Century Thought* (Philadelphia: University of Pennsyl-
vania Press, 2010), 150.

16. Gershom Scholem, "Letter to Hans Jonas of November 14, 1977," in
Briefe: 1971–1982, ed. I. Shedletzky (Munich: C.H. Beck, 2000), 160. For the relation between Scholem and Jonas, see Christian Wiese, " 'For a time I was privileged
to enjoy his friendship . . .': The Ambivalent Relationship between Hans Jonas and
Gershom Scholem," *The Leo Baeck Institute Yearbook* 49, no. 1 (2004): 25–58.

metaphysical anti-Semitism."[17] For Scholem, however, this para-doxical role of Gnosticism in Jewish mysticism proved exactly that it is essentially a subversive and antinomian force in Judaism that runs counter to its traditional religious logic:

> It was Gnosticism, one of the last great manifestations of mythology in religious thought, and definitely conceived in the struggle against Juda-ism as the conqueror of mythology, which lent figures of speech to the Jewish mystic. The importance of this paradox can hardly be exagger-ated; it must be kept in mind that the whole meaning and purpose of those ancient myths and metaphors whose remainders the editors of the book *Bahir,* and therefore the whole Kabbalah, inherited from the Gnostics, was simply the subversion of a law which had, at one time dis-turbed and broken the order of the mythical world.[18]

The ancient Gnostics took the idea of subversion at face value in a way that seems hardly defensible, let alone malleable into a rule of conduct for the modern believer. Scholem was not interested in the concrete, aggressive means through which the Sabbatians, Frankists, and Gnostics tried to achieve their redemption through sin. Rather, he was interested in the dynamic between a world-negating focus on redemption and its concrete implications for the continuation of an unredeemed life in this world. The example of Gnostic revolt shows very clearly how the way someone thinks about transcendence and salvation influences the way he behaves in the immanent world and makes sense of profane history, even if his concept of transcendence entails a radical rejection of imma-nence and history. This is the dialectic of religious nihilism.

Scholem completed this dialectic by making immanence into his primary concern: in a world where God is absent or even pure nothingness, the most pressing question is not how to reach tran-scendence but how to continue living in this unredeemed world. This might also be the meaning of the last stanza of Scholem's poem *Mit einem Exemplar von Kafkas "Prozess,"* which he included in a

---

17. "Response by Hans Jonas," in *The Bible in Modern Scholarship: Papers Read at the 100th Meeting of the Society of Biblical Literature, December 28–30, 1964,* ed. J. Philip Hyatt (Nashville: Abingdon Press, 1965), 279–93.

18. Scholem, *Major Trends,* 35.

letter to Benjamin. After lamenting God's absence, he concluded in the penultimate line of the poem: "Oh, we must live all the same" (*Ach wir müssen dennoch leben*).[19] When the pursuit of another world ultimately proves futile, we realize that we still have to lead our lives in this unredeemed world. The most immediate concern is indeed the remaining value of our life, our actions, and our communities after the initial rejection of all immanent being as meaningless. In other words, Scholem attempted to reaffirm immanence, as he could not stop short at a univocal and paralyzing negation. Nonetheless, he could no longer naïvely reaffirm the intrinsic meaning of the cosmos; he could not deny that meaning is not immediately given. In a true dialectical sense, Scholem therefore pursued an affirmation of the world that was mediated by its initial negation. This is the dialectical negation of the negation. Benjamin Lazier also understood Scholem's project along these lines: "The Gnostics of late antiquity had divorced God from the world the better to escape it. . . . Scholem also spoke of an abyss between God and the world, but . . . to save the relative autonomy of the world (a version of it) from God, and thereby to affirm it. Dualism—not so much; dialectic—yes."[20]

What was at stake for Scholem was the affirmation of this world in view of its fundamental nihilism and meaninglessness. In that sense, he attributed value to life in this world in a way that ran counter to its immanent logic. He proposed a way to live history

---

19. Gershom Scholem, "Letter to Walter Benjamin, 1934," in Benjamin and Scholem *Briefwechsel*, 156: the poem reflected on the issues that are central in this chapter: divine absence ("Sind wir Ganz von dir geschieden?"), nihilism and divine nothingness ("Nur dein Nichts is die Erfahrung, die sie von dir haben darf"), and antinomianism ("Aus dem Zentrum der Vernichtung bricht zu Zeiten wohl ein Strahl, aber keiner weist die Richtung, die uns das Gesetz befahl"). The last two lines of the penultimate stanza and the first two of the last stanza suggested that any speculation about an absent God who does not respond to our questions is in vain ("Wenn dich einer drum befragte, du versänkst in Schweigen nur."/ "Kann Solch Frage sich erheben? Ist die Antwort unbestimmt?). In this spirit, the poem concludes that we still live in this world in spite of our pursuit of another one ("Ach wir müssen dennoch leben, bis uns dein Gericht vernimmt").

20. Benjamin Lazier, *God Interrupted: Heresy and the European Imagination between the World Wars* (Princeton: Princeton University Press, 2008), 160.

against its grain and to make sense of the world as a manifestation of divine nothingness. His historical analyses of Sabbatian and Gnostic subversion implied a more complex and sublimated form of antinomianism that should be understood as an inversion of all things earthly. Stéphane Moshès also recognized the centrality of this motif of inversion in Scholem's thought and considered it to be the gist of his interpretation of Kafka. According to Moshès, Scholem found in Kafka a "meticulous presentation of a world void of the idea of the divine, yet one in which immanence itself must be read as the inverse of a lost transcendence."[21] This motif of nihilistic inversion also returned in the work of Scholem's close friend Walter Benjamin, notably in his "Theological-Political Fragment." A discussion of the fragment could spell out some of the deeper philosophical and theological implications of Scholem's historical analyses.

Walter Benjamin: World Politics as Nihilism

The "Theological-Political Fragment" is arguably Walter Benjamin's most enigmatic text. Although Benjamin's other essays are not exactly an easy read either, this text is written in an exceptionally dense and hermetic style. The fragment is not much longer than a single page, but it is nonetheless one of Benjamin's most central, and hence most commented on, texts.[22] Not surprisingly, there is absolutely no consensus about the correct interpretation of the "Theological-Political Fragment." As the fragment was never published during Benjamin's lifetime, no one even knows when exactly it was written. Scholem claimed that it was an early text, written around 1921, influenced by Scholem's own reflections on Jewish mysticism. Theodor Adorno argued that Benjamin wrote this text

---

21. Stéphane Moses, "Gershom Scholem's Reading of Kafka: Literary Criticism and Kabbalah," *New German Critique* 77 (1999): 155.

22. For an overview of the leading (theological) interpretations of Benjamin's *Fragment*, see Colby Dickinson and Stéphane Symons, eds., *Walter Benjamin and Theology* (New York: Fordham University Press, 2016).

at the end of his life after his turn to more materialist and Marxist problems. Scholem's dating and interpretation will be followed here, not because his reading is the only correct one but because it highlights certain parallels between his own theological motif of inversion and Benjamin. The "Theological-Political Fragment" can be understood as turning Scholem's religious and historical reflections more explicitly into a metaphysical understanding of profane history and politics. Benjamin showed that a radical emphasis on transcendence inevitably required a specific interpretation of the immanent world, however negative and antinomian this interpretation might be. More than that, this interpretation of the immanence, which was initially rejected, then became his main concern and even his only point of interest. Both Scholem's and Benjamin's philosophical project has been characterized accordingly as a "metaphysics of the profane."[23] Both were interested in the possibility of meaning in a radically de-divinized and nihilistic world.

It is tempting to identify Benjamin's position in the "Theological-Political Fragment" as radically dualistic. He claimed that "nothing that is historical can relate itself, from its own ground, to anything messianic."[24] This could be an almost Gnostic separation between immanence and transcendence: God is completely absent from world history, which is finite, inferior, and radically meaningless. Nonetheless, Benjamin was not dualistically concerned with the transcendent, but, like Scholem's project, Benjamin's entailed a dialectical interest in immanence. Benjamin was concerned first and foremost with the residual meaning of the profane realm from which messianic meaning is completely removed. He maintained the absolute separation between the profane and the messianic but wanted to determine the meaning of the former on the basis of its inversion of the latter: "One arrow points to the goal toward which the profane dynamic acts, and another marks

---

23. Eric Jacobson, *Metaphysics of the Profane: The Political Theology of Walter Benjamin and Gershom Scholem* (New York: Columbia University Press, 2003).

24. Walter Benjamin, "Theological-Political Fragment," in *Selected Writings*, vol. 3, *1935–1938*, ed. Howard Eiland and Michael Jennings (Cambridge, MA: Harvard University Press, 2006), 305.

the direction of Messianic intensity."[25] By virtue of this opposition, the profane has autonomy with regard to the messianic. The profane has its own logic, yet it can be understood only as a complete inversion of the logic of the messianic. This opposition does not negatively show that immanent being has no value at all but that its meaning can arise paradoxically only in the absence of the messianic or in its nihilistic constitution. Although this opposition seems initially merely negative, it can at the same time be considered a constructive force. In other words, the positive meaning of the profane does not depend on a value that has to be added to it, but it can exist only in this very meaninglessness and opposition itself. Meaning, for Benjamin, consisted in the essential transience of the profane.

In the opposition between the profane and the messianic, Benjamin dialectically recovered their interrelation: "Just as a force, by virtue of the path it is moving along, can augment another force on the opposite path, so the profane order—because of its nature as profane—promotes the coming of the Messianic Kingdom."[26] Since the relation of the profane and the messianic is one of inverse proportionality, Benjamin held that the transience of the profane is already the messianic dynamic itself: "For nature is Messianic by reason of its eternal and total passing away."[27] History and nature are messianic insofar as they are the profane in decay.

Scholem, too, understood the messianic as the inversion of the profane. He conceived the messianic logic of redemption through sin as the absolute opposition to the profane. Its antinomianism was a sinful destruction of the profane that functioned as an active realization of Benjamin's worldly decay. While Scholem's redemption though sin required an antinomian and messianic action within history, Benjamin conceived history itself as antinomian and messianic by virtue of its essential transience. As he emphasized in "On the Concept of History," history itself has "a *weak* messianic power," as it "carries with it a secret index by which it

---

25. Benjamin, "Theological-Political Fragment," 305.
26. Benjamin, 305.
27. Benjamin, 306.

is referred to redemption."[28] If this is the case, the messianic is at work in the present itself and constitutes meaning within the profane. This would have been impossible for Scholem, whose experience of profane meaning is merely one of nothingness and radical divine absence. In line with Scholem, Benjamin was interested in the dialectical implications of a radical otherworldliness for the meaning of this world, but, unlike Scholem, Benjamin's interest in otherworldliness itself became subordinated to a focus on the profane. Benjamin radicalized Scholem's dialectics to such an extent that he actually overcame Scholem's Gnostic frame of reference.

Benjamin was familiar with some Gnostic sources, but he certainly did not consider himself to be a Gnostic.[29] He made this piercingly clear in his interpretation of Kafka, whose work he described as a "struggle against Gnosticism" (*Kampf gegen die Gnosis*).[30] Although Benjamin dropped this line in the final version of his Kafka essay, he did quote a conversation on Gnosticism between Kafka and Max Brod at length:

> I remember a conversation with Kafka which began with present-day Europe and the decline of the human race. "We are nihilistic thoughts, suicidal thoughts that come into God's head," Kafka said. This reminded me at first of the Gnostic view of life: God as the evil demiurge, the world as his Fall. "Oh no," said Kafka, "our world is only a bad mood of God, a bad day of his." "Then there is hope outside this manifestation of the world that we know." He smiled. "Oh, plenty of hope, an infinite amount of hope but not for us."[31]

---

28. Walter Benjamin, "On the Concept of History," in *Selected Writings*, vol. 4, *1938–1940*, ed. Howard Eiland and Michael Jennings (Cambridge, MA: Harvard University Press, 2003), 390 (emphasis original).

29. Benjamin reputedly owned the Wolfgang Schultz's Gnosticism reader: Wolfgang Schultz, *Dokumente der Gnosis* (Jena: Eugen Diedrichs, 1910). Pierre Klossowski confirmed this in an interview, stating that "Benjamin lent me his copy of *Dokumente der Gnosis*: the collection edited by Schultz." Pierre Klossowski and Jean-Maurice Monnoyer, *Le peintre et son démon* (Paris: Flammarion, 1985), 184.

30. Walter Benjamin, "Anmerkungen zu 'Franz Kafka: Zur zehnten Wiederkehr seines Todestages'," *Gesammelte Schriften*, vol. 2.3 (Frankfurt am Main: Suhrkamp, 1977), 1268.

31. Quoted in Walter Benjamin, "Franz Kafka: On the Tenth Anniversary of His Death," in *Selected Writings*, vol. 2, pt. 2, ed. Michael Jennings, Howard Eiland, and Gary Smith (Cambridge, MA: Harvard University Press, 2005), 798.

Precisely because there is no hope for us beyond the world, profane life acquires meaning and autonomy. In view of the futility of hope, Benjamin and Benjamin's Kafka ultimately did not care about the transcendent. While Scholem's dialectics oscillated between a focus on the absent God and a return to the world, Benjamin was concerned with saving the meaning and autonomy of the world against a Gnostic transcendence. To put it in Hans Blumenberg's words, he wanted to "overcome Gnosticism."[32] Just as he was not concerned with Gnostic transcendence, Benjamin had arguably no religious interest in the end of time or the coming of the Messiah either. Although he claimed that "every second was the small gateway in time through which the Messiah might enter,"[33] he was not interested in his *actual* coming but in the eternal *possibility* of his coming, and in the way this possibility influenced our perception of time and present. In other words, not the *Messiah* as such but the *messianic* was most central in Benjamin's thought. Unlike Scholem, Benjamin did not consider the Messiah as the only instance that could truly generate meaning. The Messiah is rather a limit concept that made historical meaning possible even if his coming is eternally deferred.

For Benjamin, the experience of meaning in a world that is waiting for the Messiah was always fragmentary and never complete. But even such a fragmentary possibility of meaning in history shows that there is unity between the profane and the messianic. In this sense, the messianic is not Gnostically opposed to the profane but ultimately completes and redeems history—as the enigmatic first line of the "Theological-Political Fragment" states, "Only the Messiah completes all history."[34] In redemption, the unity of the messianic and the profane is complete, as it marks the end of history, where the absolute low point of the profane coincides with the fullness of the messianic. Only here would the historically fragmented meaning become whole again. Benjamin conceived of the

---

32. Hans Blumenberg, *The Legitimacy of the Modern Age,* trans. Robert Wallace (Cambridge, MA: MIT Press, 1983), 126.
33. Benjamin, "On the Concept of History," 397.
34. Benjamin, "Theological-Political Fragment," 305.

unity of the messianic and the profane without, however, ascribing any teleology to profane history. He emphasized that redemption is "not the goal, but the terminus" of history.[35] The presence of the messianic in history does not consist in the gradual historical progress toward redemption. If this were the case, the arrows of the messianic and the profane would point in the same direction. The meaning of history can consist only in its decay and its transience, in the fact that it brings itself to an end. In a less metaphysically charged fashion, Benjamin expressed the same ideas in *On the Concept of History*, where he radically criticized the narrative of historical continuity and progress, which he considered characteristic of the historiography of victors and rulers. For Benjamin, however, the messianic could appear only in the refusal to conform to this historical mainstream. It is the task of the historian to take the history of the repressed into account and to "to brush history against the grain."[36] Rather than a history of victory and progress, this would give rise to one of discontinuity, catastrophe, and decay.

Although human beings could not control this decay or realize the coming of the Messiah through action, Benjamin maintained, nonetheless, that one could go along with the transience of the profane through antinomian action. This antinomianism is the only meaningful comportment in the world and hence the only meaningful guideline for worldly politics. Benjamin concluded the "Theological-Political Fragment" accordingly: "To strive for such passing away—even the passing away of those stages of man that are nature—is the task of world politics, whose method must be called nihilism."[37] Scholem's redemption through sin could be a pertinent example of Benjamin's nihilistic world politics. Both conceptualized a meaningful comportment for a world where the messianic is initially completely absent, and proposed an active destruction of the profane that prefigures the coming of the Messiah. Both are obvious instantiations of religious nihilism. Although Benjamin's conception of the messianic as an inversion of the profane

---

35. Benjamin, 305.
36. Benjamin, "On the Concept of History," 392.
37. Benjamin, "Theological-Political Fragment," 306.

suited Scholem's interpretation, his political nihilism did not imply an active pursuit of redemption through sin but rather a refusal to act. For Benjamin, nihilism involved a retreat from politics. This rejection of politics, nonetheless, remained a fully political position. It is not the case that the "Theological-Political Fragment" had no political ideals at all, but rather that these ideals could be expressed only negatively in complete opposition to the current predicament. The messianic involvement with worldly politics is not one of gradual change or of improvement of the political status quo but one of revolution. Nihilistic politics must strive for radical transformation and for the complete abolishment of political lawfulness.

Benjamin did not give any examples of nihilistic politics in the "Theological-Political Fragment," but the role of political and revolutionary violence in his "Critique of Violence" can be considered as such.[38] If Scholem's dating of the "Fragment" is correct, both essays would have been written around the year 1921. Thus, it makes sense to interpret Benjamin's example of the strike in the "Critique of Violence" as an instantiation of nihilistic politics. The strike is initially purely negative: it is a mere refusal to work. Usually, this nonaction of the strike functions as the concrete means to bargain for better working conditions. Or, in the case of the general strike, the omission of action can even be a violent demand for political change. These strikes are not yet nihilistic, as they merely aim to modify and improve the current social or political situation without questioning the legitimacy of the sociopolitical order. They have a positive, lawmaking message that wants to change but not abolish politics. In this regard, the strike is a violent means to achieve very concrete political goals. However, Benjamin suggested that this logic of means and ends is absent in the revolutionary or proletarian strike. The nonaction of the strike is here genuine political nihilism. While the usual refusal to work is active in that it wants to realize certain positive contents, the revolutionary strike

---

38. Walter Benjamin, "Critique of Violence," in *Selected Writings*, vol. 1, *1913–1926*, ed. Marcus Bullock and Michael Jennings (Cambridge, MA: Harvard University Press, 2004), 236–52.

is a pure nonaction without any positive objectives and concrete ends. To put it in Benjamin's words, it is a "pure means." Only in this complete omission of action can the strike truly oppose the logic of the state. Accordingly, the revolutionary strike is not law-making or law-preserving, but law-destroying. As a nihilistic opposition to the state, it does not aim for political change but points to an anarchic justice beyond and opposite the current sociopolitical order.

Just as historical change and progress did not lead to redemption in the "Theological-Political Fragment," so did political change not lead to justice in the "Critique of Violence." Redemption and justice are on a completely different level beyond profane history and beyond the state. Accordingly, they require a catastrophic and nihilistic revolution that reverses and destroys the previous order of immanence. Nonetheless, we can never be sure, as human beings, whether our actions realize this revolution or not. Benjamin made this very clear in his discussion of revolutionary violence. Human beings are capable of violent action that is genuinely law-destroying, nihilistic, redemptive, and hence akin to what Benjamin called "divine violence,"[39] but we cannot know whether this or that specific use of violence actually leads to a state beyond immanent lawfulness. From our position within the realm of profane politics, we cannot judge whether certain uses of violence are truly revolutionary or not.[40] To return to the terminology of the "Theological-Political Fragment," there is a meaningful messianic relation to the unredeemed realm of profane possible in the form of political nihilism. This nihilism is, moreover, the antinomian and redemptive realization of worldly transience. However, it is impossible to know whether and how our concrete actions in this world meaningfully relate to the messianic and lead to redemption.

---

39. Benjamin, "Critique of Violence," 248.

40. Benjamin, 252: "But if the existence of violence outside the law, as pure immediate violence, is assured, this furnishes the proof that revolutionary violence, the highest manifestation of unalloyed violence by man, is possible, and by what means. Less possible and also less urgent for humankind, however, is to decide when unalloyed violence has been realized in particular cases."

On this point, the parallel with Scholem's redemption through sin tends to break down.

Jacob Taubes: Paul's Negative Political Theology

The question of meaning and agency in an unredeemed, nihilistic world was also an important leitmotif in the thought of Jacob Taubes. Taubes approached this question almost always from the point of view of Apocalypticism: How does the realization that there is an end to time influence the way we live in history? Not unlike Gnosticism and messianism, Apocalypticism radically put the spiritual meaning of the world in jeopardy. If God is supposed to destroy the world at the end of time, the history of the world has to be rejected as transitory, finite, and even radically evil. Nonetheless, as history has not yet come to an end, the Apocalypticist inevitably has to decide how to live in and make sense of history as a transitory period. Again, the passivity of resignation and anticipation cannot be a viable option. Although the Apocalypticist rejects profane history and politics, he cannot escape his involvement in them. In other words, he cannot escape the simple fact that he lives in history and is part of a political community.

In *The Political Theology of Paul,* Taubes argued that these are also the problems that the apostle Paul faced. On the one hand, Paul expected Christ's second coming (*parousia*), thus being convinced that salvation and the end of time were imminent. On the other hand, he wanted to establish a Christian community on the basis of his apocalyptic vision. Instead of proclaiming passive resignation in view of the imminent end, Paul wanted to gather the people who are waiting for Christ's second coming in a political association. In Taubes's view, Paul's project is political theology: he established a political community on the basis of the theological conviction that there is an end to time and that he lived in a transitory period. In this politico-theological spirit, Paul's aim was the "establishment and legitimation of a new people of God."[41] Taubes understood

---

41. Jacob Taubes, *The Political Theology of Paul,* trans. Dana Hollander (Stanford: Stanford University Press, 2004), 28.

Paul's endeavor as a repetition of Moses's establishment of the Jewish people as the people of God. In Christ's message, Paul found a new foundation for the establishment of a people that at the same time universalized the idea of God's people. The notion of the holy people no longer merely concerned the Jews but in principle included everyone. Paul was the apostle of the Gentiles.

Paul's apocalyptic community is what we still know today as the church. For obvious reasons, the church has tried to suppress its apocalyptic roots as much as possible. Since Paul believed that the end of the world was near, the political legitimacy of his community was essentially transitory. The community itself had no absolute legitimacy because it was to be abolished at the end of time together with all worldly and political affairs. According to Taubes, Paul's apocalyptic worldview delegitimized political order as such. Paradoxically, Paul's political community is premised on the apocalyptic rejection of all politics. Not unlike its more radical Gnostic variants, Paul's church prepared and even strived for its own abolishment at the end of time. The Gnostic church of Marcion portrayed the same dynamic but made the apocalyptic (self-) annihilation into a more explicit project. Marcion's community of ascetics was based on an absolute ban on sexual intercourse. Taubes interpreted this celibacy as an apocalyptic policy: "To think this through means, after all, to starve the world by withholding the seed from it. It's a church that practices, or executes, the end of the world."[42] The obvious result of this celibacy was of course the disintegration of the community itself. If the members of the Marcionite community were prohibited to reproduce, the church would eventually die out. Paradoxically, this self-annihilation was the very point of the apocalyptic political association.

As the Marcionite celibacy inverted the logic of the profane (sexual reproduction) through a complete omission of action (abstaining from sexual intercourse), it could be understood as nihilistic politics in the Benjaminian sense.[43] Unlike the dynamics of

42. Taubes, *The Political Theology of Paul*, 58.
43. In view of the discussion of Benjamin's anti-Gnostic stance in the previous section, it seems impossible to maintain Taubes's more general claim that Benjamin is a modern Marcionite: Jacob Taubes, "Walter Benjamin—ein moderner

redemption through sin that Scholem discovered, the Marcionite church did not pursue redemption through an act of transgression but through a nihilistic refusal to act. Benjamin and Taubes maintained that this refusal was nonetheless a political act, however empty, nihilistic, and antipolitical it seemed. Even the theological rejection of profane politics remained ultimately a political position on which a community could be established. In this regard, apocalypticism had a political theology, albeit necessarily a negative one: theology no longer legitimized a certain political order by showing how it represented the divine but delegitimized political order as such.[44] In view of the imminent end of time, no political community has any divine justification. This negation of politics and of every dominant political order itself becomes the cornerstone of apocalyptic politics. This was a fortiori the case for Paul and his Epistle to the Romans, said Taubes: "This is why my thesis is that in this sense the epistle to the Romans is a political theology, a *political* declaration of war on the Caesar."[45] Paul's apocalyptic theology implied a rejection of politics that targeted the dominant political order of that moment—namely, the Roman Empire. This theological rejection was from the outset also a form of political protest that can be considered illiberal, anarchic, or nihilistic. Taubes also interpreted Paul's paradigmatic criticism of the law (*nomos*) along these lines. Paul's notion of the law, for Taubes, referred not only to the religious concept of Mosaic law but primarily to the political concept of Roman law: "The concept of law—and this again is political theology—is a compromise formula of the Imperium Romanum."[46] In line with this antinomian criticism of the law, Paul conceived the end of time as the abolishment of all political law and authority. The dynamics of

---

Marcionit? Scholems Benjamin-Interpretation religionsgeschichtlich überprüft," in *Apokalypse und Politik: Aufsätze, Kritiken und kleinere Schriften,* ed. Herbert Kopp-Oberstebrink and Martin Treml (Munich: Wilhelm Fink, 2017), 286–98.

44. For the notion of "negative political theology," see Wolf-Daniel Hartwich, Aleida Assmann, and Jan Assmann, "Afterword," in Taubes, *Political Theology of Paul,* 139.

45. Taubes, *Political Theology of Paul,* 16.

46. Taubes, 23.

redemption concretely ran counter to the profane politics of the Roman Empire. Accordingly, Christ can only be the Messiah in a complete opposition to the political power of the Roman law. From the perspective of immanence and profane politics, the Messiah could appear only as the loser and the weakling. In this regard, Roman law as it were confirmed Christ's messianic status in his crucifixion. From the perspective of the messianic, however, this weakness proved that Christ is superior to the profane realm of politics: "It isn't *Nomos* but rather the one nailed to the cross by *Nomos* who is the imperator!"[47] What ultimately prevailed is not Roman law but its antinomian rejection.

Interestingly, Taubes argued that Paul established a Christian community on the basis of this antinomian rejection of politics. Paul's negative political theology of protest entailed a rule of political conduct in a transitory period. Not unlike Scholem and Benjamin, Taubes was interested in the dialectical consequences of a radical world-negation for the continuing association with this world. In his reading of Paul, this question got a very practical and political twist: "We're living in the evil Roman Empire, so how are we living there?"[48] There is a whole range of possible answers to this question, going from the Marcionite celibacy that wanted to destroy society by cutting it off from its source of human reproduction to the violent Gnostic revolutions that prefigure Sabbatian redemption through sin. Paul's alternative was certainly less revolutionary than these Gnostic answers. If the end of the world is as imminent as Paul thought it was, it seems more reasonable to keep quiet and avoid provoking the political establishment. Nonetheless, Paul did not recommend mere indifference to the world either. He rather proposed a nihilistic association with the world that kept on doing the things one used to do but in the full consciousness of their futility. This was a way of living in the world as though one does not belong to it. In this sense, it was a kind of mockery of all worldly affairs. This attitude, which Taubes recognized in Paul's notion of "as though not" (*hos me*), was a negation and

47. Taubes, 24.
48. Taubes, 40.

inversion of all the worldly relations, actions, and properties. Paul suggested doing exactly those things that one is expected to do but with an inverted valuation, thus eroding and nullifying the meaning of these actions. Taubes quoted here from Paul's Epistle to the Corinthians: "The appointed time has grown short. From now on, let even those who have wives be as though they had none, and those who mourn as though they were not mourning, and those who rejoice as though they were not rejoicing, and those who buy as though they had no possessions, and those who deal with the world as though they had no dealings with it. For the present form of this world is passing away. I want you to be free from anxieties" (1 Corinthians 7:29). These are obviously more sublimated forms of antinomian revolt against immanence than mere violent action. Nonetheless, Paul's "as though not" represented the same messianic logic of inversion as Scholem's redemption through sin. Both concepts conceived of a method to live profane history in the opposite direction. However, Paul took away the violent edge of redemption through sin by interiorizing this opposition. Taubes also emphasized the parallel between Benjamin's political nihilism and this passage from Paul's Epistle to the Corinthians.[49] According to Taubes, all the elements of Benjamin's "Theological-Political Fragment" were already present in Paul. First, Paul's assertion that the world is passing away clearly returned in Benjamin's notions of decay and transience. Moreover, the interiorized nullification and inversion of all profane actions is an obvious example of world politics as nihilism. Finally, Benjamin's metaphor of the opposing arrows of the profane and the messianic took a very concrete shape in Paul's strategy of the "as though not." The messianic is the opposite of the profane but never more than just the opposite: mourning/not mourning, rejoicing/not rejoicing, dealing/not dealing, and so on. For Paul and Benjamin alike, the messianic could be

---

49. For a critique of Taubes's interpretation of Paul and Benjamin, see Sigrid Weigel, "In Paul's Mask: Jacob Taubes Reads Walter Benjamin," in *Theological Genealogies: Reflections on Secularization in 20th-Century German Thought,* ed. Stéphane Symons and Willem Styfhals (Albany: SUNY, forthcoming).

understood or put into practice only negatively and nihilistically as the inversion of the profane.

Ultimately, Scholem, Benjamin, and Taubes were concerned with the dialectics of an initial rejection of the world, a dualistic escape into transcendence or the end of time, and a return to immanence or time. What is at stake philosophically in their preoccupation with Gnosticism, messianism, Apocalypticism, or Pauline Christianity is not the exclusive emphasis on the transcendent but the residual meaning of immanence. In his own commentary on Paul, *The Time That Remains,* the Italian philosopher Giorgio Agamben interpreted the concept of messianism in the work of Scholem, Benjamin, and Taubes along the same lines. He concluded more radically and explicitly than these three Jewish thinkers that "the messianic vocation is a movement of immanence, or, if one prefers, a zone of absolute indiscernibility between immanence and transcendence, between this world and the future world."[50] Paul's prime concern, for Agamben as well as for Taubes, was not the end of time as such but the way in which it changed the present experience of time and immanence. Accordingly, Agamben showed that "the messianic is not the end of time but the time of the end."[51] The pure orientation toward the end of time is dualistic and implies the passive attitude of eschatological indifference, whereas the messianic experience of the time of the end is dialectical and implies an active involvement in this world. Messianic time presupposes the notion of an end of time but emphasizes its implications for the continuation of our life in an unredeemed present. Not transcendence but immanence is at stake here. Taubes considered this to be Paul's most immediate concern: "In what epoch are we living, what sort of present time is this?"[52]

---

50. Giorgio Agamben, *The Time That Remains: A Commentary on the Letter to the Romans,* trans. Patricia Dailey (Stanford: Stanford University Press, 2005), 25.

51. Agamben, *Time That Remains,* 62.

52. Taubes, *Political Theology of Paul,* 53.

Toward an Overcoming of Religious Nihilism

The exploration of the twentieth-century interpretations of Jewish messianism has shown that the problem of religious nihilism goes beyond the scope of Gnosticism and concerns every eschatological religion that is confronted with the deferment of redemption and the end of time. The problem is of course more explicit in the Gnostic speculations where the separation between immanence and transcendence, between history and redemption, is as radical as it can get. The underlying nihilistic question, however, exceeds the specific case of Gnosticism: how to cope with a world that apparently has lost all its meaning in comparison to an unreachable transcendence. More than that, this question even exceeds the boundaries of religious thinking, as the same quest for meaning in a nihilistic world equally motivates the secular philosophies after the death of God. Establishing the connection between religious and secular nihilisms, Scholem, Benjamin, and Taubes interpreted it as a continuation of religious motives within secular thought.

Nihilism, in all these variants, rendered impossible any immediate acceptance of the world or any *spiritual investment in the world as it is*. In view of the absolute absence of divine meaning in this world, the immediate spiritual attachment to the world had become problematic. Scholem, Benjamin, and Taubes promoted an antinomian investment in the world that reversed the current order of the world. They pursued a spiritual investment without accepting the world as it is. This chapter indeed emphasized that their religious nihilisms did not exclude an involvement in this world but, on the contrary, provided very concrete lines of immanent action.

As such, religious nihilism does allow for a connection between the transcendent and the immanent, even if it rejects the traditional metaphysics of participation where the world reflects and parallels the beyond. This relation, however, is not one of participation but of opposition. Immanence does not parallel the transcendence order; rather, it is its mirror image. From this conception of transcendence derives a course of action that inverts the order of immanence—concretely taking shape in forms of conduct as diverse as Gnostic provocation, Sabbatian redemption through sin,

Benjaminian political nihilism, revolutionary violence, negative political theology, Marcionite asceticism, and Pauline *hos me*. In spite of its potential for extremism, religious nihilism is actually nuanced at the moment it becomes an active and immanent principle, for it precludes the risk of losing oneself in a Gnostic, world-negating transcendence and admits to the practical necessity of turning back and conforming to immanence. The return to immanence is a first step toward the overcoming of Gnosticism. While Taubes's and Scholem's interest in immanence was still premised on Gnosticism conceived dialectically, and hence on an explicitly religious motivation, Benjamin's more substantial focus on the profane already entailed an explicit rejection of Gnosticism, and hence a diminishing interest in religious transcendence.

In *The Legitimacy of the Modern Age*, Hans Blumenberg radicalized this tendency, associating the modern investment in immanence with the "overcoming of Gnosticism."[53] From a radically different perspective, Blumenberg was also interested in the dialectical implications of a Gnostic world-negation for the remaining value of life in this world. As the next two chapters show, he explored how in late medieval theology a Gnostic transcendence proved to be fundamentally inaccessible and necessitated a modern revaluation of immanence. This modern revaluation did not negate Gnosticism's nihilistic premise, for Blumenberg; rather, it made its "disappearance of order" immanently productive.[54] Modern self-assertion found in this meaninglessness the potential to intervene in the world and change it to humanity's own benefit, thus asserting the meaning of finite existence on earth in favor of the futile focus on an absent God. Gnostic transcendence even became disposable once the dialectic of a world-negating transcendence had necessitated the return to immanence. For Blumenberg, the immanent implications of Gnosticism went beyond the scope of religion proper, thus overcoming Gnosticism.

Gnosticism could trigger a modern and worldly reaction against its unworldliness but could not itself be made worldly, for

---

53. Blumenberg, *Legitimacy*, 126.
54. Blumenberg, 137.

Blumenberg. In his understanding, the Gnostic world-negation itself could not entail any substantial relation to the world. He explicitly stated this in a reply to Taubes's discussion of the relation between Gnosticism and surrealist provocation at the second gathering of the interdisciplinary Poetik und Hermeneutik research group: "Gnosticism did not know protest and revolt as forms of reaction. The call of the bearer of salvation from out of transcendence is not an appeal to any kind of behavior in relation to the world, let alone to an action against the world; rather the call exhausts itself in the actualization of anamnesis, in the restitution of the relation to the origin of human interiority."[55] Blumenberg's account of Gnosticism radically opposed Taubes's interpretation, on both conceptual and historical grounds. Blumenberg's interpretation was therefore dualistic rather than dialectical, as the Gnostic acosmism could not condition worldly behavior in and of itself. For Taubes, on the contrary, Gnostic acosmism had very concrete implications for the immanent spheres of history and politics—notably in the form of protest and revolt. The first lines of Taubes's introduction to the essay collection *Gnosis und Politik* could neither summarize his intellectual project more clearly nor make the opposition to Blumenberg more manifest: "Gnosticism and politics seem to be opposites. As an escape out of time and out of history, 'Gnosis' in all its variants posits itself against any politics. Yet, this escape itself can be pointed to historically."[56] The Gnostic hostility toward this world can and should be recuperated within this world in political and historical action. Only by virtue of this dialectic in which world-negation itself is made worldly—that is, secularized (*verweltlicht*)—could Gnosticism continue its legacy in the modern age, for Taubes. What was at stake in this disagreement between Taubes and Blumenberg was not just a historical interpretation of

---

55. Hans Blumenberg, "Reply to Notes on Surrealism," in Jacob Taubes, *From Cult to Culture: Fragments toward a Critique of Historical Reason*, ed. Charlotte Elisheva Fonrobert and Amir Engel (Stanford: Stanford University Press, 2010), 117.

56. Jacob Taubes, "Vorwort," in *Gnosis und Politik*, ed. Jacob Taubes (Berlin: Wilhelm Fink, 1984), 5.

Gnosticism but also the nature of the modern. This becomes particularly clear in the next two chapters. For Taubes, Gnosticism could return and be secularized in modernity because it could be made worldly. Against Taubes, Blumenberg stated that modernity had to overcome Gnosticism precisely because it resisted such secularization or *Verweltlichung*.

5

EPOCH

The Gnostic Age

The issue of modern Gnosticism crystallized, in postwar German philosophy, in a very concrete debate between Eric Voegelin and Hans Blumenberg. The relevance of Gnosticism for the under-standing of specific modern evolutions and thinkers had been dis-cussed prior to them, as the previous chapters have shown. Yet, the relation between Gnosticism and modernity had never been understood as explicitly and in as all-embracing a manner as in Voegelin's and Blumenberg's work. Rather than discussing specific examples of Gnostic revival, they connected it to an entire epoch. They used the concept of Gnosticism to get a grip on something as hazy and general as "the modern age" (*Neuzeit*) itself. How-ever, their views on the relation between Gnosticism and moder-nity were radically different from each other. Whereas Voegelin argued that the "modern age . . . would better be named the Gnos-tic age,"[1] Blumenberg made the opposite claim in *Die Legitimität der Neuzeit* (*The Legitimacy of the Modern Age*): "The modern

---

1. Eric Voegelin, "The Oxford Political Philosophers," *Philosophical Quarterly* 11, no. 3 (1953): 111.

age is the second overcoming of Gnosticism."[2] Blumenberg did not define modernity as the return of Gnosticism but as a reaction against its return. To summarize Blumenberg's complex historical picture, Gnosticism was overcome a first time in Augustine's refutation of Manichaeism, returned in late medieval nominalism, and was overcome a second time in modern thought. In short, modernity was Gnostic for Voegelin, anti-Gnostic for Blumenberg.

Before Voegelin and Blumenberg developed these interpretations of the modern age, the notion of Gnosticism had already been excised from its immediate historical and theological meaning and used metaphorically to make sense of specific modern phenomena. Precisely because the connection between Gnosticism and its original historical meaning loosened, Voegelin and Blumenberg were able to extend its metaphorical use to define an entire epoch. As a result of this, not only did Gnosticism lose the conceptual connection to its original meaning, but it also became absolutely unclear what Voegelin and Blumenberg meant exactly when they associated Gnosticism with the modern age. For much the same reason, it is unclear how Voegelin's and Blumenberg's theories relate to each other or can be opposed to each other. For, in spite of their opposed interpretations of modernity and Gnosticism, a real debate between Voegelin and Blumenberg did not take place. One can only guess what they thought about each other's interpretation of Gnosticism and modernity. Nonetheless, Blumenberg would have very likely dismissed Voegelin's position as the umpteenth example of secularization theory, which tries to make sense of secular modernity by showing how it unconsciously remains indebted to theological structures.

---

2. Hans Blumenberg, *Die Legitimität der Neuzeit* (Frankfurt am Main: Suhrkamp, 1966); Hans Blumenberg, *Die Legitimität der Neuzeit,* 2nd rev. ed. (Frankfurt am Main: Suhrkamp, 1976), 138; English translation: Hans Blumenberg, *The Legitimacy of the Modern Age,* trans. Robert Wallace (Cambridge, MA: MIT Press, 1983), 126. For unknown reasons, Blumenberg omitted the word "second" in this quote in the revised edition of 1976. Robert Wallace reintroduced it in his translation.

This chapter primarily aims to reconstruct Voegelin's interpretation of philosophical and political modernity by investigating the meaning of his claim that Gnosticism is "the nature of modernity" and exploring how his concept of Gnosticism is related, or not, to its original historical meaning.[3] This discussion then allows for a more substantial comparison between Voegelin and Blumenberg that proceeds from a shared structural understanding of Christianity. Blumenberg's interpretation of the overcoming of Gnosticism will be developed more extensively in the next chapter.

Jacob Taubes and the Voegelin-Blumenberg Debate

Voegelin and Blumenberg never made an effort to discuss their opposed interpretations of modernity, and they neither met nor corresponded. The main reason why they never debated their opposed positions is that the obvious terminological resemblances of their theories did not imply a shared conceptual framework. First, they had a very different historical understanding of the modern epoch itself. Voegelin, on the one hand, had an extremely broad and generalist conception of modernity. The modern age, in which we supposedly still live today, began for Voegelin in the twelfth century with Joachim of Fiore. There is a tendency in Voegelin's work to call everything modern that deviated in some way from traditional Christian or ancient thought. Accordingly, late medieval heresy, seventeenth-century science or philosophy, nineteenth-century progressivism, and totalitarian politics were all equally modern for Voegelin. Blumenberg, on the other hand, had a more precise and generally accepted understanding of modernity. What he called *Neuzeit* is basically a paradigm in intellectual history that largely coincided with modern philosophy and began with Descartes. In addition, Voegelin and Blumenberg had very different conceptions of Gnosticism. Whereas Blumenberg referred to Marcionism and emphasized Gnosticism's dualistic metaphysics, Voegelin's

---

3. Eric Voegelin, *The New Science of Politics: An Introduction* (Chicago: University of Chicago Press, 1952), 107.

conception of Gnosticism had a clear Valentinian twist and focused on its mystical conception of knowledge (gnosis).

Blumenberg and Voegelin also hardly referred to each other's work. Voegelin developed his thesis about the Gnostic nature of modernity mainly in his *New Science of Politics* of 1952.[4] As the book was published several years before Blumenberg's *Legitimacy of the Modern Age* (1966), Voegelin obviously could not have referred to him at the time of writing, but even after 1966 he never made an effort to defend his own position against Blumenberg or even to refer to him in his later writings on Gnosticism. Blumenberg, in turn, never mentioned Voegelin's name in *The Legitimacy of the Modern Age*. However, when Blumenberg referred to "*he who says that the modern age would better be entitled the Gnostic age*," he obviously had Voegelin in mind. Although Blumenberg reversed the latter's claim, he explicitly considered Voegelin's thesis as programmatic for his own understanding of modernity: "The thesis I intend to argue here begins by agreeing that there is a connection between the modern age and Gnosticism, but interprets it in the reverse sense: the modern age is the second overcoming of Gnosticism." Blumenberg did take up Voegelin's suggestion but was ultimately not concerned with the philosophical complexities of Voegelin's theory: "I am not particularly interested in determining what the author in fact meant by this phrase."[5] Accordingly, he neither quoted Voegelin nor entered into further discussion with him. In this regard, it might be conceivable that Blumenberg did not even read *The New Science of Politics*. Voegelin's provocative thesis was well known in the German intellectual world of the 1960s, and the few sentences that are dedicated to Voegelin in *The Legitimacy of the Modern Age* did not require more than the general familiarity with his thesis that most German intellectuals must have had.[6]

---

4. Voegelin, *New Science of Politics*, 107–32.

5. Blumenberg, *Legitimacy*, 126.

6. Moreover, Blumenberg actually refers to the wrong text in his only footnote on Voegelin. Instead of referring to *The New Science of Politics*, he refers to a short review essay on political philosophy where Voegelin mentions the issue of the

Although Blumenberg and Voegelin did not immediately recognize the potential for an intellectual debate in their opposed definitions of modernity, their common acquaintance and correspondent Jacob Taubes did. Only a few months after the publication of *The Legitimacy of the Modern Age,* Taubes asked Blumenberg in a letter: "What would you think if I invited you and Voegelin in Berlin, or ask Voegelin to invite us in Munich to discuss your Gnosticism-thesis in his circle?"[7] Voegelin seemed genuinely interested in a discussion, but Blumenberg declined Taubes's invitation. He did not feel like discussing issues that he felt done with after working on them for so many years. Taubes, however, insisted, and Blumenberg eventually gave in. He agreed to come to Berlin for a conference that Taubes hosted in November 1967, but by that time Voegelin was no longer able to participate.[8]

Although the meeting between Voegelin and Blumenberg never took place, Taubes's idea of bringing them together initiated, in and of itself, an influential intellectual debate. Taubes, as it were, construed the debate by emphasizing the opposition between two interpretations of modernity and Gnosticism in which the representatives of both positions were hardly interested. The fact that Blumenberg and Voegelin never engaged in this debate themselves does not mean that it is an irrelevant one. The debate was mainly construed in the reception of their respective works, first and foremost by Taubes himself but also by other postwar German

---

Gnostic nature of the modern age only in passing: Blumenberg, *Legitimacy,* 126; Eric Voegelin, "Philosophie der Politik in Oxford," *Philosophische Rundschau* 1, no. 1 (1953): 41.

7. Jacob Taubes, "Letter to Hans Blumenberg of December 14, 1966," in Hans Blumenberg and Jacob Taubes, *Briefwechsel 1961–1981,* ed. Herbert Kopp-Oberstebrink and Martin Treml (Berlin: Suhrkamp, 2013), 110.

8. See Eric Voegelin, "Letter to Jacob Taubes of January 23, 1967," in *Selected Correspondence: 1950–1984* (Columbia: University of Missouri Press, 2007), 519–20. In this letter, Voegelin said: "I am very sorry to hear that Mr. Blumenberg apparently finds himself in a state of depression at the moment, because I would really have enjoyed meeting with him in order to have to opportunity for a conversation. Next winter such a conversation will hardly be possible, at least as far as I am concerned, since I will have a sabbatical semester which I will spend in America."

thinkers.[9] Voegelin's and Blumenberg's relevant texts on modern Gnosticism were, for example, taken up and opposed to each other in an anthology of Gnostic texts complied by leading contemporary philosopher Peter Sloterdijk.[10] Moreover, philosophers like Odo Marquard and Jacob Taubes himself or, more recently, Michael Pauen and Richard Faber developed their own Gnostic readings of modernity in explicitly referring to Voegelin's and Blumenberg's opposed positions.[11] As such, the "Voegelin-Blumenberg debate" played an absolutely central role in the postwar reflections on Gnosticism and in postwar German philosophy more generally.

Taubes's role in the debate between Voegelin and Blumenberg he had in mind was clearly not reducible to that of a passive organizer. As pointed out, he had an active role in conceiving a confrontation between two thinkers who did not present their ideas as such. Unlike the more systematic philosophers Blumenberg and Voegelin, Taubes was essentially a polemical thinker. He was the kind of intellectual who always looked for opportunities for confrontation and debate. Throughout his academic career, Taubes had always been concerned with the practical transposition of ideas that were presented in monological or monographic form into the more dialogical academic mediums of debate, commentary, seminar, colloquium, essay collection, and correspondence. Not surprisingly, Blumenberg called Taubes "someone who is made for inter-subjectivity."[12] Taubes's intellectual style seemed completely

---

9. Almost twenty years later, Taubes even dedicated an edited volume to the Voegelin-Blumenberg debate: Jacob Taubes, ed., *Gnosis und Politik* (Munich: Wilhelm Fink, 1984).

10. Thomas Macho and Peter Sloterdijk, eds., *Weltrevolution der Seele: Ein Lese- und Arbeitsbuch der Gnosis von der Spätantike bis zu der Gegenwart*, 2 vols. (Lahnau: Artemis und Winkler, 1991).

11. See Odo Marquard, "Das Gnostische Rezidiv als Gegenneuzeit," in *Gnosis und Politik*, ed. Jacob Taubes (Munich: Wilhelm Fink, 1984), 31–36; Michael Pauen, *Dithyrambiker des Untergangs: Gnostizismus in Ästhetik und Philosophie der Moderne* (Berlin: Akademie, 1994); Richard Faber, *Politische Dämonologie: Über modernen Marcionismus* (Würzburg: Königshausen und Neumann, 2007).

12. See Herbert Kopp-Oberstebrink, "Affinitäten, Dissonanzen: Die Korrespondenz zwischen Hans Blumenberg und Jacob Taubes," in Blumenberg and Taubes, *Briefwechsel*, 304–11.

opposed to that of Blumenberg, who was the typical secluded philosopher writing bulky volumes in complete isolation and avoiding
direct confrontation and discussion.[13] It is hardly surprising, in this
regard, that Blumenberg declined Taubes's invitation.

In addition to his intellectual inclination to debating, Taubes
had more philosophical reasons for being actively involved in this
debate. He was indeed genuinely interested in the relation between
Gnosticism and modernity himself. In *Occidental Eschatology*,
Taubes discussed the role of Gnosticism and Gnostic Apocalypticism in the Western intellectual tradition from antiquity to modernity. Nonetheless, he never treated this topic as systematically and
explicitly as Voegelin and Blumenberg did. Thus, Taubes discovered in the Voegelin-Blumenberg debate the systematic framework
in which he could express his own ideas on gnosis and modernity.
In other words, Taubes wanted not only to organize a debate between the two thinkers but also to actively take a position in this
debate himself. Interestingly, Taubes would take up a third position, in between those of Blumenberg and Voegelin. On the one
hand, he agreed with Voegelin that modernity is the Gnostic age;
on the other hand, he supported Blumenberg's defense of the legitimacy of modern thought.

Voegelin was very critical of modern culture in general and believed that Gnostic modernity entailed an illegitimate secularization
of Christian theology. Modern thought, he argued, *immanentizes*
the Christian promise of a transcendent salvation into the controllable pursuit of this-worldly redemption. This heretical and illusory attempt to draw such a religious mystery, which by definition
transcends human understanding, into the realm of human action
was also characteristic of the ancient Gnostic mind-set. For Voegelin, this process of immanentization was ultimately responsible for
the rise of the political religions of communism and Nazism in the

---

13. In a letter to Taubes on *The Legitimacy of the Modern Age* he explicitly stated this: "Es gibt Stellen, an denen ich Namen nicht genannt habe, weil ich
den Anschein der Polemik fürchtete." This is one of the reasons why he declined
Taubes's invitation to debate with Voegelin and why he barely mentioned Voegelin's name in the first place. Hans Blumenberg, "Letter to Jacob Taubes of January 9, 1967," in Blumenberg and Taubes, *Briefwechsel*, 120.

twentieth century. Blumenberg, on the contrary, wanted to defend the legitimacy of modernity by showing how it did not imply a secularization or continuation of religious and, more specifically, Gnostic contents. Modern thought, for Blumenberg, had its own autonomous logic that was not reducible to religious developments but that arose in dynamic relation to such developments. Taubes ultimately subscribed to Voegelin's secularization thesis but evaluated the continuity between Gnosticism and modernity much more positively. In contrast to Voegelin, Taubes did not fear Gnosticism's destructive potential, which he recognized in the modernist avantgarde or in revolutionary politics. He was indeed fascinated by the world-negating potential of Gnosticism and its radical implications for action within the immanent world. Taubes elucidated his middle position between Voegelin and Blumenberg in the letter in which he invited Voegelin to debate his Gnosticism thesis:

> Hans Blumenberg's *The Legitimacy of the Modern Age* recently appeared. A book that immediately concerns your, I would almost say our (although, where you put minus, I sometimes put plus), main thesis about modernity as the Gnostic age. *The New Science of Politics* provocatively challenged the legitimacy of modernity. In Blumenberg's book now arises a defense of modernity. I think we should discuss this among the three of us. What would you think if you and Blumenberg came to a colloquium in Berlin, first to treat the Gnosticism-thesis in the context of the history of religion, and later the problem of the legitimacy of modernity in a hermeneutical context.[14]

Taubes made clear that there were more fundamental questions at stake in the opposition between Voegelin and Blumenberg than a mere historical discussion about the return of Gnosticism in the modern age. At stake were the very same questions that characterized the German secularization debates: Does the rise of the modern epoch entail cultural decay or intellectual progress? How legitimate is the project of modernity? And is modernity as secular as it thinks it is?

---

14. Jacob Taubes, "Letter to Eric Voegelin of January 6, 1967," in Blumenberg and Taubes, *Briefwechsel*, 116.

De-divinization and Re-divinization

Voegelin's *New Science of Politics* is ultimately concerned with the question of secularization. What he called the Gnostic age is actually "a secular age," to use a more contemporary phrase.[15] In line with Jacob Taubes and Karl Löwith, he was interested in the way theological contents were secularized in modern thought. Unlike Taubes and Löwith, Voegelin did not explore the different modern examples of secularization in detail. Rather, he sought to find out how and why the immanentization of Christian theology could have taken place in modernity. Voegelin showed how secularization has its origins in the inner constitution of Christianity itself, and more specifically in its radical de-divinization of the world. Gnosticism's and modernity's failure to cope with this withdrawal of the divine from the cosmos forced them to re-divinize the world through the immanentization of Christian eschatology.

Christianity is a religion of de-divinization, argued Voegelin in *The New Science of Politics*. Unlike the polytheistic and mythical religions, the Christian believer no longer considers the divine to be immediately and univocally present within this world. Rather, God is fundamentally withdrawn from it. Accordingly, the cosmos appears as a de-divinized world that is nonetheless created and ordered by this world-transcendent God. Christianity thus portrayed an evolution from the "compact" experience of the divine within nature to a "differentiated" experience of a God outside of the cosmos.[16] This Christian tendency toward de-divinization, however, was from the outset accompanied by the heretical desire for a re-divinization of the world. This re-divinization, which characterized both ancient Gnosticism and modern secularism according

---

15. Charles Taylor, *A Secular Age* (Cambridge, MA: Harvard University Press, 2007).

16. Voegelin introduces the notions of compactness and differentiation to conceive the difference between mythical and philosophical worldviews: Voegelin, *New Science of Politics*, 157. These concepts become central categories in his analyses of the intellectual history of the West in his five-volume project *Order and History*: Eric Voegelin, *Order and History*, vol. 1, *Israel and Revelation* (Columbia: University of Missouri Press, 2001).

to Voegelin, attempted to draw the divine back into the cosmos by immanentizing Christianity's theological framework. Gnosis, in this regard, was a mystical knowledge that allowed for direct access to the divine from within the immanent world itself.

To the extent that *The New Science of Politics* was mainly concerned with political theory and with the nature of political representation, the implications of Christianity's de-divinization were for Voegelin first and foremost political. In Christian society, "the sphere of power is radically de-divinized; it has become temporal," Voegelin said.[17] In other words, worldly politics no longer represented a higher religious order or truth. The emperor, for example, could no longer be considered the representative or incarnation of God on earth. While losing its religious legitimation, worldly politics also attained autonomy with regard to religion. Politics and religion became separated for the first time in history and henceforth had their own independent logic. For Voegelin, Christianity therefore marked the end of political theology. The religious message of Christianity itself had no political meaning, only a spiritual one.[18] Christianity offered no guidelines for political action, only the expectation of salvation. The de-divinization of politics had its origins in Christianity's conception of eschatology. Christianity's redemptive end of time was not to be conceived in any apocalyptic, millennial, or chiliastic sense as the political realization of a perfect society. Following Augustine's conception of the end of time, Voegelin did not consider the Christian kingdom of God as the final stage of political history but as a spiritual condition that lies beyond the immanent spheres of politics and history. In other words, Christian eschatology has no political or historical significance whatsoever: it allows for neither a political theology nor a

---

17. Voegelin, *New Science of Politics*, 106.

18. In the famous debate between Carl Schmitt and Eric Peterson on the possibility of political theology in Christianity, Voegelin takes the side of Peterson. He explicitly agrees with Peterson that political theology cannot exist in (orthodox) Christianity: Voegelin, *New Science of Politics*, 106, 102n76. See also György Géréby, "Political Theology versus Theological Politics: Eric Peterson and Carl Schmitt," *New German Critique* 35, no. 3 (2008): 7–33.

philosophy of history. The eschatological de-divinization of politics thus coincided with a de-divinization of history.

Although the immediate presence of the divine in history and society had become problematical in Christianity, Voegelin would certainly not have argued that Christianity's ahistorical and apolitical message could not be represented here on earth. It should be represented, however, by a spiritual organization that renounces, at least in principle, its claim for political power—that is, by the church. In this regard, the church is the only remnant of a divine presence within Christian society. Because the church, as the representative of an eternal but apolitical truth within history, cannot itself have any political power, there has to be another institution that is responsible for the political organization of society—that is, the state. The latter, however, has to renounce any religious justification of its power. The emperor can no longer rule by divine right, nor can the state be the representative of a higher truth or transcendent order. They are merely responsible for the political organization of society in a purely immanent sense. Thus losing its divine legitimation, the state also acquires its own autonomous sphere of power over which the church has no authority at all. Voegelin considered this separation between church and state to be fundamental for every Christian society. He summarized it as follows:

> This left the church as the universal spiritual organization of saints and sinners who professed faith in Christ, as the representative of the *civitas Dei* in history, as the flash of eternity into time. And correspondingly it left the power organization of society as a temporal representation of man in the specific sense of that part of human nature that will pass away with the transfiguration of time into eternity. The one Christian society was articulated into its spiritual and temporal orders. In its temporal articulation it accepted the *conditio humana* without chiliastic fancies, while it heightened natural existence by the representation of spiritual destiny through the church.[19]

The separation between church and state was, in Voegelin's perspective, characteristic of Christian society during the Middle

---

19. Voegelin, *New Science of Politics*, 109.

Ages. The rise of modernity was then marked by the collapse of this separation through the re-divinization of the political sphere, which was caused, in turn, by a re-divinization of history. This modern re-divinization began, for Voegelin, as early as the twelfth century with Joachim of Fiore's Trinitarian philosophy of history. Joachim basically applied the theological structure of the Trinity to the course of profane history by dividing it into three successive epochs—respectively, the ages of the Father, the Son, and the Holy Spirit. In his theory of the three ages, the course of profane history got a divine meaning that it could not have had in orthodox Christianity. Thus, Joachim's philosophy of history broke radically with the traditional, Augustinian interpretation of world history as a purposeless succession of meaningless events. In the Augustinian view, only the history of salvation, which transcends profane history, has a clear meaning and eschatological direction. According to Voegelin, Joachim confused profane history with transcendent history because he applied the structure of the history of salvation to the history of the world: "The Joachitic speculation was an attempt to endow the immanent course of history with a meaning that was not provided in the Augustinian conception. And for this purpose Joachim used what he had at hand, that is, the meaning of transcendental history."[20] In other words, Joachim re-divinized history by immanentizing or secularizing Christianity's transcendent eschatology.

Voegelin explained how this process of secularization is radicalized in modern philosophies of history. Modernity's secular eschatologies transformed the hope for transcendent salvation into a progress toward an immanent state of perfection, often presented in the form of a pursuit of a perfect political society that is attainable within profane history itself. This situation becomes potentially dangerous when a society either believes it has already reached such a condition, or worse, when it claims to know the means to realize it. Virtually every political action, however immoral it may be, can be justified to reach this secular eschaton,

---

20. Voegelin, 119.

which is posited as the only and absolute goal of society. If a particular political order makes such absolutist claims, society is re-divinized according to Voegelin. Unlike Christian politics, these societies no longer recognize the relativity and temporality of their political legitimacy, but claim to have an absolute justification to the extent that they represent some kind of pseudo-religious truth. In modern thought and especially in the philosophy of Hegel and Marx, the absolute no longer appeared as an abstract ideal beyond this world but had become an identifiable position within history. This philosophical fallacy of confusing the merely immanent and relative with the absolute coincided for Voegelin with a real political danger.

The political implications of secularization, already present in nuce in the nineteenth-century philosophy of history, culminated in twentieth-century totalitarianism. In communism and Nazism, Voegelin argued, the immanent eschaton became a very real political goal, in the form of the classless society and the *Dritte Reich*, respectively. Only in such a context, where politics had set itself an absolute goal, could a concept like the "final solution" become politically conceivable. For Voegelin, political actions and solutions could never be never "final" or absolutely justified, unless they were guided by an absolute ideal lying beyond the domain of immanent politics. Political action, in its modern and totalitarian form, was no longer confined to its immanent function of ruling and representing a society but recovered its lost religious function by claiming to represent or even realize a pseudo-divine truth here on earth. Voegelin indeed characterized the totalitarian movements as political religions.[21] As totalitarianism completed the modern re-divinization of society, it is hardly surprising that it made use of (pseudo-)religious symbolism. It is often argued, in this regard, that the *Führer* had an almost divine status in Nazi Germany or that the totalitarian mass meetings resembled pagan rituals. Voegelin himself focused on the very specific example of the continuity of

---

21. Eric Voegelin, "The Political Religions," in *The Collected Works of Eric Voegelin*, vol. 5, *Modernity without Restraint*, ed. Manfred Henningsen (Columbia: University of Missouri Press, 2000), 19–73.

Joachitic symbols in totalitarianism: "In his Trinitarian eschatology Joachim created the aggregate of symbols which govern the self-interpretation of modern political society to this day."[22] He elaborated, for example, on the return of the Trinitarian structure of Joachim's historical speculation in the political and historical self-understanding of the Nazi empire as the *Dritte Reich* or, much earlier, of Moscow as the third Rome.

Voegelin now connected the modern re-divinization to the return of Gnosticism: "These Gnostic experiences, in the amplitude of their variety, are the core of the re-divinization of society."[23] This claim is surprising, to say the least. Voegelin's interpretation of Gnosticism as a religion of re-divinization and immanentization completely disregarded and even contradicted Hans Jonas's generally accepted understanding of Gnosticism as radically world-negating. The Gnostics paradigmatically emphasized the absolute transcendence of the divine and its fundamental absence from this world. Rather than a re-divinization, Gnosticism seemed to entail the most radical de-divinization of world, history, and society. As one commentator of Voegelin correctly noted, "His picture of Gnosticism is, of course, simply inaccurate. . . . The Gnostic god— at least the higher or father god—far from being a world-immanent god, was more radically world-transcendent than anything Christianity had ever envisioned."[24] Curiously, Voegelin never took this obvious interpretation of Gnosticism into account in *The New Science of Politics* (he did do so in his later writings, as will be shown).

Nonetheless, the connection between Gnosticism and modern immanentization is not completely out of place if one takes another central feature of the Gnostic religiosity into account. In spite of the absolute transcendence of the Gnostic God, a select company of believers—the Gnostic sectarians—claimed to have privileged

---

22. Voegelin, *New Science of Politics*, 111.
23. Voegelin, 124.
24. Russell Nieli, "Eric Voegelin's Evolving Ideas on Gnosticism, Mysticism, and Modern Radical Politics," *Independent Journal of Philosophy* 5 (1988): 96. See also James L. Wiser, "From Cultural Analysis to Philosophical Anthropology: An Examination of Voegelin's Concept of Gnosticism," *Review of Politics* 42 (1980): 92–104.

access to God's mind through the mystical knowledge of gnosis. Gnosis allowed for direct contact with the divine from within the world, in spite of God's absence from this world. Although communication between human beings and God was certainly not obliterated in orthodox Christianity's de-divinized world, it always remained mysterious and uncertain. Communication with a transcendent God was only possible through faith, and the only knowledge one could have about him was based on the tenuous relation of faith and trust. Gnosis (Greek for "knowledge") functioned as a heretical alternative to this uncertain Christian *cognitio fidei* (cognition through faith) because it allowed for a direct and certain knowledge of transcendence. In Voegelin's perspective, this meant that Gnosticism took the Christian de-divinization absolutely seriously and even radicalized it, but at the same time tried to regain an immediate access to the divine for which the Christian perspective did not allow. Thus, Gnosticism did not entail a merely divinized worldview; rather, it *re*-divinized immanent existence after its initial de-divinization through Christian orthodoxy: "The attempt at immanentizing the meaning of existence is fundamentally an attempt of bringing our knowledge of transcendence in to a firmer grip than the cognitio fidei, the cognition of faith will afford; and the Gnostic experiences offer this firmer grip insofar as they are an expansion of the soul to the point where God is drawn into the existence of man."[25] In spite of its ostensible historical inaccuracy, this quote from *The New Science of Politics* dovetailed with Hans Jonas's interpretation of Gnosticism. Although Jonas emphasized the importance of a metaphysical dualism, which is disregarded in Voegelin's account, he also allowed for the direct unity of the human and the divine that Voegelin suggested: "The dualism is between man and the world, and concurrently between the world and God. . . . In this three-term configuration—man, world, God—man and God belong together in contraposition to the world, but are in spite of their essential belonging-together, in fact separated precisely by the world."[26] This Gnostic unity of the human and the divine as well as the possibility of absolute knowledge that this

---

25. Voegelin, *New Science of Politics*, 124.
26. Hans Jonas, *The Gnostic Religion* (Boston: Beacon Press, 1958), 326.

unity guarantees was fundamental to Voegelin's interpretation of Gnosticism and its return in modern culture.

In Christianity, this certain and absolute knowledge about the divine was fundamentally impossible for Voegelin. As he provocatively put it, "Uncertainty is the very essence of Christianity."[27] He argued that the Christian believer is always in doubt about the transcendent purpose of existence, about the meaning of world, history, and society, and about the possibility of salvation. Gnosis pursued an existential certainty that Christianity could not guarantee. This very pursuit of certainty was ultimately also the driving force of modern secularization. Modern thought, said Voegelin, could not cope with these uncertainties about the most fundamental questions. In order to overcome them it reverted to a forgotten heretical potential that lay hidden within the Christian tradition itself. In this regard, secularization is no mere negation or corruption of religion but finds its origin in a tension within Christianity itself. The uncertainties that destabilized orthodox Christianity from within tended toward resolution and stabilization in Gnostic heresy. As long as Christianity exists, said Voegelin, there will be people "who do not have the spiritual stamina for the heroic adventure of the soul that is Christianity."[28] The possibility of Gnosticism can therefore never be rooted out completely. Gnosticism, in Voegelin's perspective, is the eternal, structural counterpart of orthodox Christianity. In order to overcome the Christian uncertainties, gnosis and modernity made the divine univocally present in the immanent world. The modern immanentization of Christian eschatology was therefore an attempt to capture and control the meaning of existence, and by extension also the meaning of history and the possibility of salvation. In modernity, the meaning of reality is no longer to be found in an unattainable salvation or in a world beyond, but can be discovered within the evolution of profane history itself. Modernity radicalizes the ancient Gnostic immanentization by ultimately denying transcendence itself. While the ancient Gnostic experience merely made the divine accessible for the immanent perspective by mystically drawing it

---

27. Voegelin, *New Science of Politics*, 122.
28. Voegelin, 123.

into the soul of the Gnostic believer, modernity is the complete immanentization of the divine to the point where transcendence itself is lost.

Gnosticism and the Inner-Christian Tension

In Voegelin's reflections on secularization, uncertainty appeared as the destabilizing factor in Christian orthodoxy that tended toward stabilization in Gnostic heresy and modern secularism. As such, uncertainty was not something to be avoided for Voegelin. On the contrary, it should be embraced, in religion as well as in philosophy, as the only sincere human relation to the beyond. Modern philosophy, argued Voegelin, could not cope with this incertitude and opted for the illusory certainty of gnosis rather than the uncertain truth of Christianity. Voegelin considered the philosophical and Gnostic attempts to overcome this uncertainty illusory because the finite human perspective did not allow for an absolute knowledge in his view: "The leap over the bounds of the finite into the perfection of actual knowledge is impossible. If a thinker attempts it, he is not advancing philosophy, but abandoning it to become a Gnostic."[29]

The Christian uncertainty appeared as the existential or epistemological implication of a deeper philosophical tension within the human condition itself. This tension was first revealed in the process of de-divinization, which Voegelin connected not only to Christianity, but in his later works to the entire range of intellectual and spiritual breakthroughs that are commonly associated with the "axial age." Voegelin, however, preferred the notion of "hierophanic events," which he borrowed from Mircea Eliade, to Karl Jasper's concept of axiality: "By letting man become conscious of his humanity as existence in tension toward divine reality, the hierophanic events engender the knowledge of men's existence in the

---

29. Eric Voegelin, "Science, Politics, and Gnosticism," in Henningsen, *Collected Works of Eric Voegelin*, 5:272.

divine-human In-between, in Plato's Metaxy."[30] Human existence is characterized by this middle position between this world and the beyond. Although human beings are directed toward the beyond, they can never have an absolute grip on it. This subtle balance between this world and the beyond that marks human nature is lost in Gnosticism and modernity, according to Voegelin.

This anthropological tension also has metaphysical implications that become particularly obvious in Christianity, and more specifically in its hesitation between this world and the beyond. In Christianity's de-divinized worldview, Voegelin maintained, the meaning of the divine for immanent being is highly ambiguous and indeed uncertain. *The New Science of Politics* mainly emphasized the political implications of this ambiguity: political society is completely de-divinized, but that does not mean there are no spiritual reasons for forming a community, for example, in a church. In his later works, Voegelin described this ambiguity more philosophically as a tension between immanence and transcendence: although God is absent from this world, immanent being is certainly not void of divine meaning in Christianity. De-divinization rendered the immediate mythical presence of the divine in the cosmos problematic, but it certainly did not abolish the meaning of the cosmos. Reality no longer coincides with the divine that now transcends it, but the divine did create and govern reality, Voegelin emphasized: "The new truth can affect the experience of divine reality as the most adequate symbolization of cosmic-divine reality, but it cannot affect the experience of divine reality as the creative and ordering force in the cosmos."[31] The experience of the divine is now "differentiated" between immanence and transcendence—between the Beginning and the Beyond, to use Voegelin's concepts from *The Ecumenic Age*: "Although divine reality is one, its presence is experienced in the two modes of the Beyond and the Beginning. The Beyond is present in the immediate experience of movements in the psyche, while the presence of the divine Beginning is mediated through the

---

30. Eric Voegelin, *Order and History*, vol. 4, *The Ecumenic Age* (Columbia: University of Missouri Press, 2000), 50.

31. Voegelin, *Order and History*, 4:53.

experience of the existence and intelligible structure of things in the cosmos. The two modes require two different types of language for their adequate expression."[32] The unity of these two divine aspects is a religious mystery that is rationally unfathomable. One can speak independently of a divine presence within this world and of God's radical absence from this world, but they cannot be brought together in one coherent discourse.

For Voegelin, the resolution of this ambiguity was possible only by abandoning the differentiated experience of the divine and reverting to more simplistic and "compact" experiences of the divine that characterized Gnostic heresy. Gnosticism accepted the de-divinized worldview and its conception of a transcendent God but struggled with the religious mystery that the divine is both absent from this world and present within it as a creative force. If one should direct spiritual attention toward a divine beyond, why would the meaning of this world still matter, the Gnostic asks. Or formulated more theologically, why has God created a world at the beginning of time from which he has to save us at the end of time? Voegelin conceived the issue as follows: "The intensely experienced presence of the Beyond brings the problem of the Beginning to intense attention. When the formerly unknown god of the Beyond reveals himself as the goal of the eschatological movement in the soul, the existence of the cosmos becomes an ever more disturbing mystery. . . . A Cosmos that moves from its divine beginning toward a divine beyond of itself is mysterious indeed; and there is nothing wrong with the question as such."[33] The real problem with Gnosticism, Voegelin argued, was that it wanted a definitive answer to this question. The attempt to systematically grasp the relation of the Beginning and the Beyond denied the religious mystery: "The fallacy at the core of the Gnostic answers to the question is the expansion of consciousness from the Beginning to the Beyond."[34] Ancient Gnosticism brought these two aspects together in a single theological narrative that unambiguously dissociated the

---

32. Voegelin, 4:63.
33. Voegelin, 4:64.
34. Voegelin, 4:65.

evil god of creation (Beginning) from the good God of redemption (Beyond). Accordingly, it univocally opted for the beyond and completely discarded the meaning of the cosmos. The Christian balance between both was lost.

Voegelin's interpretation of Gnosticism in his later works dovetailed better with the traditional dualistic interpretation than his earlier views in *The New Science of Politics*. Voegelin, moreover, linked Gnosticism to the same Christian ambiguities Hans Blumenberg also emphasized in his reflections on the early Gnostic thinker Marcion in *The Legitimacy of the Modern Age*: "The fundamental thought that underlies Marcion's Gnostic dogmatics is, I think, this: A theology that declares its God to be the omnipotent creator of the world and bases its trust in this God on the omnipotence thus exhibited cannot at the same time make the destruction of this world and the salvation of men from the world into the central activity of this God."[35] On this point, Voegelin's and Blumenberg's positions were surprisingly similar. For both, Gnosticism was the attempt to overcome an inner-Christian tension between the immanence of creation and the transcendence of salvation by univocally choosing the latter option. Their respective evaluations of this tension itself, however, were radically different. For Voegelin, on the one hand, this Christian tension was a subtle balance that reflected the human condition as being between the divine and the worldly. Blumenberg, on the other hand, had a philosophically more neutral interpretation. He maintained that orthodox Christian theology was marked by a structural instability, a paradox even, that historically tended toward stabilization. Ancient Gnosticism was one of these stabilizations; late medieval nominalism, he argued, was another.

Not unlike Voegelin, Blumenberg showed that Gnosticism resurfaced at the end of the Middle Ages after its seeming disappearance in the early centuries of medieval Christianity. Blumenberg did not refer to Joachim of Fiore as the main representative of this Gnostic return but to another Franciscan—namely, William of Ockham.[36]

---

35. Blumenberg, *Legitimacy*, 129.

36. For the Franciscan legacy in the German secularization debates, see Guido Vanheeswijck, "De dubbele Franciscaanse Erfenis: Een ontbrekende Schakel in het

Moreover, Blumenberg did not recognize the return of Gnosticism in the alleged re-divinization of history but rather in the radical emphasis on divine transcendence that was implied in Ockham's nominalism. Nominalism is a philosophical theory that denies the existence of ontological entities (universals) that correspond to abstract notions. Although universal concepts like "human being" have meaning to us, there is nothing that corresponds to them in reality. These concepts are nothing but the names (*nomines*) we give to a collection of individuals. Blumenberg pertinently noted that the motivation behind Ockham's nominalism was theological, and more specifically the theological emphasis on God's absolute and inscrutable omnipotence. If universals exist, even if God himself created them, God's creative power is limited. Rather than creating ex nihilo, God would create the world by repeating the structure of the universal in the individual existence of worldly beings. Blumenberg summarized: "The concept of the *potentia absoluta*, however, implies that there is no limit to what is possible, and this renders meaningless the interpretation of the individual as the repetition of the universal."[37] Moreover, the existence of universals would imply that human beings ultimately share God's rationality. If human concepts reflect the universals that God used to create the world, the human and the divine mind are fundamentally alike. Nominalism could not accept this, and emphasized the transcendent omnipotence of God at the expense of the immanent rationality of creation. To rephrase this idea in Voegelin's words, the Beginning becomes a problem in view of an intense experience of the Beyond.

The inner-Christian tension between this world and the beyond that Marcion already discovered in early Christianity returned in medieval Christianity as a paradox between the immanent rationality of the world and the transcendent omnipotence of God's will. Blumenberg put it like this: "Here was the common ground of all the paradoxes of Scholasticism: It could not remove from the

Löwith-Blumenberg-debat (The Double Franciscan Legacy: A Missing Link in the Löwith-Blumenberg Debate)," *Tijdschrift voor Filosofie* 74, no. 1 (2012): 11–44.
    37. Blumenberg, *Legitimacy*, 153.

world anything that was essential to the functioning of the system of proofs of God's existence, but neither could it commit divinity to this world as the epitome of its creative capacity."[38] In other words, medieval Scholasticism wanted to unite two mutually exclusive concepts of the divine: on the one hand, it understood the divine as present in this world in order to retain the rationality of the cosmos; on the other hand, it had a concept of divine absence that excluded the possibility that God coincided with this rational cosmos in order to retain his omnipotence. Not unlike ancient Gnosticism, Ockham's nominalism tipped this unstable balance to the latter side of a divine absence. In line with Gnostic cosmology, this emphasis on transcendence also devalued the meaning of immanence. In the nominalist worldview, the structure and existence of the world were deprived of their rational necessity and uniqueness. The world could have been created in an entirely different way; or worse still, it could not have existed at all. Moreover, one cannot know how God created the world: he might have created a good and rational cosmos, but he could have created just as well the evil and irrational world-prison of Gnosticism. In view of God's absolutely free will, the world becomes absolutely contingent.

Interestingly, the resolution of this inner-Christian tension in favor of a univocal emphasis on transcendent omnipotence ultimately triggered the genesis of modern thought, for Blumenberg. In this regard, it is not just an insignificant theological possibility that is manifested in rather marginal phenomena like ancient Gnosticism or late medieval nominalism, but an absolutely critical shift in the intellectual history of the West. Modernity should be understood as a reaction against late medieval divine absolutism and its implied return of Gnosticism—hence, Blumenberg's claim that "the modern age is the second overcoming of Gnosticism."[39] The radical emphasis on transcendence left the world and human existence void of meaning. Just as the reliability of reality was no longer guaranteed by the rationality of its creator, the possibility of salvation from this world was contingent upon an inscrutable

38. Blumenberg, 160.
39. Blumenberg, 126.

divine will. The only possibility that remained for modern human beings in such a threatening existential situation was the immanent assertion and development of their own finite lives here on earth. Modernity did not stabilize the inner-Christian tension by tipping the balance toward either a Gnostic transcendence or the opposite side of a pure immanence. Rather, it dialectically resolved the tension by presenting a third option. The modern reaction to theological absolutism entailed a return to immanence without, however, reverting to the Greek or Scholastic ideal of a rational and reliable cosmos. The immanent world as such remained utterly meaningless, but now human self-assertion constituted meaning in relation to this world.

Voegelin's understanding of secularization followed a similar logic, albeit a far less complex one. Whereas Blumenberg understood modernity as a dialectical reaction to the Gnostic resolution of an inner-Christian tension, Voegelin considered modernity to be identical with it. For Blumenberg there was an alternative to the Gnostic stabilization of Christianity; for Voegelin there was not. The loss of balance between the Beginning and the Beyond was for Voegelin by definition Gnostic. In whatever historical configuration the Christian balance was lost, Gnosticism resurfaced. Only in this regard were phenomena as diverse as ancient heresy, late medieval theology, and modern thought equally conceivable as Gnostic. Modern secularization therefore was nothing more than the Gnostic resolution of the Christian tension between immanence and transcendence—this time not in the direction of radical transcendence but of radical immanence. The way the balance was tilted was of secondary importance for Voegelin. For even if it tilted toward transcendence, it still entailed a re-divinization and immanentization.

As an ostensible radicalization of de-divinization, Gnosticism's exclusive emphasis on transcendence inadvertently re-divinized the world, according to Voegelin. As indicated above, the axial de-divinization formed the historical background of the Gnostic speculations, but gnosis recovered the divinized worldview of the preaxial religions by reestablishing a (mystical) unity between the human and the divine. The Gnostic claim that God is absolutely absent from this world paradoxically made him more accessible to human understanding. God was no longer ambiguously mixed up with this world, as a being that is mysteriously both immanent and transcendent. In the Gnostic worldview, it was very clear where God is and even more so where he is not. In this regard, certain knowledge of the divine was possible, even if it was initially merely negative—the divine should be understood as the complete opposite of the world. This negative theology then made an immediate and unambiguous relation with the divine possible through the experience of gnosis. To the extent that God is completely accessible from within this world, the divine is drawn into the immanent existence of human beings.

Evil and Gnostic Self-Salvation

If Gnosticism's radical de-divinization ultimately entailed a re-divinization of the world, Voegelin's concept of Gnostic immanentization did not contradict the radically world-negating dynamics of Gnostic heresy. Paradoxically, world-negation actually caused the re-divinization of politics and history. Voegelin believed that Gnosticism's negative theology brought God closer to immanent politics because a very concrete course of negative political action derives from divine absence. Because the world of Gnosticism is godless, evil, and corrupted, politics gains a divine justification to the extent that it rejects and destroys the present world order. In antiquity, the antinomian or libertine rejections of all moral, religious, and political standards were characteristic of Gnostic politics; in modernity, they took the shape of political revolution, which can be liberal as well as Marxist or totalitarian. Both in ancient Gnosticism and in modernity, politics was re-divinized because political action was no longer indifferent to the transcendent truths of religion but explicitly wanted to realize salvation. In the Gnostic worldview, destructive action prepared the establishment of a redemptive future, Voegelin claimed: "However the phases of salvation are represented in the different sects and systems, the aim is always destruction of the old world and passage to the new."[40]

As indicated above, the Gnostic re-divinization of politics coincided with a re-divinization of history, for Voegelin. Re-divinization did not entail the immediate divine justification of the present. On the contrary, the divinization of history meant that the divine was manifested in the historical evolution from an evil present to a perfect future. Gnosticism indeed considered the present to be radically meaningless and even evil. Because it could not accept the world as it currently is, Gnosticism projected salvation into the future, Voegelin argued: "From this follows the belief that the order of being will have to be changed in a historical process. From a wretched world a good one must evolve historically."[41] In antiquity, this Gnostic re-divinization of history took shape in an apocalyptic eschatology that conceived salvation as a revolutionary and destructive change at the end of profane history. In modernity, Voegelin argued, this Gnostic eschatology was secularized in the philosophy of history, where historical change can bring about an immanent absolute.

The connection between Gnosticism, Apocalypticism, and modernity strongly aligned Voegelin with Jacob Taubes's *Occidental Eschatology*.[42] Although Voegelin completely subscribed to Taubes's analysis of modern culture as a return of Gnosticism and

---

40. Voegelin, "Science, Politics, and Gnosticism," 256.

41. Voegelin, 297.

42. Voegelin referred to Taubes once in *New Science of Politics* (111n8). Voegelin was arguably not well acquainted with Taubes's work until they started corresponding in 1953. See Voegelin, *Selected Correspondence*; Jacob Taubes and Eric Voegelin, *Briefwechsel*, ed. Herbert Kopp-Oberstebrink (Munich: Wilhelm Fink, forthcoming). It was possibly Leo Strauss who referred Voegelin to Taubes. In a letter to Strauss of 1950, Voegelin elaborated on Joachim of Fiore and on his own Gnosticism thesis, which he published two years later in *New Science of Politics*. Strauss replied that he recognized Taubes's *Occidental Eschatology* in Voegelin's thesis: Leo Strauss, "Letter to Eric Voegelin of December 10, 1950," in *Faith and Political Philosophy: The Correspondance between Leo Strauss and Eric Voegelin, 1934–1964*, trans. and ed. Peter Emberly and Barry Cooper (Columbia: University of Missouri Press, 2004), 74–75. In his later writings on modern Gnosticism, Voegelin cited Taubes's *Abendländische Eschatologie* as an important source: Voegelin, "Science, Politics and Gnosticism," 253.

its apocalyptic eschatology, their respective evaluations of this process were opposed. While Voegelin criticized Gnosticism, Taubes embraced it. Upon meeting Taubes, Voegelin reputedly remarked with a sense of dread: "Today I met a Gnostic in the flesh!"[43] What Voegelin feared most about the Gnostic return in modernity, was for Taubes its main attraction: its radical world-negation and its appetite for destruction. In other words, Voegelin's main reproach to Gnostic modernity and to Taubes, for that matter, was their lack of *spiritual investment in the world as it is.*

Voegelin's diagnosis of modern culture was of course pertinent. Since the rise of modern science and philosophy, the intrinsic meaning of the world has been denied ever more radically. Being no longer has a primal sense of goodness but is considered neutral and indifferent. In a world void of meaning, human beings can no longer have any spiritual relation to the reality that surrounds them. In view of this lack of spiritual investment, the world itself ultimately becomes disposable. If this world without intrinsic meaning does not fit our human aspirations any longer, nothing keeps us from changing or even destroying it and creating it anew. For reasons discussed above, the consequences of this Gnostic line of thought can be very dangerous, especially when applied in modern politics. For Voegelin, the dangerous political attempt to abolish the existing situation rather than compromise with it ultimately negated the nature of political action. On a more fundamental level, it even relied on an illusory and too simplistic ontology. On the one hand, the modern Gnostic ontology overestimated the scope of human political action; on the other hand, it underestimated the substantiality of the world: "The world, however, remains as it is given to us, and it is not within man's power to change it. In order—*not,* to be sure, to make the undertaking possible—but to make it *appear* possible, every Gnostic intellectual who drafts a program to change the world must first construct a world picture from which those

---

43. Wolf-Daniel Hartwich, Aleida Assmann, and Jan Assmann, "Introduction," in *From Cult to Culture: Fragments toward a Critique of Historical Reason,* ed. Charlotte E. Fonrobert and Amir Engel (Stanford: Stanford University Press, 2010), xxiv.

essential features of the constitution of being that would make the program appear as hopeless and foolish have been eliminated."[44] For Voegelin, the Gnostic construction of such a world picture first presented reality as fundamentally evil and subsequently conceived human beings as capable of saving themselves from this evil world. Gnosticism thereby negated the finite condition of human existence as well as the constitution of being as meaningful in itself.

Against the Gnostic-modern degradation of the world, Voegelin wanted to safeguard the dignity of the cosmos. For Voegelin, the world was meaningful in and of itself. The meaning of immanent being had surely become problematic after Greek philosophy and Christian revelation discovered a truth beyond this reality, but it could not disappear altogether. The Greek concept of cosmos as well as the Christian notion of creation indeed accounted for the mysterious divine meaning of being. In this respect, Voegelin claimed that the Gnostic interpretation of the world as meaningless or evil artificially negated being's primal sense of goodness. Failing to cope with the ambiguous and mysterious presence of the divine in this world, the Gnostic rather discarded the value of immanent reality altogether. The illusion of a complete absence of meaning allowed the Gnostic to find meaning univocally and exclusively beyond this world. It allowed human beings, moreover, to blame the existence of evil in this world on a cosmological corruption rather than on their own failures.

In this regard, Voegelin lamented that the belief in salvation could no longer be understood in the Christian sense as an uncertain hope for individual forgiveness of our own human sins. Rather, salvation appeared as a straightforward escape from immanence that human beings could realize themselves through destructive and revolutionary action. Against the passivity of Christian faith, gnosis is an active concept that allows human beings to have control of salvation. Unlike Christian grace, modern and ancient Gnostic salvation is considered by Voegelin to be within the reach of our human capacities. The redemptive knowledge of gnosis is

---

44. Voegelin, "Science, Politics, and Gnosticism," 305.

not just something modern human beings hope for; it is something they pursue. Paradigmatically, knowledge is what we attain ourselves; it is not something we just passively receive. Since Voegelin emphasized that modern human beings did not want to depend on the uncertain and uncontrollable transcendent redemption of Christianity, the Gnostic alternative fitted the modern mind perfectly. Gnosticism allowed the moderns to gain control of their own salvation through the intervention, improvement, and recreation of reality. Gnosis is the knowledge that is needed to change the structure of reality. For Voegelin this structural change took many different forms in modernity: he considered it characteristic of scientific knowledge, which allowed for intervention in nature as well as for totalitarianism that wanted to revolutionize political reality. In all its different forms, modern thought was conditioned by the dynamics of self-salvation. The modern Gnostic, argued Voegelin, believed "that a change in the order of being lies in the realm of human action, that this salvational act is possible through man's own effort."[45] This Gnostic self-salvation is by definition immanent salvation. If salvation does not come from beyond this world, it can be realized within profane history itself. In Voegelin's picture, modernity secularized or immanentized Christian eschatology. Modernity's immanent salvation was necessarily also a historical salvation. If the present is unredeemed and if salvation cannot come from beyond according to the modern, salvation has to take place in the future. Because human beings determine the process of profane history through action, it is believed that humanity can realize its salvation in the historical change from an evil to a perfect world.

Because modern human beings thus believed themselves to be their own savior, Voegelin ultimately argued that they took over God's position. Modernity reached its apogee when "[man] becomes conscious that he himself is God, when as a consequence man is transfigured into superman."[46] If man becomes an earthly, secular God, the position of the Christian deity itself is secularized.

---

45. Voegelin, 298.
46. Voegelin, *New Science of Politics*, 125.

Voegelin typically recognized this divinization of man in Nietzsche's Übermensch or in Hobbes's earthly God, the Leviathan,
but this divinization was ultimately a Gnostic motif for him: "The
Gnostic experiences . . . are an expansion of the soul to the point
where God is drawn into the existence of man."[47] Gnosis, in Voegelin's view, installed an immediate connection between the human
and the divine that ultimately enabled the modern divinization of
man. Only by becoming God can modern human beings attain an
absolute certainty and control of salvation.

This Gnostic divinization of the human was for Voegelin radically suspect. If human beings think they are able to take over
God's place, modernity fundamentally disregards the human condition. Voegelin maintained that doubt and uncertainty are simply essential features of human existence. Human beings are finite
creatures that oscillate between immanence and transcendence
without ever being able to appropriate the truth of transcendence
definitively. In order to attain certainty about salvation, modernity
has to change this human condition. The dangerous consequences
of this illusory attempt to change human nature were, for Voegelin, most obvious in totalitarian politics. In *The Origins of Totalitarianism,* Hannah Arendt also elaborated on this topic, discussing
the totalitarian experiments with changing human nature in the
concentration camps.[48] In his review of Arendt's book, Voegelin
connected these ideas to his own reflections on modern eschatology: "Totalitarian movements do not intend to remedy social evils
by industrial changes, but want to create a millennium in the eschatological sense through transformation of human nature." In a
very different way than Arendt, he emphasized the danger of mess-
ing around with human nature: "A 'nature' of a thing cannot be
changed or transformed; a 'change of nature' is a contradiction of
terms; tampering with the 'nature' of a thing means destroying the
thing."[49] The illusory attempt to change human nature and realize

---

47. Voegelin, 124.
48. Hannah Arendt, *The Origins of Totalitarianism* (New York: Harcourt
Brace, 1951), 437–59.
49. Eric Voegelin, "The Origins of Totalitarianism" (review of Hannah
Arendt's *Origins of Totalitarianism*) *Review of Politics* 15 (1953): 74.

salvation paradoxically destroyed human nature. Voegelin took this destruction in a very literal sense. In the case of Nazism, it referred to mass murder and genocide. In his essay "Science, Politics, and Gnosticism," Voegelin returned to this idea, which he had introduced in the review of Arendt: "The nature of a thing cannot be changed; whoever tries to alter its nature destroys the thing. Man cannot transform himself into a superman; the attempt to create a superman is an attempt to murder man. Historically, the murder of god is not followed by the superman, but the murder of man: the deicide of the Gnostic theoreticians is followed by the homicide of the revolutionary practitioners."[50]

Secularization and Human Nature

Voegelin's pessimism about the modern age aligned his project in some significant ways with Karl Löwith's theory of secularization. Voegelin's argument that modernity secularized or immanentized Christianity's transcendent eschatology is taken almost entirely from Löwith's *Meaning in History*.[51] Löwith was deeply critical of this process of secularization and of modern culture in general, albeit less explicitly so than Voegelin. Both agreed that the modern attempt to overcome human finitude and open up a redemptive infinity within immanence grievously wronged human nature. Both argued that human beings are essentially related to an infinite otherness that cannot be recuperated, controlled, or secularized. In antiquity, this otherness took the shape of a harmonious and eternal cosmos; in Christianity, it was the divine truth of transcendence. In modernity, this relationship was lost because human beings identified themselves with this infinite, immanent absolute, thus shutting the door to the constitutive experience of a meaningful heterogeneity. Compared to Christian and classical thought, modernity

---

50. Voegelin, "Science, Politics, and Gnosticism," 284.

51. Karl Löwith, *Meaning in History: The Theological Implications of the Philosophy of History* (Chicago: University of Chicago Press, 1949). Voegelin refers extensively to this book: Voegelin, *New Science of Politics*, 111–19; see therein notes 8, 9, 21, and 22.

was therefore a historically illegitimate paradigm of thought for Löwith: "It sees with one eye of faith and one of reason. Hence its vision is necessarily dim in comparison with either Greek or biblical thinking."[52]

This relation between Voegelin and Löwith can offer insight into the relation between Voegelin and Blumenberg, and their opposing interpretations of Gnosticism's role in the modern age. In *The Legitimacy of the Modern Age,* Löwith was the main target of Blumenberg's criticism of secularization.[53] Löwith's theory, for Blumenberg, was exemplary of the secularization theorem in general, which delegitimized specific modern ideas by showing their substantial continuity with theological contents—modern idea X is actually *secularized* theological content Y. Since Blumenberg's elaborate criticism of Löwith was actually directed at this entire secularization narrative, and since Voegelin relied specifically on Löwith and on this very narrative, Blumenberg's criticism of Löwith immediately applied to Voegelin as well. Although Blumenberg did not discuss Voegelin directly, his famous debate with Löwith made it piercingly clear that he would have immediately dismissed Voegelin's understanding of modernity as well. Indeed, he would not only have criticized Voegelin to the extent that he relied on Löwith's theory of secularized eschatology, but rejected his interpretation of the epochal relation between Gnosticism and modernity as well, characterizing modernity instead as the "overcoming of Gnosticism." Unlike Löwith and Voegelin, Blumenberg did not recognize a substantial continuity between specific religious contents and modern thought. Accordingly, he accepted neither the continuity between eschatology and the modern philosophy of history nor the unmediated relation between the ancient Gnostic

---

52. Löwith, *Meaning in History,* 207.

53. Blumenberg, *Legitimacy,* 37–51. For an overview of the renowned Löwith-Blumenberg debate: Robert M. Wallace, "Progress, Secularization, and Modernity: The Löwith-Blumenberg Debate," *New German Critique* 22, no. 1 (1981): 63–79; Jean-Claude Monod, *La querelle de la sécularisation: Theologie politique et philosophies de l'histoire de Hegel à Blumenberg* (Paris: Vrin, 2012).

religion and the modern age. The modern epoch had its own orig-inal and legitimate contents that were not reducible to religious developments but arose in a more complex, dialectical relation to them. Indeed, the modern age is not characterized by the return of Gnosticism but by an overcoming of this return.

This different historical picture also implied a different and less pessimistic anthropology of modern humanity, for Blumenberg. In contrast to Voegelin, Blumenberg did not interpret the modern tendency to control and change the world as an eschatological or Gnostic attempt to save human beings from an ontological evil. For Blumenberg, the modern intervention in nature was merely an attempt to make life possible and bearable in a world that is indif-ferent to human aspirations. Consequently, modern human beings did not take up God's position in Blumenberg's view. When human beings no longer need to save themselves they do not need the illicit perspective of an earthly god either. On the contrary, Blumenberg's anthropology of modern humanity was based on human finitude rather than on a supposedly accessible infinity. Unlike Voegelin, who argued that the modern Gnostic pretended to have access to a divine truth, Blumenberg had indeed emphasized that the rela-tion between the human and the divine had become fundamentally unbridgeable at the end of the Middle Ages and the beginning of modernity. Thus, human beings were utterly powerless in view of a remote and unintelligible transcendence, realizing that the ulti-mate truth about their existence and salvation was inaccessible. The only possibility that remained in such an awkward existen-tial situation was the immanent assertion of finite human existence here on earth—and, as the next chapter shows, a modest embrace of the world. Not surprisingly, the project of human self-assertion is the cornerstone of Blumenberg's interpretation of the modern worldview. From this follows that the immanent world does not just serve as means for the survival of human beings, but that it becomes the material in which human existence realizes itself: "Self-assertion," said Blumenberg, is "an existential program ac-cording to which man posits his existence in a historical situation and indicates to himself how he is going to deal with the reality surrounding him and what use he will make of the possibilities that are open to him."[54] Instead of negating human nature, as Voegelin argued, modernity rather accounted for it, in Blumenberg's view. Perfectly in the spirit of Blumenberg's criticism of Löwith's and Voegelin's positions, and also defending the legitimacy of (political) modernity against implied religious continuities, the French philosopher Marcel Gauchet denied the modern divinization of man: "The death of God does not mean that man becomes God by reappropriating the conscious absolute self-disposition once attributed to God; on the contrary, it means that man is categorically obliged to renounce the dream of his own divinity. Only when the gods have disappeared does it become obvious that men are not gods."[55] Blumenberg similarly believed that when God disappeared in secular modernity, human beings did not occupy the empty infinity.[56] Rather, human beings could now become conscious of their radical finitude for the first time. Modernity, for Blumenberg, was the fundamental assertion of this finitude and the exploration of its worldly potential.

---

54. Blumenberg, *Legitimacy,* 138.

55. Marcel Gauchet, *The Disenchantment of the World: A Political History of Religion,* trans. Oscar Burge (Princeton: Princeton University Press, 1999). 199. For the relation between Gauchet and the German secularization debates, see Daniel Steinmetz-Jenkins, "French Laïcité and the Recent Reception of the German Secularization Debate into France," *Politics, Religion, and Ideology* 12, no. 4 (2011): 433–47; André Cloots, "Modernity and Christianity: Marcel Gauchet on the Christian Roots of the Modern Ways of Thinking," *Milltown Studies* 61 (2008): 1–30.

56. "The supposed migration of the attribute of infinity." Blumenberg, *Legitimacy,* 77.

Theodicy

Overcoming Gnosticism, Embracing the World

Hans Blumenberg's most explicit treatment of the relation between Gnosticism and modernity can be found in the first chapter of the second part of *The Legitimacy of the Modern Age,* entitled "The Failure of the First Attempt at Warding Off Gnosticism Ensures Its Return."[1] In the chapter, he approached Gnosticism from the perspective of theodicy. Simply put, the philosophical project of theodicy aimed to defend the goodness of the monotheistic God against the apparent existence of evil in his creation. In other words, theodicy wanted to give an answer to the question of why evil exists in a world that is created by a benevolent God. Blumenberg explained how Gnosticism—and Marcion of Sinope, in particular—came up with an answer to the Christian question *unde malum* (Where does evil come from?). Gnosticism proposed a simple, albeit heretical solution for this question by denying that the transcendent God had created the world. In radically dissolving the relation between God and world, Gnosticism blamed the creation of the world and all worldly evils on another, fallen or inferior deity. In an attempt

---

1. Hans Blumenberg, *The Legitimacy of the Modern Age,* trans. Robert Wallace (Cambridge, MA: MIT Press, 1983), 127–36.

to restore the creative power of the transcendent God without risking his fundamental goodness, Saint Augustine developed a theodicy that blamed the existence of evil on the corrupted free will of human beings rather than on an evil Gnostic demiurge. For Blumenberg, this Augustinian transposition of evil from the creator to human beings marked the beginning of the Christian Middle Ages as a *first* overcoming of Gnosticism. However, he also argued that Augustine's attempt at theodicy ultimately proved untenable. A return of Gnosticism and its conception of evil were thus possible at the moment the limits of the Augustinian worldview became clear, that is, at the end of the Middle Ages and the beginning of modernity. Modernity, then, was constituted by a new—now *second*—overcoming of Gnosticism, according to Blumenberg.

This chapter aims to show how, in Blumenberg's thinking, this modern overcoming of Gnosticism could again be understood as a theodicy. In this respect, one could argue that the early modern philosophical project of theodicy is constitutive for modern thought in general; or, to put it even more boldly, that theodicy is the essence of modernity, as Blumenberg's friend and colleague Odo Marquard has often argued. Although Blumenberg never made such a strong claim himself, his genealogy of modernity in the second part of *The Legitimacy of the Modern Age* arguably endorsed such a conjecture. In a letter to Blumenberg, for example, Jacob Taubes emphasized the centrality of "the problem of theodicy in Christian theology on which your second part of *The Legitimacy of the Modern Age* is founded."[2] More interesting, in this regard, was Odo Marquard's reading of Blumenberg's analysis of modernity as the second overcoming of Gnosticism: he argued that "theodicy—the second refutation of Marcion—would be and remains to be necessary for the foundation of modernity."[3] Although Blumenberg never made the connection between theodicy,

---

2. Jacob Taubes, "Letter to Hans Blumenberg of August 30, 1967," in Hans Blumenberg and Jacob Taubes, *Briefwechsel 1961–1981*, ed. Herbert Kopp-Oberstebrink and Martin Treml (Berlin: Suhrkamp, 2013), 130.

3. Odo Marquard, "Das Gnostische Rezidiv als Gegenneuzeit," in *Gnosis und Politik*, ed. Jacob Taubes (Munich: Wilhelm Fink, 1984), 34.

modernity, and Gnosticism as explicitly as Marquard, he recognized theodicy's significance for modern thought in his later *Genesis of the Copernican World*, stating that "the modern age begins with an act of theodicy."[4]

In Blumenberg's reading, theodicy entailed neither a complete justification of the goodness of the world and its creator nor an absolute legitimation of modernity. He even stated explicitly that "the legitimacy of the modern age is not the legitimation of its specific constituent elements under all possible circumstances."[5] Accordingly, the main function of modern theodicy, for Blumenberg, was not the theological vindication of the creator and its creation but the modest justification of the world as it is. Such a project could be called an *a-theological theodicy*, and this chapter shows how, for Marquard as well as for Blumenberg, this modern, atheological theodicy was exemplary of modernity's investment in the world in general. If Gnosticism ultimately implied the impossibility of *spiritual investment in the world as it is*, modernity paradigmatically countered Gnosticism by developing new modes of investment in the world. Theodicy appeared as one of the concrete means through which modernity overcame the evil and oppressive cosmos of Gnosticism, thus embracing rather than abolishing the present world. In its most fundamental sense, theodicy demonstrated that evil could not corrupt reality by showing that the world is reliable for human beings.

This emphasis on the modern attempt to overcome the Gnostic world-negation by embracing the world could not make the contrast between Blumenberg's project and Taubes's reading of modernity clearer. As the previous chapters have shown, Taubes pointed time and again to the different afterlives of the Gnostic world-negation in modernity. In line with ancient Gnosticism, the revolutionary movements of Western modernity were supposedly motivated by a protest against the world and by the attempt to abolish it. While the oppressive and evil cosmos of ancient

---

4. Hans Blumenberg, *The Genesis of the Copernican World,* trans. Robert M. Wallace (Cambridge, MA: MIT Press, 1987), 262.

5. Blumenberg, *Legitimacy,* 240.

Gnosticism returned in the determinism of the modern scientific worldview, the Gnostic pursuit of redemption returned in the Romantic, artistic, and political world-negations. Taubes stated this explicitly in one of the many debates he had with Blumenberg at the meetings of the Poetik und Hermeneutik research group: "The Gnostic doctrine of redemption is a protest against a world ruled by *fatum* or *nomos*. This fatum presents itself in the mythological style of Gnosticism as personified powers: astrological determinism. The world as it is represented by the interpretation of modern science and technology and against which modern poetry turned in varying phases since romanticism, regains a mythical coherence as a unified whole: natural-scientific determinism."[6] For Blumenberg, by contrast, the moderns neither experienced the world as evil or oppressive nor protested against its immanent lawfulness. Rather, the rational lawfulness of reality that had been secured by theodicy and modern science guaranteed the reliability of the world against the uncertainty and arbitrariness of Gnosticism's evil creator. In a direct reply to Taubes's claim at the second meeting of Poetik und Hermeneutik, Blumenberg stated: "Modern law of nature cannot be compared with the Gnostic heimarmene because it was designed against the arbitrariness of the miracle and the abysmal uncertainty of the *creatio continua*. From this origin stems its solid, positive quality of consciousness."[7] In other words, modern lawfulness was neither oppressive nor limiting to human freedom, because it was an invention of human self-assertion that gave meaning to the world and made human freedom possible in the first place.

Odo Marquard explicitly sided with Blumenberg's criticism of Taubes. Rather than abolishing the world as Gnosticism attempted, modernity wanted to conserve and defend it, Marquard argued.

---

6. Jacob Taubes, "Notes on Surrealism," in *From Cult to Culture: Fragments toward a Critique of Historical Reason*, ed. Charlotte Elisheva Fonrobert and Amir Engel (Stanford: Stanford University Press, 2010), 103.

7. Hans Blumenberg, "Reply to Notes on Surrealism," in Taubes, *From Cult to Culture*, 118. The discussions were originally published in the proceedings of the second meeting of Poetik und Hermeneutik: Wolgang Iser, ed., *Immanente Ästhetik, ästhetische Reflexion: Lyrik als Paradigma der Moderne; Kolloquium Köln 1964: Vorlagen und Verhandlungen* (Munich: Wilhelm Fink, 1966), 429–52.

In order to do this, modern thought had to refute Gnosticism's basic premise that the world and its creator are intrinsically evil. This, for Marquard, was the function of modern theodicy. However, if modernity failed at some point in accepting the world as it is, the project of theodicy would be abolished and the Gnostic conception of the world as radically evil would resurface. As Marquard considered theodicy to be constitutive of the modern age, such a failure of theodicy would imply the end of modernity.

The debates between Blumenberg, Marquard, and Taubes about the scope of Gnosticism and theodicy in modernity function in this chapter as a key to understanding Blumenberg's enigmatic definition of modernity as the overcoming of Gnosticism.[8] These debates, it will be shown, took root in concrete discussions between the three thinkers at the meetings of Poetik und Hermeneutik.[9]

Odo Marquard Reads Hans Blumenberg's Gnosticism Chapter

Odo Marquard was a German philosopher who is traditionally associated with the conservative Ritter-Schule. His essays were

8. These discussions are much more central, at least with regard to the early reception of Blumenberg's *Legitimacy,* than his debates with Karl Löwith and Carl Schmitt, which have been (over)emphasized in the secondary literature on Blumenberg's book: Robert M. Wallace, "Progress, Secularization, and Modernity: The Löwith-Blumenberg Debate," *New German Critique* 22 (1981): 64; Martin Jay, "Review of *The Legitimacy of the Modern Age,*" *History and Theory* 24 (1985): 192; Laurens Dickey, "Blumenberg and Secularization: Self-Assertion and the Problem of Self-Realizing Teleology in History," *New German Critique* 41 (1987): 152; Pini Ifergan, "Cutting to the Chase: Carl Schmitt and Hans Blumenberg on Political Theology and Secularization," *New German Critique* 37 (2010): 149–171; Celina María Bragagnolo, "Secularization, History, and Political Theology: The Hans Blumenberg and Carl Schmitt Debate," *Journal of the Philosophy of History* 5 (2011): 84–104; Timo Pankakoski, "Reoccupying Secularization: Schmitt and Koselleck on Blumenberg's Challenge," *History and Theory,* 52 (2013): 214–45.

9. For an intellectual history of Poetik und Hermeneutik, see Julia Amslinger, *Eine neue Form von Akademie: "Poetik und Hermeneutik"—Die Anfänge* (Munich: Wilhelm Fink, 2017).

always sharp, full of clever neologisms, and written in an unusual, humorous style. He was arguably one of the few twentieth-century philosophers with a sense of humor. One of the many recurring motifs in his writings was the interest in the problem of theodicy. His essays on theodicy almost always discussed the intrinsic relation between theodicy and philosophical modernity: "Where theodicy is, modernity is; where modernity is, theodicy is."[10] Nonetheless, he never treated this topic systematically. As a fierce opponent of German idealism's absolutist discourse and a self-proclaimed skeptic, Marqaurd was indeed wary of any philosophical systematization. As a brief colleague but longtime friend of Blumenberg, Marquard was also an avid reader and admirer of Blumenberg's work. He seemed to be one of the few prominent philosophers who really put Blumenberg's conceptual framework into use in his own thought. For this reason, it is not always clear where Marquard's commentary on Blumenberg's work stopped and where his own thinking began. This was also true of his interpretation of Blumenberg's overcoming of Gnosticism. Marquard always understood Blumenberg's definition of modernity as the second overcoming of Gnosticism as a theodicy, even though Blumenberg rarely discussed the constitutive role of theodicy for modernity explicitly.

If the relation between modernity, Gnosticism, and theodicy that Marquard suggested is to be taken seriously, the scope of his notion of theodicy should be clarified further. The mere fact that theodicy was a central concept in early modern philosophy obviously does not entail that it was a paradigmatically modern project, let alone that it constituted modern thought. The notion of theodicy was coined by Gottfried Wilhelm Leibniz in his *Essais de Théodicée*,[11] but it was Immanuel Kant who gave this concept its clearest definition. The latter understood theodicy as "the defense of the highest wisdom of the creator against the charge

---

10. Odo Marquard, "Entlastungen: Theodizeemotive in der neuzeitlichen Philosophie," in *Apologie des Zufälligen* (Stuttgart: Reclam, 1986), 14.

11. Gottfried W. Leibniz, *Theodicy: Essays on the Goodness of God, the Freedom of Man, and the Origin of Evil*, ed. and trans. E. M. Huggard (La Salle: Open Court, 1985).

which reason brings against it for whatever is counterpurposive in the world."[12] In short, theodicy exonerates God with regard to the existence of evil in the world. Since in the Christian tradition God is considered both the benevolent and the almighty creator of the world, theodicy cannot argue, as Gnosticism actually did, either that he deliberately created evil or that he was incapable of avoiding it. If God created evil, he would not be benevolent; if he was not able to avoid it, he would not be almighty. Paradigmatically, theodicy sought to defend God's goodness either by a denial of evil's substantiality (what we experience as evil is actually not so) or by a rational guarantee that evil does not corrupt reality in a fundamental way (evil might exist but in the end the world is fundamentally good). Being explicitly concerned with the defense of God's goodness, theodicy endorsed that reality, in the most fundamental sense, cannot be evil. Marquard's use of the notion of theodicy seemed especially concerned with this last connotation: theodicy, as Hegel also understood it in his philosophy of history, is the rational guarantee that "evil has not prevailed . . . in any ultimate sense."[13]

In the cosmologies of Gnosticism, however, evil ultimately did prevail. Unlike Christian orthodoxy, Gnosticism paradigmatically rejected the goodness of the world and its creator. Gnosticism's radically dualistic cosmology entailed an unbridgeable separation between the world and the transcendent God, who neither governs nor created this world. Rather, the world was brought into being by a fallen or inferior deity, either out of ignorance or even out of sheer malignancy. This Gnostic demiurge created a fundamentally evil world from which salvation is possible only through mystical knowledge (gnosis) of the God of transcendence. In Marquard's perspective Gnosticism and theodicy were therefore radically opposed: if Gnosticism claimed that evil corrupts the very

---

12. Kant, "On the Miscarriage of All Philosophical Trials in Theodicy," in *Religion and Rational Theology,* ed. and trans. Allen Wood and George Di Giovanni (Cambridge: Cambridge University Press, 1996), 24.

13. Georg W. F. Hegel, *Introduction to the Philosophy of History,* trans. Leo Rauch (Cambridge: Hackett, 1988), 18.

roots of reality, theodicy was the attempt to overcome Gnosticism's "radical" evil. Theodicy, Marquard argued, was the refutation of Gnosticism.[14]

Marquard now applied this connection between Gnosticism and theodicy to Blumenberg's suggested definition of modernity as the overcoming of Gnosticism. If theodicy is the overcoming of Gnosticism and if the overcoming of Gnosticism needs a theodicy, the project of theodicy appears to be constitutive for the modern age. The question of course remains why theodicy occupied such a central place in modern thought. In other words, why did Marquard maintain that theodicy is a specifically modern phenomenon that was absent or at least less urgent in antiquity or the Middle Ages? Going beyond Marquard's position, one could argue that the importance of theodicy in modern thought can be explained only by some kind of resurgence of the problem of evil or by an acute experience of counterpurposiveness at the beginning of the modern age. The question of theodicy would not arise, in this regard, in medieval Scholasticism, where evil was thought in terms of *privatio boni,* and was not experienced as a substantial ontological problem.[15] Only the threat of radical evil, endangering the goodness of the world and its creator, could explain the necessity of the project of modern theodicy. In Blumenberg's perspective, the possibility of this experience of evil and the need for theodicy are clearly related to the return of Gnosticism at the end of the Middle Ages.

In line with the traditional view, Blumenberg maintained that Saint Augustine had dealt a death blow to Gnosticism at the beginning of the Middle Ages. In an attempt to defend the goodness of the world and its creator against Gnostic heresy, Augustine developed a theodicy that blamed the existence of evil on human beings' corrupted free will rather than on an evil Gnostic demiurge.[16]

---

14. Marquard, "Das Gnostische Rezidiv," 34.

15. For Thomas Aquinas's interpretation of evil as the "privation of the good": Thomas Aquinas, *Summa Theologica: Volume I-Part I* (New York: Cosimo, 2007), art. 49.

16. See Aurelius Augustine, *On the Free Choice of Will, On Grace and Free Choice, and Other Writings,* ed. Peter King (Cambridge: Cambridge University Press, 2010).

As Augustine's attempt at theodicy ultimately failed for Blumenberg, he argued that Gnosticism and its conception of evil returned at the moment the limits of the Augustinian worldview became clear, that is, at the end of the Middle Ages. As the title of *The Legitimacy of the Modern Age*'s chapter on Gnosticism states, "the failure of the first attempt at warding off Gnosticism ensures its return."[17] Modernity therefore needed a new, "second overcoming of Gnosticism."[18]

By merely transposing the responsibility for evil's existence from the Gnostic demiurge to humanity's corrupted free will, Augustine had not solved the problem of evil. For this reason, Blumenberg did not consider the orthodox Christian solution to this problem to be a real theodicy. Not only did it fail to eradicate the Gnostic conception of evil, but it would eventually also fall short in exonerating God. In Augustine's alleged refutation of Gnosticism, the world itself remained as evil as it used to be for the Gnostics. The only difference was that human beings were now held responsible for this evil. As Blumenberg put it, "The mortgage of Gnosticism falls on man."[19] This responsibility, however, was imposed upon humanity as an original sin for which individual human beings could not be held accountable. Accordingly, Blumenberg argued that the Augustinian dogma of original sin ultimately reintroduced God's responsibility for evil: "For this sin, with its universal consequences, in the end only the original ground of everything could be held responsible—all the massa damnata had to do was to suffer the consequences."[20] If the dogma of original sin designated a human condition that goes beyond the individual free action, God—after all, the creator of human beings—is responsible for evil. For Blumenberg, this divine responsibility de facto entailed the return of Gnosticism and its conception of an evil creator.

Blumenberg argued that the illicit Augustinian theodicy, combined with the optimistic cosmology that Scholasticism borrowed

17. Blumenberg, *Legitimacy*, 127.
18. Blumenberg, 126.
19. Blumenberg, 305.
20. Blumenberg, 25.

from ancient philosophy, was successful in keeping the problem of evil at bay during the Middle Ages. Latent rather than solved, however, the Gnostic conception of evil eventually returned in the late medieval emphasis on divine absolutism: "The Gnosticism that had not been overcome but only transposed returns in the form of the hidden God and his inconceivable absolute sovereignty."[21] Such a radical emphasis on divine transcendence rendered the world vulnerable again for the Gnostic threat of evil, as the omnipotent and remote God (*Deus absconditus*) of late medieval nominalism no longer guaranteed the fundamental goodness and dependability of creation. Blumenberg maintained that the exclusive focus on the omnipotence and inscrutability of God's will made it impossible for human beings to know that the world was created for their sake, and to be certain that it is rational and good. If God's will is absolutely free and if he truly has the power to do whatever he wants, the act of creation could not have been limited by the ideals of rationality or goodness. In view of this divine absolutism, the meaning of creation became purely contingent for human beings: God might have created a good and rational world, but he could just as well have created a radically evil one. Since the absolutist interpretation of divine transcendence could not guarantee that evil does not prevail in any ultimate sense, the Gnostic conception of evil returned at the end of the Middle Ages. Ultimately, the meaning of the late medieval world, deprived of its intrinsic goodness, consisted in the possibility of its destruction at the end of time. In this perspective, salvation became much more urgent than it used to be in the Scholastic tradition.

Unlike in ancient Gnosticism or Apocalypticism, however, the possibility of eschatological salvation from evil itself became uncertain in view of the late medieval emphasis on divine absolutism. Blumenberg argued that Gnosticism returned under "aggravated circumstances."[22] If human beings had no access to God's reasons for creating the world, neither could they know God's criteria for judging and redeeming humanity. Accordingly, salvation also

---

21. Blumenberg, 135.
22. Blumenberg, 137.

became contingent. Since human beings had absolutely no clue whether they would be saved at the end of time, the possibility of their salvation became practically arbitrary. Accordingly, if salvation was uncertain and eternal damnation likely, Blumenberg maintained that "the basic eschatological attitude of the Christian epoch could no longer be one of hope for the final events but was rather one of fear of judgment and the destruction of the world."[23] In view of divine absolutism, not only did the created world become vulnerable to the threat of radical evil, but salvation from this world was rendered as unreliable as the world itself. In line with Blumenberg, Marquard paradoxically concluded that "the salvation from evil itself is presented as evil."[24] This double manifestation of the problem of evil was the first reason why theodicy was necessary at the beginning of the modern age: it had to prove that the absolute will of a remote God did not necessarily endanger the goodness of reality.

Focusing more on the internal dynamics of modern thought, a second explanation for the modern necessity of theodicy could be found in the worldview of modern science. As a result of the nominalist critique of the Scholastic conceptions of God and creation, Blumenberg maintained that new possibilities for approaching reality were conceivable in modernity. Since the human mind had absolutely no access to the will of God, the modern scientist lacked the categories to understand the reasons behind God's creation. Accordingly, nature could no longer be conceived anthropomorphically, and modern science paradigmatically disposed of the categories of beauty, purposefulness, order, and goodness. Blumenberg termed this process, in which reality is regarded more and more as mere meaningless facticity, the "disappearance of order."[25] Disposing of premodern cosmology, modern science lost the traditional philosophical framework that guaranteed the goodness of the world. Consequently, if the ontological optimism of Greek philosophy and medieval Scholasticism was no longer

---

23. Blumenberg, 44.
24. Marquard, "Entlastungen," 16.
25. Blumenberg, *Legitimacy*, 137.

convincing, the medieval account of evil as *privatio boni* also failed. This Scholastic interpretation of evil as the mere absence of the good was rendered meaningless at the moment the existence of the good itself became questionable. The concept of *privatio boni* made sense only in an optimistic cosmology, where the threat of radical evil, corrupting the roots of reality, was a priori dismissed. Obviously, the absence of the good did not necessarily imply the existence of evil. On the contrary, if the modern world is indifferent and purposeless, it is neither good nor bad. Nevertheless, the failure of the medieval privative conception of evil paved the way for the possible Gnostic resurgence of a substantial and radical evil. In this respect, modern theodicy could function as a kind of precautionary measure: if one could no longer believe that the world is fundamentally good, one had to avoid at all costs that it became fundamentally evil. The omnipresence of the problem of evil in the works of early modern philosophers, such as Malebranche, Arnauld, Bayle, Spinoza, and Leibniz, all explicitly promoting the modern scientific worldview, proved that the threat of evil was indeed very real at the beginning of the modern age, at least on a theoretical level.[26]

Gnosticism, Myth, and the Absolutism of Reality

Blumenberg was obviously not interested in the problem of evil and theodicy in the strict *philosophical* sense, but these concepts proved to be useful in his essentially *historical* analysis of the early modern age. For Blumenberg, the notions of theodicy and "overcoming Gnosticism" functioned as the concrete historical means through which early modern thought legitimized and constituted itself. In light of the supposed historical resurgence of Gnosticism at the beginning of the modern age, he understood the project of modern thought as an attempt to disarm the Gnostic evil

---

26. For an overview of the early modern debate about the problem of evil and theodicy, see Steven Nadler, *The Best of All Possible Worlds: A Story of Philosophers, God, and Evil* (Princeton: Princeton University Press, 2010).

that would eventually endanger the very possibility of human existence. Precisely because an existential and anthropological concern was at stake, modernity's genesis was both necessary and legitimate. The late medieval powerlessness of human beings in the light of divine absolutism was ultimately unbearable. Having the Gnostic thinker Marcion's metaphor of the *cellula creatoris* (the cell of the creator) in mind, Blumenberg suggested that late medieval humanity was imprisoned in a depraved world where every possible escape was blocked.[27] The emphasis on divine omnipotence had practically rendered God's creation and salvation unreliable, even downright frightening. In such a reality that refused, in an absolute way, to take humanity into account, human life was impossible. In view of divine absolutism, reality itself now tended to become absolute because it overwhelmed human beings and left no room for their existence. In *Arbeit am Mythos* (*Work on Myth*), Blumenberg had termed this aspect that renders human life impossible the "absolutism of reality."[28]

Reality, in its absolute and barest sense, was for Blumenberg too unpredictable and too powerful to allow for human existence. The direct confrontation with such a reality, unmediated by any kind of human categorization, would leave human beings in an unbearable and constant state of anxiety. The absolutism of reality was an indefinite power that overwhelmed and paralyzed human beings uninterruptedly. Only by countering this primordial absolutism of power and by keeping it at a distance could human life first become possible. This distancing of reality was the function of myth, and the continuous process of reducing the absolutism of reality was what Blumenberg called "work on myth." By means of stories, names, and metaphors, work on myth made the world approachable by categorizing reality's indefinite otherness. Blumenberg cryptically summarized: "What has become identifiable by means of a name is raised out of its unfamiliarity by means of metaphor and

27. Blumenberg, *Legitimacy*, 135.

28. Hans Blumenberg, *Arbeit am Mythos* (Frankfurt am Main: Suhrkamp, 1979); English translation: Hans Blumenberg, *Work on Myth*, trans. Robert M. Wallace (Cambridge, MA: MIT Press, 1985), 3.

is made accessible, in terms of its significance, by telling stories."[29] In this regard, the indefinite absolute power of reality was divided into definite, familiar, and eventually even controllable mythical instances. Blumenberg paradigmatically recognized this mythical "separation of powers" in the polytheistic religions that "distribute a block of opaque powerfulness, which stood over man and opposite him, among many powers that were played off against one another, or even cancel one another out."[30]

Although *Work on Myth* introduced the concept of the absolutism of reality in the context of mythology, every system of thought, whether it is mythical or rational, has to deal with this absolutism and is essentially a mode of work on myth. In this regard, Blumenberg explicitly criticized the traditional distinction between myth and reason. Since both have exactly the same function, that is, to reduce the absolutism of power and to make reality reliable, there is a fundamental continuity between myth and reason. Notwithstanding their different strategies, both can be equally successful in realizing this reduction of the absolute. Reason is therefore not altogether unmythical, just as myth is not altogether irrational. On the contrary, said Blumenberg, "myth itself is a piece of high-carat work of logos."[31]

From these observations can be inferred that Blumenberg interpreted the history of Western thought in terms of the changes in the human reduction of the absolutism of reality. In other words, Blumenberg's historical analyses, in almost all of his works, and especially in *The Legitimacy of the Modern Age,* assumed the anthropological presupposition that human beings cannot confront reality as such.[32] For Blumenberg, there was no point of view from which one can know, experience, or even live reality in an absolute sense: "Whatever starting point one might chose, work

29. Blumenberg, *Work on Myth*, 6.
30. Blumenberg, 14.
31. Blumenberg, 12.
32. For Blumenberg's philosophical anthropology, see Hans Blumenberg, *Beschreibung des Menschen* (Frankfurt am Main: Suhrkamp, 2006); Felix Heidenreich, *Mensch und Moderne bei Hans Blumenberg* (Munich: Wilhelm Fink, 2005).

on the reduction of the absolutism of reality would already have begun."[33] In *Work on Myth,* this claim was thoroughly existential: the confrontation with the absolute makes human existence impossible. As the title of the first chapter of this book suggested, human existence is possible only *"after* the absolutism of reality."[34] In his *In Memoriam* for Blumenberg, Odo Marquard emphasized the importance of this train of thought in Blumenberg's philosophy in general: "The fundamental idea of Hans Blumenberg's philosophy seems to me the idea of a discharge of the absolute *(Entlastung vom Absoluten).* The human being cannot withstand the absolute. In very different forms, he has to distance himself from it."[35] This observation applied not only to *Work on Myth* and its notion of absolutism of reality but also to the central role of divine absolutism in *The Legitimacy of the Modern Age.*

Not unlike the two major works discussed, a similar concern with the absolute was at stake in Blumenberg's early methodological work, *Paradigmen zu einer Metaphorologie (Paradigms for a Metaphorology).*[36] Compared to *Work on Myth,* Blumenberg's position in *Paradigms* was more epistemological, and lacked the former's explicit anthropology. Presenting an interpretation of metaphor's role in philosophical thought, *Paradigms* maintained that

---

33. Blumenberg, *Work on Myth,* 7.

34. Blumenberg, 3 (my emphasis).

35. Odo Marquard, "Entlastung vom Absoluten: In memoriam," in *Die Künst des Überlebens: Nachdenken über Hans Blumenberg,* ed. Franz Josef Wetz and Hermann Timm (Frankfurt am Main: Suhrkamp, 1999), 20. For other interpretations of the role of the absolute in Blumenberg's work, see Barbara Merker, "Bedürfnis nach Bedeutsamkeit: Zwischen Lebenswelt und Absolutismus der Wirklichkeit," in Wetz and Timm, *Die Künst des Überlebens,* 68–98; Philipp Stoellger, "Die Passion als 'Entlastung vom Absoluten': Negative Christologie im Zeichen der Tränen Gottes," in *Permanentes Provisorium: Hans Blumenbergs Umwege,* ed. Michael Heidgen, Matthias Koch, and Christian Köhler (Munich: Wilhelm Fink, 2015), 225–58.

36. Hans Blumenberg, *Paradigmen zu einer Metaphorologie* (Frankfurt am Main: Suhrkamp, 1997); English translation: Hans Blumenberg, *Paradigms for a Metaphorology,* trans. Robert Savage (Ithaca: Cornell University Press, 2010). For a comparative analysis of the role of the absolute in *Work on Myth* and *Paradigms for a Metaphorology,* see Kirk Wetters, "Working over Philosophy: Hans Blumenberg's Reformulations of the Absolute," *Telos* 158 (2012): 100–118.

the absolute conceptual knowledge of reality is an illusion. Blumenberg indeed assumed that every philosophical discourse used certain "absolute metaphors" that could not be translated back into absolute conceptuality.[37] At some point, every philosophical system is confronted with the failure of conceptuality in grasping reality, and it is precisely this "logical perplexity, for which metaphor steps in."[38] For Blumenberg, the existence of absolute metaphors did not imply that every concept is necessarily metaphorical, let alone relative. Rather, he maintained that a fully transparent conceptual philosophy that knows reality in an absolute way cannot exist because every conceptual structure assumes an irreducible metaphorical context or background. Blumenberg's notion of absolute metaphor implied a criticism of the illusory absolutist pretentions of conceptual knowledge: "Absolute metaphor leaps into a void, inscribing itself on the *tabula rasa* of theoretical unsatisfiability."[39] In other words, our access to reality can never be absolute, for it is essentially mediated by metaphors, that is to say, by categories of the human imagination rather than by absolute concepts.

By the time Blumenberg was writing *Work on Myth,* he interpreted these metaphorical tools that make our knowledge of reality possible as the very tools we need to make human existence itself possible. Since these tools are merely metaphorical and do not grasp reality as such, their account of reality is by definition deficient. Accordingly, the mythical and metaphorical reductions of the absolutism of reality are fallible, and never final. Although some stories or theories are more convincing than others, Blumenberg argued that "every story gives an Achilles' heel to sheer power."[40] The moment such a story, metaphor, or theory failed, a new one had to take—*re-occupy*—its place in order to continue its function of containing the absolutism of powers. In Blumenberg's account, intellectual history was the sum total of these modifications or *re-occupations* (*Umbesetzung*). *The Legitimacy of the Modern Age*

---

37. Blumenberg, *Paradigms*, 3.
38. Blumenberg, 3.
39. Blumenberg, 132.
40. Blumenberg, *Work on Myth*, 16.

and especially the chapter on Gnosticism were concerned with a particular moment in the history of these modifications. Blumenberg was interested here in the moment when the metaphorical framework of the Middle Ages lost its grip on the absolutism of reality, and modern thought had to re-occupy its functional position.

In view of Blumenberg's conceptual framework of *Work on Myth,* it was hardly a coincidence that he blamed the overemphasis on divine absolutism for the dissolution of the Middle Ages. In *Work on Myth*'s chapter on dogma, he even suggested that the monotheistic attempt at countering the absolutism of reality by introducing a new absolute in the guise of a single, unfathomable, and omnipotent God was from the outset bound to fail.[41] Unlike the polytheistic separation of powers, which seemed fundamental for myth, monotheistic dogma merely translated the absolutism of reality into a static absolutist discourse. Not only its conception of God, but virtually every claim dogma made about reality, was posited as absolute, unfathomable, and inaccessible. Accordingly, dogma did not allow for elaborate stories to be told about the divine. As Blumenberg also put it in a short, unpublished fragment on Gnosticism: "The concept of absolute divine power excludes telling myths about it."[42] Blumenberg thus made a radical distinction between dogma and myth, implying that dogma was less successful in reducing the absolutism of reality than myth. To the extent that Christianity historically adopted aspects of mythical thought, this deficiency of dogma did not immediately become obvious. But the question for Blumenberg remained whether the radicalization of dogma could ultimately meet the human need of reducing the absolutism of reality: "Has a theism ever been able to afford to contradict human needs, to renounce everything in favor of the absolute priority of the concept?"[43] In *The Legitimacy of the Modern Age,* the answer would certainly be yes—namely,

---

41. Blumenberg, 215–62.

42. Hans Blumenberg, "Hans Jonas: Prognostiker der Wiedergefundenen Gnosis," Blumenberg Nachlass, DLA Marbach: "Der Begriff der absoluten göttlichen Macht schliesst aus, von ihr einen Mythos zu erzählen."

43. Blumenberg, *Work on Myth,* 229.

the theism of Gnosticism and late medieval nominalism. The Gnostic-nominalistic emphasis on divine absolutism coincided with a dangerous minimum of human self-assertion. In this regard, late medieval divine absolutism represented the failure of reducing the absolutism of reality—a failure of work on myth. By allowing for the possibility of a Gnostic evil, both at the beginning (creation) and at the end (salvation) of the world, divine absolutism made human life practically impossible.

Gnostic Myth or Gnostic Dogma

In *The Legitimacy of the Modern Age,* Gnosticism appeared as the radicalization of the Christian emphasis on divine absolutism, and hence as an extreme form of dogmatic thought. To the extent that dogma was intrinsically incapable of successfully reducing the absolutism of reality, Gnosticism, both in its ancient and in its late medieval guise, represented the ultimate failure of dogma. In this regard, Gnosticism was a category of illegitimacy for Blumenberg. Accordingly, it is only by overcoming Gnosticism that modernity guaranteed its own legitimacy. The Gnostic failure of dogma destabilized the Christian Middle Ages from within, and demanded resolution in the modern age. In other words, it necessitated the genesis of the modern paradigm of thought that applied new tools to reducing the absolutism of reality.

In the second part of *Work on Myth,* however, Blumenberg introduced a very different picture of Gnosticism. In opposition to his account in *Legitimacy,* Gnosticism no longer appeared as an extreme form of dogma, but rather as a legitimate paradigm of work on myth. Accordingly, it no longer represented the ultimate failure of the reduction of the absolutism of reality; on the contrary, the Gnostic narratives succeeded in the mythical separation of the absolutism of powers. Unlike dogma, Gnosticism did not posit one God as the single absolute principle; rather, it speculated about a cosmological battle and separation between good and evil powers. For Blumenberg, "this dualistic model is pregnant with

myth."[44] Except for Marcion's more systematic speculations, the
Gnostic cosmologies were indeed typically formulated in a mythical language. These myths differed from the ancient myths to the
extent that they were artificially composed allegories rather than
pure narratives that arose out of a long historical process where
stories were told, gradually changed, and adapted to their listen-
ers. Ancient myths were neither consciously composed nor did they
have a real author; rather, they intrinsically belonged to a tradition without anyone knowing where these stories came from. The
significance of ancient myths indeed depended to a large extent on
this long evolutionary process that spanned many different genera-
tions of storytellers. Although the Gnostic "art myths," as Blumenberg called them, did not meet these requirements, they could fulfill
the same function as more traditional myths.[45]

Blumenberg's interpretation of Gnosticism appeared to be rather
confusing: on the one hand, Gnosticism was an extreme form of
dogma; on the other hand, it could also be mythical. More than
that, Gnosticism even heretically countered the early Christian dogmatization by means of myth. In this regard, Robert Buch noted
that "Blumenberg's appeal to Gnosticism is overall ambivalent."[46]
Consequently, it did not seem to make sense to characterize modernity both as the reaction against Christian dogma and as the
overcoming of Gnosticism. Considering the mythical meaning
of Gnosticism, both were clearly not the same. Buch pertinently
added: "Blumenberg legitimizes modernity as the defense against
Gnosticism, which, however, in its turn undermines dogma that
questions the legitimacy of the modern age." Thereupon, he emphasized the ambiguity in Blumenberg's conception of Gnosticism

44. Blumenberg, 179.
45. Blumenberg, 174.
46. Robert Buch, "Gnosis," in *Blumenberg Lesen*, ed. Robert Buch and Daniel
Weidner (Berlin: Suhrkamp, 2014), 87. Also see Felix Heidenreich, "Unvermittelte
Gegensätze: Blumenbergs Analyse des gnostischen Denkens," in *Prometheus gibt
nicht auf: Antike Welt und modernes Leben in Hans Blumenbergs Philosophie*, ed.
Melanie Möller (Munich: Wilhelm Fink, 2015), 141–54.

again: "Gnosticism is both the elaboration of the tensions in early Christianity and the objection against this development."[47]

This ambiguity in Blumenberg's reference to Gnosticism, however, reveals a more structural problem in his account of the relation between myth and dogma. In the essay "Wirklichkeitsbegriff und Wirkungspotential des Mythos," which appeared well before *Work on Myth* in the proceedings of the fourth gathering of the Poetik und Hermeneutik group in 1968, Blumenberg already explicitly opposed myth to dogma: "Our categories for describing the mythical stand in contrast to theology."[48] The question, however, is whether the rigid distinction between both is ultimately tenable. Especially with regard to Gnosticism, such a distinction between myth and dogma seems very artificial. In response to Blumenberg's essay, Jacob Taubes criticized the former's opposition between both exactly on this account.[49] In this reply, published as "Der dogmatische Mythos der Gnosis" (The Dogmatic Myth of Gnosticism) in the same proceedings, Taubes even argued that Gnosticism was a prime example of a system of thought that is both dogmatic and mythical.[50] Taubes thereby allowed for a more complex and dialectical relation between myth and monotheistic dogma than Blumenberg's opposition.

According to Taubes, Gnosticism was both a product and a rejection of the monotheistic tradition: it radicalized the monotheistic rupture between the transcendent god and the immanent world into an extreme form of cosmological dualism, but it equally attempted to overcome this rupture through its mystical conception of redemption. In the mystical experience of gnosis, the dualistic

---

47. Buch, "Gnosis," 98.

48. Hans Blumenberg, "Wirklichkeitbegriff und Wirkungspotential des Mythos," in *Terror und Spiel: Probleme der Mythenrezeption,* ed. Manfred Fuhrmann (Munich: Wilhelm Fink, 1971), 42.

49. For an overview of this discussion between Taubes and Blumenberg, see Herbert Kopp-Oberstebrink, "Between Terror and Play: The Intellectual Encounter of Hans Blumenberg and Jacob Taubes," *Telos* 158 (2012): 119–34.

50. Jacob Taubes, "Der dogmatische Mythos der Gnosis," in *Terror und Spiel: Probleme der Mythenrezeption,* ed. Manfred Fuhrmann (Munich: Wilhelm Fink, 1971), 145–56; English translation: Jacob Taubes, "The Dogmatic Myth of Gnosticism," in Taubes, *From Cult to Culture,* 61–75.

separation between transcendence and immanence was unified again. In Taubes's perspective, Gnostic mysticism sought to re-establish a mythical sense of unity that was destroyed in the mono-theistic separation between immanence and transcendence:

> Gnostic myth takes up again the theme of archaic mythologemes. It sig-nifies the repetition of mythic experiences on a new plane: on the plane of a consciousness that presupposes the rupture of gods and worlds, of god and world. The unity of mythic consciousness, which, however one might understand it, presupposes, in varying metamorphoses, the pres-ence of the divine and his commerce with the world and with man, is destroyed. It can only be regained at a specific prize, achieved by the as-cent of the pneuma [spirit] that out-runs, out-plays, and out-tricks the infinite distance of worlds and eons.[51]

Taubes's concept of myth itself had arguably few affinities with Blumenberg's theory. In particular, the sense of a mythical unity of transcendence and immanence was not prominent in Blumen-berg's thought. Taubes's conceptions of mythical unity relied in-stead on Gershom Scholem's understanding of mysticism in *Major Trends in Jewish Mysticism*. Scholem basically defined mysticism here as a dialectical return to myth, mediated by the monotheis-tic separation of the mythical unity between the human and the di-vine.[52] Gnosticism's mythical tools and ambitions notwithstanding, Taubes maintained that it essentially belonged to the dogmatic tra-dition. Gnosticism wanted to revive the mythical worldview, but it was undeniably marked by the dogmatic idea that there can be only one true doctrine. Gnosticism was ultimately shaped by the philosophical and theological notion of truth that did not exist as such in the mythical era.[53] Unlike the ancient myths, Taubes main-tained, Gnostic stories were mere allegories of a single underlying dogmatic truth. Although there was an enormous variety of Gnos-tic myths, all these stories were ultimately expressions of a single theological doctrine.

---

51. Taubes, "Dogmatic Myth of Gnosticism," 68.
52. Gershom Scholem, *Major Trends in Jewish Mysticism* (New York: Schocken Books, 1946), 7.
53. Taubes, "Dogmatic Myth of Gnosticism," 69.

Taubes's different understanding of myth certainly did not invalidate his critique of Blumenberg's rigid opposition between myth and dogma. Taubes's example of Gnostic myth forced Blumenberg to return to this topic in *Work on Myth*, which was published several years after the Poetik und Hermeneutik meeting. Although he never mentioned Taubes, Blumenberg devoted an entire chapter to Gnosticism in *Work on Myth* that can be read as a response to Taubes's critique. In this chapter, Blumenberg amended his radical distinction between myth and dogma by elaborating on the possible ways in which both interpenetrated in Gnostic thought. He granted: "The disjunction between the mythical and the dogmatic frame of mind is not complete."[54] Initially, Blumenberg emphasized the univocal mythical nature of Gnosticism. Dismissing Taubes's allegorical interpretation of Gnostic myth, he showed how the variety of mythical themes in Gnosticism did not presuppose an underlying common dogma but a fundamental mythical structure. For Blumenberg, such a "fundamental myth" functioned as a synthetic principle that underlay the variety of Gnostic myths and consisted in the narrative of a dualistic struggle between two cosmological powers. This struggle was often presented through a caricatured inversion of ancient and Jewish creation myths. In these Gnostic myths, the creator was no longer fundamentally good but was rather presented as an evil demiurge, opposed in every respect to the benevolence of the transcendent God.

Although its internal dynamics were essentially mythical, Gnosticism's rivalry with church dogma forced it to adopt the dogmatic mode of expression. Blumenberg showed that Gnosticism's essential concern with gnosis (knowledge), and hence with truth, was already a direct result of its confrontation with metaphysical and dogmatic thought. Here, Blumenberg clearly took up Taubes's suggestion: "In Gnostic myth, the search for truth appears in a much more urgent form than in archaic myth. Philosophy and revelation have already formed criteria for truth that the Gnostic myth cannot dismiss."[55] Taubes's position differed here from Blumenberg's only

---

54. Blumenberg, *Work on Myth*, 184.
55. Taubes, "Dogmatic Myth of Gnosticism," 69.

to the extent that he took Judaism's role in the genesis of Gnosticism into account. Taubes argued that Jewish dogma determined Gnosticism's modes of expression from the outset, whereas Blumenberg ignored this possible Jewish influence and maintained that Gnosticism's origins were primarily mythical. Since Gnosticism was only later confronted with a strong Christian dogmatization, its dogmatic nature was only secondary for Blumenberg. Borrowing the concept from Hans Jonas, Blumenberg termed this dogmatization of the Gnostic myth its "secondary rationalization."[56]

This rationalization essentially transformed the primary mythical structure of Gnosticism into dogma's rational framework of questions and answers. An essential feature of Blumenberg's interpretation of myth was the conviction that myths were *not* told in order to answer questions or even to reveal the truth. In contrast to both dogma and philosophy, myth preceded such a problem-oriented framework: "Myth does not need to answer questions," said Blumenberg. "It makes something up, before the question becomes acute and so that it does not become acute."[57] Thus, myth was concerned with dispelling fear, uneasiness, and discontent, and with the projection of stability and reliability into the life-world in order to make human existence possible. However, the contents of the Gnostic art myths were presented as answers to the theological questions it inherited from church dogma's frame of reference, after Gnosticism's secondary rationalization. In this regard, Blumenberg agreed with Taubes that Gnosticism could be at the same

56. Blumenberg, *Work on Myth*, 185.

57. Blumenberg, 197. Blumenberg's main criticism of the traditional interpretation of myth concerns exactly this misunderstanding of myth as an answer to a question. Christianity and Enlightenment anachronistically conceive myths as preliminary answers to supposedly eternal problems that will later be solved in a more serious way, either by theology or by science and philosophy. Such a misunderstanding of myth essentially approaches the archaic stories from the perspective of their epistemological failure. Blumenberg, in his turn, wanted to approach myth from the point of view of what it actually achieves—that is to say, he wanted to grasp myth's function. Blumenberg explicitly opposed this functional understanding of myth to Ernst Cassirer's account of myth as a symbolic form (168). The function of myth for Blumenberg is obviously the reduction of the absolutism of reality.

time mythical and dogmatic. Accordingly, the initial ambiguity discovered in Blumenberg's use of the notion of Gnosticism represented a historical ambiguity in Gnostic thought itself: on the one hand, Gnosticism had a strong "tendency to mythicization"; on the other hand, it was also exposed "to the conjecture that it could be demythologized."[58] Although Gnosticism was essentially mythical, this latter tendency to demythologize or rationalize is intrinsic to Gnosticism as well. The mythical struggle between two gods, for example, could easily be reformulated in the philosophical or theological language of dualism. Such a rationalization was obviously not possible with every myth.

When Blumenberg elaborated on Gnosticism in *The Legitimacy of the Modern Age,* he was particularly mindful of this last meaning of Gnosticism, that is, Gnosticism as a dogmatic mode of thought after its secondary rationalization. It is also in this perspective that Gnosticism's fundamental influence on medieval dogma can be understood. For not only did dogma change Gnostic myth, but Gnosticism itself left a profound mark on Christian theology as well. Only in this perspective was a later return of Gnosticism at the end of the Middle Ages conceivable for Blumenberg. After Gnosticism's secondary rationalization, Gnostic myth slipped into church dogma. Blumenberg termed this process in which Gnosticism itself disappeared but continued its legacy within medieval Christianity its "tertiary re-occupation." Only after this process could the ultimate scope of Gnosticism's underlying theological problems and questions become obvious. These problems—theodicy being one of them—were already implied in Gnosticism's mythical guise but as such never became explicit:

> So if this [tertiary re-occupation] does not display the questions that precede Gnostic mythology historically, it does display the problem-concerns that the mythology had made acute and that it leaves behind it, as soon as it perishes as a result of the abundance of its narrative contradictions and the discipline of the Roman Church's dogma. The fundamental myth, which is reduced here to the formula that approaches abstraction, does not simply vanish along with the epoch to which it

---

58. Blumenberg, *Work on Myth,* 187.

belongs; rather it challenges the succeeding epoch to satisfy the needs it had effortlessly aroused. I have already mentioned the theodicy problem, in which this inheritance from Gnosticism and the effort of re-occupying the framework of positions that carries its imprint are really deposited.[59]

The Gnostic legacy implicitly challenged Christian dogma through the problems of evil and theodicy. In this conceptual form, these problems did not belong to the fundamental (mythical) structure of Gnosticism proper, but they were crystallized in the confrontation between Gnosticism and Christian dogma. These problems were the dogmatic reformulations of essentially mythical contents. Only in its tertiary re-occupation did it make sense, for Blumenberg, to associate Gnosticism with the problem of evil and with theodicy.

In an attempt to determine the scope of the essential Gnostic remainder in medieval Christian thought, Blumenberg's Gnosticism chapter in *The Legitimacy of the Modern Age* was primarily interested in this tertiary re-occupation. His main argument here was that Augustine's emphasis on free will and on the dogma of original sin was the (tertiary) re-occupation of the functional position of the Gnostic demiurge. Augustine's theodicy aimed to absolve the creator of the world of responsibility for the existence of what is bad in the world by blaming evil on the free will of human beings. No longer speculating mythically about the inferiority of the world and its creator, or about the dualistic struggle between two cosmological powers, Augustine's moralization of evil considered evil for the first time as a problem in the strict philosophical sense of the word. As already indicated, Augustine's theodicy failed to solve this problem, as he merely transposed evil from the demiurge to human beings' free will. This epochal failure to overcome Gnosticism's legacy ensured, for Blumenberg, its return at the end of the Middle Ages and the beginning of the modern age. To the extent that the problem of evil was essentially entwined with the (medieval) dogmatic tradition, modernity did not try to solve it. Rather, it wanted to get rid of the problem itself. Since any solution to this

---

59. Blumenberg, 187.

problem would essentially remain within the limits of the dogmatic paradigm of thought, Blumenberg showed that modernity overcame the problem itself by overcoming Gnosticism and the entire dogmatic frame of reference.

Modernity's Atheological Theodicy

The detour around *Work on Myth* has provided a more profound framework for understanding the central dynamics of Blumenberg's interpretation of modernity. If the modern age arose out of the dissolution of the medieval frame of reference, it was confronted with dogma's epochal failure to reduce the absolutism of reality—concretely taking shape in the resurgence of Gnosticism and the problem of evil. As the Augustinian rejection of Gnosticism marked the structural beginning of the medieval paradigm of thought, for Blumenberg—"The formation of the Middle Ages can only be understood as an attempt at the definitive exclusion of the Gnostic syndrome"[60]—the Middle Ages end with a return of Gnosticism and with a failure of the Augustinian solution for the problems of evil and theodicy. The epochal task of modernity was therefore to develop a new metaphorical framework that reduced the absolutism of reality and made human existence possible again. This process took shape in the (second) overcoming of Gnosticism by both disarming its conception of evil and by making the world reliable. Not surprisingly, this was exactly the function of modern theodicy, especially in the traditional Leibnizian sense: theodicy demonstrated that evil could not radically corrupt reality by proving the rationality and reliability of the world and its creator.

If the Middle Ages were founded on Augustine's theodicy, the failure of his attempt would require a new theodicy that constituted a new era. However, this central role of theodicy would imply that secular modernity is ultimately founded on a theological project. This is indeed what Marquard suggested when he discussed

---

60. Blumenberg, *Legitimacy*, 130.

the constitutive role of theodicy for modern thought in his essay "Idealismus und Theodicee" (Idealism and Theodicy).[61] Written in 1965, a year before the publication of *The Legitimacy of the Modern Age*, the essay unmasked German idealism's emphasis on the autonomy of the subject as an implied form of theodicy. Marquard argued that German idealism, despite its secularist and atheist aspirations, was unconsciously premised on the theological project to acquit God of his responsibility for evil. Human beings rather than God were held responsible for the existence of evil in the world, since reality is ontologically dependent upon human subjectivity in German idealism. In *The Legitimacy of the Modern Age,* Blumenberg heavily criticized Marquard's position as a tacit variant of the traditional secularization narrative, which tried to understand modern phenomena by tracing them back to their alleged theological origins.[62] For Blumenberg, the rise of modernity is related to certain theological dynamics but never as a mere continuation or secularization of theology. In this perspective, modernity could not be understood as a continuation of the theological project of theodicy. Rather, Blumenberg understood modernity as overcoming the dogmatic frame of reference, from which the problem complex of theodicy derived its meaning.

This criticism seems to invalidate Marquard's conjecture that Blumenberg's understanding of the modern overcoming of Gnosticism implies a theodicy. However, it also indicates that Marquard's reflections on theodicy should not be understood as just a simple commentary on Blumenberg's ideas, but, rather, as the result of a long-standing debate between both thinkers that had

---

61. Odo Marquard, "Idealismus und Theodizee," *Philosophisches Jahrbuch* 73 (1965): 33–47. For the later reprint, see Odo Marquard, *Schwierigkeiten mit der Geschichtsphilosophie* (Frankfurt am Main: Suhrkamp, 1973), 52–65.

62. In the academic year 1965–66, Marquard and Blumenberg were colleagues for a short time in Gießen. This might explain why Blumenberg could include a reflection on Marquard's position on such short notice. In the first edition of *Die Legitimität der Neuzeit* (Berlin: Suhrkamp, 1966), he devoted only four pages to Marquard: 37–40. In the second revised edition of 1976, he included an entire chapter on Marquard and theodicy: Hans Blumenberg, *Die Legitimität der Neuzeit,* 2nd rev. ed. (Suhrkamp: Berlin, 1976), 63–72; Blumenberg, *Legitimacy,* 53–62.

already started before the publication of *The Legitimacy of the Modern Age*. Moreover, Blumenberg did not criticize Marquard so much for interpreting German idealism as a theodicy, but for equating theodicy with theology. Strangely enough, modern theodicy had for Blumenberg nothing to do with theology. Not unlike Marquard, he recognized the constitutive role of theodicy in early modern thought, as well as in German idealism, but he claimed that something more was at stake here than the mere theological justification of God's goodness. Blumenberg maintained that modern theodicy's primary concern was not the exoneration of God, but rather the development of a worldview that makes nature reliable: "In fact the Enlightenment's interest in theodicy is certainly not primarily related to the question of righteousness; its problem is that of a reliability that . . . provides a guarantee of the autonomous lawfulness of the world process, undisturbed by miracles."[63] If the absolutely unpredictable and "miraculous" will of the late medieval God made human existence in the world futile and unreliable, modernity had to develop a worldview that guaranteed the predictability and rationality of reality. Accordingly, modern theodicy was, for Blumenberg, "already outside any theological function." What Blumenberg had in mind was an atheological theodicy. It is only to the extent that theodicy went beyond the scope of dogmatic theology that it could serve the human need of reducing the absolutism of reality. Rather than an advocacy of God, theodicy was therefore "an indirect advocacy of human interests."[64] Modern theodicy's most important function was the conception of a worldview that made reality as reliable as necessary for the possibility of human existence and self-assertion. In this sense, theodicy was a specific mode of work on myth, and did not belong to the dogmatic tradition of theology.

Blumenberg similarly opposed theodicy to theology in a discussion with Jacob Taubes at the third meeting of the Poetik und Hermeneutik group in 1966 in Lindau, and later came back to it in a

---

63. Blumenberg, *Legitimacy*, 58–59.
64. Blumenberg, *Legitimacy*, 58–59.

letter to Taubes.[65] This observation reflects Blumenberg's preoccupation with this distinction at the time he was finishing *The Legitimacy of the Modern Age*. In the discussion, Taubes had explicitly criticized Blumenberg's distinction between theology and theodicy as being "idiosyncratic."[66] Although Taubes later apologized for the inappropriate tone of his comment, Blumenberg's conception of theodicy indeed sounds rather unusual. Traditionally, theodicy was never associated with the anthropological concern to guarantee the reliability of the world but always with an explicitly theological motivation. In a letter to Marquard, Taubes came back to the issue, suggesting he had won the discussion with Blumenberg: "The question of 'Idealism and Theodicy' unintentionally took center stage in Lindau. Reluctantly Blumenberg had to acknowledge his defeat to you and me."[67] In spite of his criticisms, Taubes considered the distinction between theology and theodicy a very fertile one. In 1967, he even hosted a conference in Berlin on this issue of theodicy and its role in *The Legitimacy of the Modern Age*, with Blumenberg himself as one of the keynote speakers.[68] Referring to

---

65. The discussion was centered on the paper Taubes delivered. Both the paper and the transcription of the discussion were published: Jacob Taubes, "Die Rechtfertigung des Hässlichen in urchristilicher Tradition," in *Die nicht mehr schöne Künste: Grenzphänomene des ästhetischen,* ed. Hans R. Jauss (Munich: Wilhelm Fink, 1968), 169–88; Hans Blumenberg, Jacob Taubes, et al., "Erste Diskussion: Kanon und Lizenz in Antiker Literatur," in Jauss, *Die nicht mehr Schönen Künste,* 531–48; Hans Blumenberg, Jacob Taubes, et al., "Vierte Diskussion: Gibt es eine 'Christliche Ästhetik'?" in Jauss, *Die nicht mehr Schönen Künste,* 583–611; Hans Blumenberg and Jacob Taubes, "Auszug aus der Diskussion um Taubes' 'Die Rechtfertigung des Hässlichen in urchristlicher Tradition'," in Hans Blumenberg and Jacob Taubes, *Briefwechsel 1961–1981,* ed. Herbert Kopp-Oberstebrink and Martin Treml (Berlin: Suhrkamp, 2013), 241–46; Hans Blumenberg, "Letter to Jacob Taubes of September 20, 1967," in *Briefwechsel,* 134.
66. Taubes, "Erste Diskussion," 545.
67. Jacob Taubes, "Letter to Odo Marquard of September 13, 1966," unpublished letter, Jacob Taubes Archiv, ZfL-Berlin: "Ohne dass wir es wollten, wurde die Frage der *Idealismus und Theodizee* in Lindau vorrangig. Blumenberg musste also gegen seinen Willen wohl Ihnen und mir das Problem abtreten."
68. See Jacob Taubes, "Einladungsschreiben zum Berliner Colloquium über Blumenbergs *Die Legitimität der Neuzeit* (1967)," in Blumenberg and Taubes, *Briefwechsel,* 247–51. Probably intimidated by Taubes's harsh criticisms during the Poetik und Hermeneutik gathering, Blumenberg was not pleased with Taubes's

the conference in a letter to Blumenberg, Taubes stated: "That you struck oil with your distinction validates, after all, our project that we plan in Berlin."[69] Not unlike Marquard, who also participated in the conference, Taubes seemed to have considered the notion of theodicy key to understanding the second part of *The Legitimacy of the Modern Age*. It is hardly a coincidence that Marquard's essay "Das Gnostische Rezidiv als Gegenneuzeit" (Gnostic Return as Countermodernity), in which he explicitly connected Blumenberg's interpretation of Gnosticism to theodicy, appeared in an essay collection that was edited by Taubes.[70]

In the debate with Taubes that started at the third meeting of Poetik und Hermeneutik, continued in their correspondence, and finally led to the colloquium in Berlin, Blumenberg understood theodicy as the attempt to justify and assure the existing order of reality by appealing to a transcendent being. He stated that theodicy "will prove that God guarantees this order and that the existing reality is the manifestation of this order." Blumenberg continued: "This method will either have to ignore and eliminate everything that does not 'suit' humanity, that is, suffering and ugliness, or balance it out in harmony with a higher justice." In other words, theodicy either denied evil's substantiality or justified it as a necessary aspect of reality that is ultimately good and harmonious. This interpretation of theodicy surely did justice to the traditional Leibnizian concept. In contradistinction to theodicy, theology opposed such a rational justification of reality, for Blumenberg. Theology wanted to emphasize rather than deny or justify the existence of evil and ugliness, because it "finds proof of God's rationally

---

idea to have a conference organized on this topic and initially refused to come. In a letter to Marquard, Taubes explained how he eventually convinced Blumenberg to speak at the conference anyway. Testifying to the growing personal tensions between Blumenberg and himself, Taubes did not hide his frustration: "Ersparen Sie mir, Ihnen über die letzten Episoden mit Blumenberg zu berichten. Ich glaube er kommt zum Colloquium, aber es hat Geduld und viel Takt gebraucht . . . , aber sicher bin ich noch nicht, ob der Chef kommt." Jacob Taubes, "Letter to Odo Marquard of October 19, 1967," unpublished letter, Jacob Taubes Archiv, ZfL-Berlin.

69. Jacob Taubes, "Letter to Hans Blumenberg of September 26, 1967," in Blumenberg and Taubes, *Briefwechsel*, 140.

70. Marquard, "Das Gnostische Rezidiv," 31–36.

unfathomable will in this offensiveness of reality."[71] Blumenberg argued that theology, of which Gnosticism was the most radical example, is concerned with the human submission to the absolute will of God and, accordingly, with its manifestation in reality's unruliness. In this regard, it is opposed to the project of theodicy that was concerned with a dependable order of reality and, accordingly, with the rational God that guaranteed it. For Blumenberg, both perspectives were therefore mutually exclusive: in theology "where everything is oriented towards sheer submission, even the minimum of rationality that is implied in the concept of theodicy is out of the question."[72]

In view of Blumenberg's distinction between theology and theodicy, modern theodicy was atheological and actually functioned as "cosmodicy."[73] Cosmodicy would be the defense of the rationality of the world against the threat of an unpredictable divine will that tended to make the world unreliable or radically evil. In this regard, a shift took place in modern theodicy from a premodern, dogmatic emphasis on the will of God to a modern emphasis on his justice and rationality.[74] Similarly, Marquard argued in "Idealism and Theodicy" that in theodicy "no longer the gracious God but the just God is of central importance."[75] This shift implied that God's will had to conform to the demands of reason rather than vice versa. Only from such a point of view did it make sense at all to do theodicy, and to bring God before the court of reason. In this sense, theodicy's explicit theological function was subordinated to a secular and anthropological one. Theodicy legitimized a reliable conception of the world, and was founded on an ability that is accessible and even belongs to the human mind—namely, rationality. Eventually, theodicy no longer needed the detour of God to prove the coherence, goodness, and predictability of the world. Human

---

71. Blumenberg, "Erste Diskussion," 536.

72. Blumenberg, 547.

73. Blumenberg, *Legitimacy*, 142.

74. The debate about the nature of God's will was obviously a central theme in early modern philosophy. See Nadler, *The Best of All Possible Worlds*.

75. Marquard, "Idealismus und Theodizee," 171n20.

reason sufficed. Marquard showed how the radicalization of theodicy could indeed dismiss God. Paradoxically, he said, theodicy is "Atheismus ad maiorem gloriam Dei" (atheism for the greater glory of God).[76] On this point, Marquard's reflections already agreed to a large extent with Blumenberg. In his later essays, Marquard further harmonized his views on theodicy and modernity with Blumenberg's overwhelming reflections on these issues and developed his own interpretation of modernity in dialogue with Blumenberg's concept of overcoming Gnosticism.

With the atheological function of theodicy in mind, it can be determined more precisely how modern theodicy actually disarmed the threat of a radical Gnostic evil. In Marquard's perspective, modern theodicy "neutralizes" evil. In order to overcome radical evil, modern theodicy did not revive the good and harmonious cosmos of Greek or Scholastic philosophy. Rather, it developed a worldview that was neither good nor evil, but merely neutral and indifferent. Marquard termed this modern process of neutralization, in almost untranslatable ways, *Malitätsbonisierung* (the making-better-of-evil) or *die moderne Entübelung der Übel* (the modern de-eviling of evil). In the same vein, he also showed how Leibniz's God differed considerably from the traditional picture of a benevolent creator. The God of modern theodicy was a neutral and rational God who had created the world almost bureaucratically by applying the rules of reason as systematically as possible. In this sense, neither the world nor its creator was intrinsically or anthropomorphically good in the way the ancient cosmos or the Christian God used to be. Leibniz's God was not good as such; he was just the rationally best possible God. Leibniz thus disarmed the threat of radical evil by a rational neutralization of the creator. According to Marquard's interpretation, "God is not evil, but neither is he just a kind-hearted creator."[77]

This neutralization in fact invalidated the philosophical problem of evil itself. In Blumenberg's perspective, the problem of evil was essentially entwined with the medieval, dogmatic tradition.

---

76. Marquard, "Idealismus und Theodizee," in *Schwierigkeiten*, 65.
77. Marquard, "Entlastungen," 17.

Accordingly, modernity did not try to solve it, for such an attempt would inevitably remain within the boundaries of dogmatic thought. Since dogma was not able to solve the problem of evil internally, modern thought dismissed the problem itself. This was certainly an important connotation of Blumenberg's phrase "overcoming Gnosticism": modern thought overcame Gnosticism and the problem of evil by overcoming the entire dogmatic frame of reference. In this regard, Blumenberg certainly did not interpret evil as a universal or eternal philosophical problem. The notion of evil was maybe not completely absent in modern thought, for Blumenberg, but the problem had lost its metaphysical poignancy: "The evil of the world no longer appears as a metaphysical mark of the quality of the world principle or punishing justice but rather as a mark of the 'facticity' of reality. In it man appears not to be taken into consideration, and the indifference of the self-preservation of everything in existence lets evil appear to him as whatever opposes his own will to live."[78] In other words, evil still existed but modern thought guaranteed, against Gnosticism and against Augustine, respectively, that it did not corrupt reality or human beings in any ultimate sense. While the radical threat of metaphysical and moral evil made human existence virtually impossible at the end of the Middle Ages, modern theodicy attempted to take the sting out of this dogmatic conception of radical evil.

Marquard added that this *Entübelung* (de-eviling) of evil also neutralized Gnosticism's apocalyptic eschatology. With regard to Gnosticism, theodicy proved that the world is not created by an evil god and that evil does not corrupt the world in any fundamental sense. If the world is no longer dominated by such a Gnostic evil, eschatological salvation also becomes less and less urgent. In the light of this overcoming of eschatology, Marquard called

78. Blumenberg, *Legitimacy*, 138 (translation modified). See also Buch, "Gnosis," 92: "In der Tat spielt das Böse nach seiner Abfertigung durch mehrfache Umbesetzung in der *Legitimität der Neuzeit* keine signifikante Rolle mehr. Diese thematische Abwesenheit muss jedoch nicht heissen, dass in Blumenbergs Konstruktion das Böse einfach aus der Welt verschwindet, es verliert aber seine Aura. Eine solche Entschärfung ist deshalb noch nicht gleichbedeutend mit Überwindung oder Auflösung."

modernity a "conservative" epoch because it literally tried to conserve and defend the legitimacy of the world against the possibility of its abolishment at the end of time. Eschatology typically had a progressive, utopian, and even revolutionary potential; it tried to fundamentally alter and destroy the present world order. If, in modernity, human existence is bearable because the world is rationally reliable, the meaning of the world does not have to depend on such a progressive and eschatological destruction at the end of time anymore. Rather, it can be determined here and now.

This is exactly how Blumenberg also characterized modernity in *The Legitimacy of the Modern Age.* In the modern age, the meaning and reliability of existence are not determined by an external, transcendent intervention either at the beginning or at the end of time, but solely depend on immanent human subjectivity. As soon as divine meaning became uncertain or even completely absent in a world indifferent to human values, nature became the sphere of activity of human beings who were no longer constrained by the untouchable holiness of the Greek cosmos or the Christian creation: "The more indifferent and ruthless nature seemed to be with respect to man, the less it could be a matter of indifference to him, and the more ruthlessly he had to materialize, for his mastering grasp, even what was pregiven to him as nature, that is, to make it available and to subordinate it to himself as the field of his existential prospects."[79] By studying, controlling, and even using reality in favor of human existence—by becoming "master and possessor of nature"[80]—modern science and politics revalued the immanent meaning of the world, according to Blumenberg. In modernity, nature did not just serve as the means for the survival of human beings but became the material in which human existence realized and asserted itself.

Against the unpredictable God of the late Middle Ages, and against the radically evil world of Gnosticism that humanity could

79. Blumenberg, *Legitimacy,* 182.

80. René Descartes, "Discourse on Method," in *The Philosophical Writings of Descartes,* vol. 1, ed. and trans. John Cottingham, Robert Stoothoff, and Dugald Murdoch (Cambridge: Cambridge University Press, 1985), 111–51.

not hope to escape, self-assertion made the world meaningful and reliable by investing it with structures that come from within human subjectivity itself. In this sense, self-assertion was the cornerstone of theodicy and the modern overcoming of Gnosticism. Blumenberg emphasized theodicy's anthropological nature not only because it fulfilled the human need for reliability, but also because the modern subject was the very guarantee of this reliability. In modernity, the subject itself rather than God or any other power ultimately determined the meaning of the world. In the court of modern theodicy, human rationality was the judge that exonerated God from blame for the existence of evil. In the end, modern human beings succeeded in making reality reliable and productive through the immanent assertion of their finite existence here on earth without any reference to an external set of powers. Paradoxically, theodicy's reference to God was for Blumenberg just an unnecessary detour in giving rational meaning to the world.

In other words, self-assertion was the modern solution for the late medieval failure to deal with the absolutism of reality. Thus, modern rationality's work on myth fundamentally differed from the ancient myths. While the mythical human beings only reduced the absolutism of reality by distributing its power over different subforces, and maintained "the relative predominance of reality over his consciousness and his fate," the moderns reversed the absolutism of reality "into the supremacy of the subject."[81] Although theodicy and modern rationality continued the function of work on myth, their mastery and control over reality were unknown to mythical thought. In Blumenberg's perspective, modern theodicy actually reversed the traditional power relation between God and human beings. Theodicy realized what he considered in *Work on Myth* the ultimate goal of mythical thought, that is, not just to mediate the relation between the gods and human beings through stories but to have complete control over reality and the gods:

> From this perspective it becomes evident that theodicy . . . fulfill[s] myth's most secret longing not only to moderate the difference in power

---

81. Blumenberg, *Work on Myth*, 9.

between gods and men and deprive it of its bitterest seriousness but also to reverse it. As God's defender, as the subject of history, man enters the role in which he is indispensable. It is not only for the world that, as its observer and actor, indeed as the producer of its "reality," he cannot be imagined as absent, but also indirectly, by way of this role in the world, for God as well, whose "fortune" is now suspected of lying in man's hands.[82]

For Blumenberg, the question obviously remained whether human beings are ever in this position where they can absolutely justify God and the world, and whether reality can ever be completely dependent on human subjectivity. This would mean that a "final myth" were possible that "brings myth to an end" once and for all.[83] Certain movements in modern thought have, in any case, pretended to have found such a final myth. Blumenberg, for example, mentioned the "myth" of German idealism, where the absolutism of reality is reversed into the absolutism of the subject. Here, the subject is no longer overpowered by an external reality, but all reality is constituted through autonomous subjectivity. Although Blumenberg regarded such a final and all-encompassing myth as the structural goal of work on myth, he also doubted whether it could ever be truly realized. Is there not always something that would escape such absolute constructions of reality? Even the best myths, stories, theories, or indeed theodicies leave us with the question with which Blumenberg enigmatically concluded *Work on Myth*: "But what if there were still something to say, after all?"[84]

Applying this question to theodicy, it is clear that there will always be confrontations with extreme evils that simply refuse to be fitted into its rationalist and seemingly foolproof narrative. The prime example of such an evil that radically problematized theodicy's absolute justification of the world is of course that of the Holocaust. Many Jewish philosophers, such as Theodor Adorno and Emmanuel Levinas, indeed considered theodicy impossible

82. Blumenberg, 32.
83. Blumenberg, 266.
84. Blumenberg, 636.

and even blasphemous after the Second World War.[85] If, for Blumenberg and Marquard, theodicy constituted the modern age, its failure could bring an end to modernity. It is hardly a coincidence that the thinkers who criticized theodicy all explicitly addressed the limits of modern thought as well. Moreover, this failure of theodicy and the supposed end of modernity could also entail a return of Gnosticism. This is indeed what Odo Marquard argued, expanding Blumenberg's understanding of Gnosticism and modernity with a theory of countermodernity.

Gnostic Return as Countermodernity

It is almost commonplace in postwar Continental thought that theodicy had become impossible after the Holocaust. Theodicy's attempt to reconcile the existence of concrete evils with an abstract optimism about the world and its creator fundamentally failed to take the horrors of the Holocaust seriously. These events are indeed considered so horrific that they simply refuse to be glossed over in a rational, optimistic picture of reality. In the same vein, many postwar philosophers, also rejected the nineteenth-century philosophy of history, according to which even the most horrible events could have a meaning and a justification insofar as they took part in the realization of the ultimate purpose of history. Therefore the philosophy of history framed by German idealism has often been considered a continuation of the modern project of theodicy. As Hegel himself noted in the introduction to his *Lectures on the Philosophy of History*, "Our method is a theodicy, a justification of God, which Leibniz attempted metaphysically, in his way, by undetermined abstract categories. Thus the evil in the world was to be comprehended and the thinking mind reconciled with it. Nowhere, actually, exists a larger challenge to such reconciliation than

---

85. See Emmanuel Levinas, "Useless Suffering," in *The Provocation of Levinas: Rethinking the Other*, ed. Robert Bernasconi and David Wood (London: Routledge, 1988), 156–67; Theodor Adorno, *Negative Dialectics*, trans. Ernst Basch (New York: Continuum, 1983), 361–408.

in world history."[86] German idealism's theodicy actually justified the existence of evil in the present world by situating the world's negative aspects in a meaningful and progressive course of history, thus subordinating evil to the ultimate purpose of history. In other words, the philosophy of history solved theodicy's problem of evil by historicizing it: although one might experience evil in the present, history will prove that evil "cannot ultimately prevail."[87] It is only in the light of the historical evolution from an evil to a good world that the negative aspects of the world can be overcome, and that creation and world history can be justified. After Auschwitz, however, such a historical synthesis functioning as theodicy had become inconceivable. Hegel's question "To what principle, to what final purpose, have these monstrous sacrifices been offered?" was not only utterly disrespectful to the victims of the Holocaust, but given the unprecedented nature of this evil, the question had also become meaningless.[88]

In the collection of essays *Schwierigkeiten mit der Geschichtsphilosophie* (*Difficulties with the Philosophy of History*), Odo Marquard initially endorsed the relation between theodicy and the philosophy of history. In line with Hegel's understanding of theodicy, he showed in the essay "Idealism and Theodicy" how the project of theodicy is radicalized in the idealistic philosophy of history. Going beyond Hegel, however, Marquard argued that this radicalization ultimately brought the project of theodicy itself to an end by solving the underlying problem: "The problem of theodicy was not discussed at this very moment because it was no longer a problem, that is, it was solved."[89] Except for Hegel's renowned quote, the notion of theodicy was absent in German idealism. In an essay entitled "On the Miscarriage of All Philosophical Trials in Theodicy," Kant had proclaimed the impossibility of any (doctrinal) theodicy. As its idealistic solution had made the problem of theodicy itself redundant, Marquard argued that the

---

86. Hegel, *Philosophy of History*, 18.
87. Hegel, 18.
88. Hegel, 24.
89. Marquard, "Idealismus und Theodizee," in *Schwierigkeiten*, 58.

philosophical project of theodicy had disappeared. Unlike his Jewish contemporaries, Marquard did not attribute the impossibility of theodicy to its failure after Auschwitz but rather to the overwhelming success of the solution for the problem of theodicy provided by German idealism.

For Marquard, the solution for the problem of theodicy was intrinsically related to German idealism's dismissal of God in favor of its exclusive focus on human subjectivity and autonomy. Paradoxically, German idealism solved the problem of theodicy by refusing to talk about God. If human autonomy rather than God was the cornerstone of idealistic metaphysics, human beings could be held responsible for both the existence and the overcoming of evil. Accordingly, the idealistic focus on subjectivity functioned as a solution for the problem of theodicy, which unconsciously determined the structure of idealistic philosophy. In order to make human beings the keystone of theodicy, Marquard further maintained that German idealism historicized theodicy. If, in German idealism, the ontological constitution of the world revolved around subjectivity, human beings rather than the creator God controlled, mastered, and (re)created reality. For Marquard this mastery was essentially historical: human beings can change and control reality only to the extent that they recreate and improve it over the course of time. Since human beings can determine and create the future themselves, we control reality insofar as it is a historical development, that is to say, insofar as the world is (Hegelian) world history. Humanity's intervention in reality could therefore justify the present existence of evil, as this intervention is progressively oriented toward the immanent creation of a better future. By the same token, this historical progress justified the initial shortcomings of God's creation through a continuation of his creative act within immanent history itself. At the moment the Leibnizian optimism was no longer convincing, theodicy needed human beings to guarantee the ultimate goodness of reality historically.

As a consequence of this historicization of theodicy, the existence of reality could be justified only to the extent that immanent progress could overcome the present evils. This does not imply that the present as such was rendered intrinsically good; on the contrary,

Marquard even maintained that the idealistic philosophy of history conceived the present as fundamentally depraved. In other words, progress appeared as the redemptive process that ideally resulted in the future salvation from the present evil. In this regard, Marquard fundamentally subscribed to Jacob Taubes's and Karl Löwith's eschatological analysis of the philosophy of history.[90] Both maintained that the modern philosophies of history were secularized continuations of Judeo-Christian eschatology's belief in the end of time and the salvation of humankind. Marquard's position, however, also deviated from their point of view. He did not recognize in the idealistic philosophies of history so much as a transformation or secularization of eschatology, but rather eschatology's plain and simple return. For this reason, Marquard did not consider the philosophy of history to be truly modern; rather, it was a modern regression into premodernity. Or, as he himself cryptically put it, "a modern premodernity" (*eine datierungsmässig neuzeitliche Vorneuzeitlichkeit*).[91] In contrast to Taubes and Löwith, he therefore maintained that secular modernity failed in the philosophy of history, "that secularization does not take place in it, or not enough, that it did not succeed in it."[92]

For similar reasons, Marquard's relation to Blumenberg's interpretation of modernity was equally ambiguous. On the one hand, Marquard subscribed to the latter's rejection of Löwith's theory of secularization, and hence to his noneschatological, non-Gnostic account of modernity. On the other hand, he did not consider the philosophy of history to be truly modern, as Blumenberg obviously did. On this point, Blumenberg himself radically criticized Marquard's position. Although the latter's interpretation of the philosophy of history as a univocal relapse into premodernity explicitly rejected the notion of secularization, Blumenberg nonetheless considered it to be one of the worst examples of the secularization

---

90. For Löwith and Taubes on the secularization of eschatology, see chapter 2.

91. Odo Marquard, "Aufgeklärter Polytheismus: Auch eine politische Theologie?," in *Der Fürst dieser Welt: Carl Schmitt und die Folgen,* ed. Jacob Taubes (Munich: Wilhelm Fink, 1983), 80.

92. Marquard, *Schwierigkeiten,* 16.

theorem. "Without keeping its name, Marquard has reduced the secularization thesis to its most extreme and most effective form: what remains is no continuity of contents, of substance, of material, but only the naked identity of a subject, whose survival through changes in clothing and in complete anonymity, against all importunities, both gross and subtle, is assured."[93] To the extent that Marquard's interpretation of the philosophy of history deviated from Blumenberg, he also amended Blumenberg's interpretation of Gnosticism. Marquard basically accepted his definition of modernity as the overcoming of Gnosticism, but recognized in the idealistic relapse into premodernity a return of Gnosticism: "If modernity—according to Blumenberg's definition—is the second overcoming of Gnosticism, the philosophy of history is the revenge of Gnosticism against its second overcoming."[94] Not unlike Taubes, Marquard recognized a return of Gnosticism in the pessimistic worldview that underlay the philosophy of history's orientation toward the future. But while Taubes was fascinated by this denial of the value of the present in favor of a redemptive future, Marquard radically criticized it. Accordingly, he was absolutely astounded that Taubes could claim to have *no spiritual investment in the world as it is.*

For Marquard, German idealism's solution for the theodicy problem failed because it could not guarantee the goodness of the present world. Rather than improving the present itself, the idealistic philosophy of history could justify the existence of evil in the present and the past only through the figuration of a better world beyond the present. In line with the Gnostic and eschatological tradition, the philosophy of history combined a pessimistic attitude to the present (*Negativierung der Welt*) with the emphasis on another and better world to come (*Positivierung der Weltfremdheit*).[95] For Marquard, this tendency opposed the fundamentally modern emphasis on the meaning of the here and now (*Positivierung der Welt*) that discarded the appeal of another reality beyond (*Negativierung*

---

93. Blumenberg, *Legitimacy*, 59.
94. Marquard, *Schwierigkeiten*, 16.
95. Marquard, "Das Gnostische Rezidiv," 31, 35.

der Weltfremdheit)—as either a transcendent or a future world.[96] In this regard, Marquard even defined the philosophy of history as "countermodernity" *(Gegenneuzeit)*.[97] Since he maintained that theodicy constituted modern thought, the idealistic failure of theodicy also brought an end to modernity.

For Marquard, German idealism's solution for the problem of theodicy was clearly a pseudosolution. The philosophy of history did not solve the problem of evil by transposing the responsibility for the existence and the overcoming of evil to an unfathomable future. Nor could it solve the problem by holding human beings rather than God himself responsible for the existence or annihilation of evil. In the end, the idealistic theodicy unconsciously reintroduced what it attempted to eradicate—namely, Gnosticism: "This 'death of God' theodicy, which implied the autonomy of the human being as a transcendental being or a superhuman—from Kant to Nietzsche—turned theodicy through its radicalization into its opposite: into the neo-Gnostic, neo-Marcionite eschatology."[98]

In other words, Marquard considered the idealistic historicization of theodicy through human autonomy to be highly illegitimate. First of all, the philosophy of history could not justify or atone for the present; on the contrary, it emphasized its radical depravity. As an explicitly conservative thinker, Marquard was more interested in a modest justification of the current state of affairs than in an absolute progressive or eschatological orientation toward the future. Furthermore, in Marquard's perspective, German idealism repeated Augustine's fallacy of making human beings' free will fully responsible for the existence and the atonement of evil. As Blumenberg had already noted, the Augustinian moralization of evil was not able to solve the Gnostic problem of evil because it merely transposed evil from the demiurgic creator to the moral will of human beings. Both in Blumenberg's and in Marquard's perspective, such a transposition of evil to humankind ultimately entailed the return of the Gnostic problem of evil. In this regard,

---

96. Marquard, 33.
97. Marquard, 36; Marquard, *Schwierigkeiten*, 16.
98. Marquard, "Das Gnostische Rezidiv," 34.

Marquard showed how human autonomy becomes a problem for itself rather than a solution. Discussing Marquard's position, Blumenberg made a similar observation:

> One should not forget here that since Augustine's turning away from Gnosticism, the concept of evil in the world had been displaced and continues up to the present to be displaced continually further and further: evil in the world appears less and less clearly as a physical defect of nature and more and more (and with less ambiguity, on account of the technical means by which we amplify these things) as the result of human actions. To that extent, the philosophy of history already reflects a situation in which man suffers less and less from the defects of nature and more and more from the productions of his own species. That would have to produce a new variety of Gnosticism and, no less necessarily, a new conception of revolt against it.[99]

This is the only passage in *The Legitimacy of the Modern Age* where Blumenberg suggested a possible return of Gnosticism within modernity itself. If the human subject became the absolute foundation of all reality in German idealism and in its philosophy of history, it also became absolutely responsible for the existence of evil. As a result of this idealistic focus on subjectivity, Blumenberg's self-assertion turned into its opposite. No longer a solution for the evils that hamper human existence, this self-assertion that underlay technical science as well as German idealism became the very foundation of evil. Although technology was initially motivated by the needs of human self-assertion, the absolutization of this human project made the dynamics of technology independent of human motivations up to the point that it even became an uncontrollable and destructive force. In this stage, evil could become as necessary and inescapable as it used to be in Gnosticism. Unlike Marquard, Blumenberg never developed this line of thought, and one can only speculate about what he could have meant by this "new variety of Gnosticism." However, it is clear that the idealistic and technological absolutization of the subject touches upon the limits of the modern paradigm.

---

99. Blumenberg, *Legitimacy*, 56–57 (translation modified).

For Marquard, this picture of human beings as fully capable of controlling reality was simply too ambitious and therefore not genuinely modern. It negated the essential finitude of the human condition, which he considered to be one of the crucial insights of philosophical modernity. In this regard, his discontent with German idealism was mainly concerned with its illegitimate absolutism of the autonomous subject. He rather subscribed to Blumenberg's modest notion of modern self-assertion that was explicitly based on human finitude. Not unlike Blumenberg's, Marquard's philosophy is essentially antiabsolutist. He was indeed a self-proclaimed skeptic and pluralist, preferring contingency to necessity, fate to control, polytheism to monotheism, skepsis to dogma, and human finitude to absolute knowledge. In an essay on Marquard and Blumenberg, Eva Geulen similarly emphasized the importance of these philosophical motives in both thinkers: "Born in the 1920s, they belong to what Helmut Schelsky termed the 'Skeptical Generation,' and, in fact, they share several skeptical traits: high awareness of the limits of human cognition, deep distrust of all versions of speculative philosophy of history, significant room for contingencies."[100] Although Marquard was more explicitly negative about the absolutist pretensions of German idealism, Blumenberg essentially shared Marquard's concern. Blumenberg's description of the idealistic myth that brought work on myth to an end was an implied criticism of the idealistic absolutism of the subject.

If, according to Marquard, the absolutism of nineteenth-century philosophy had made theodicy impossible and was thus confronted with a return of Gnosticism, the legitimacy of modernity was fundamentally at risk. Accordingly, the project of Marquard's thought can be understood as the attempt to reestablish modernity against the legacy of the Gnostic and countermodern philosophy of history. In Marquard's perspective, such a reestablishment of the modern against the return of Gnosticism would need a new theodicy, and hence a new overcoming of Gnosticism. Less abstractly, this means that Marquard pursued a new foundation for philosophical

---

100. Eva Geulen, "Passion in Prose," *Telos* 158 (2012): 10.

optimism that legitimized and justified the present after the philosophy of history. Against German idealism and against progressive and revolutionary thought, his philosophy promoted a new investment in the world as it is. The truly modern legitimization of the world did not seek a univocal solution for theodicy, but it retained the problem itself by means of a more pluralistic and skeptical approach: "Someone who cannot find the answer to a problem eventually loses the problem; that's no good. Someone who has just one solution to a problem believes to have solved the problem and easily becomes dogmatic; that's no good either. What is best is to give too many answers: that—as is the case in theodicy—conserves the problem without actually solving it."[101] Central to the reestablishment of the modern was then the rejection of the philosophy of history's absolutist and univocal solution. Marquard refused to reduce history and the world to a single and absolute story but wanted to account for its irreducible narrative plurality. In his own terminology, he explicitly preferred the "polymythical" structure of the novel or the historical sciences to the "monomythical" philosophy of history.[102] Dismissing the dogmatic structure of monotheism and German idealism, Marquard, not unlike Blumenberg, favored the pluralistic and mythical worldview of polytheism.

With regard to theodicy, such a pluralistic approach was based on compensation, a notion that was omnipresent in Marquard's philosophy.[103] In his perspective, true theodicy does not solve the problem of evil but rather compensates for singular instantiations of evil. Accordingly, Marquard described compensation as a recurring motif in modern philosophy. In twentieth-century philosophical anthropology, for example, human beings were considered to be creatures that were poorly adjusted to their environment but at

---

101. Marquard, "Entlastungen," 29.

102. See Marquard, "Aufgeklärter Polytheismus," 84; Odo Marquard, "Lob der Polytheismus: Über Monomythie und Polymythie," in *Abschied vom Prinzipiellen: Philosophische Studien* (Stuttgart: Reclam, 1981), 91–116.

103. See Odo Marquard, "Inkompetenzkompensationskompetenz? Über Kompetenz und Inkompetenz der Philosophie," in *Abschied vom Prinzipiellen,* 23–38.

the same time able to compensate for these original deficiencies.[104] In line with Leibniz, Marquard granted that evil might exist but that theodicy proved that good and evil balance each other out. The good compensates for evil. In a more philosophically modest way than German idealism, Marquard maintained that evil could not be overcome definitively but that it could be neutralized: "Evil plus compensating good = zero."[105]

Odo Marquard's interpretation of Gnosticism and modernity should be understood as an emendation of Blumenberg's account. Although he fundamentally agreed with Blumenberg's interpretation, Marquard elaborated on a second return of Gnosticism in German idealism after its first return in the late Middle Ages. Modernity as such had nothing to do with Gnosticism for either Blumenberg or Marquard. The latter did recognize the return of this ancient heresy in German idealism, which he did not consider to be truly modern on that account. Blumenberg's *second* overcoming of Gnosticism did not suffice for Marquard. In an effort to establish the continuing legitimacy of an "a-gnostic" modernity, Marquard's philosophical project could be understood as an attempt to overcome this legacy of Gnostic idealism a *third* time.

After Modernity?

Unlike Marquard and many of his other philosophical contemporaries, Blumenberg never discussed what it could mean for the modern age to come to an end. Nonetheless, the question of the end of modernity is a crucial one if we want to understand what is at stake in Blumenberg's reflections on modern thought. Clearly, modernity could not bring myth to an end and could not be an absolute end point of history, for Blumenberg. Accordingly, there had to be limits to the modern narrative and to modernity's work on myth. This would also imply that the end of modernity is conceivable as an

---

104. Marquard, "Entlastungen," 26.
105. Marquard, 25.

internal failure of its metaphorical tools in reducing the absolutism of reality. If theodicy's second overcoming of Gnosticism is for Blumenberg one of these tools that constituted modern thought, the end of modernity might have something to do with the failure of theodicy, and hence with the return of the Gnostic concept of evil.

It is hardly a coincidence that this is exactly what many of Blumenberg's contemporaries had argued—all of them explicitly addressing the limits of modern thought. Eric Voegelin, Hans Jonas, and indeed Odo Marquard himself all argued that modernity, and the twentieth century in particular, were haunted by a Gnostic threat that radically endangered the project of modern thought. In this regard, Gnosticism could not be overcome definitively, but kept on returning at the very moments of cultural and historical crisis. In a fascinating fragment from Blumenberg's *Nachlass,* entitled *Gnostischer Fehltritt der Tierfabel* (*The Gnostic Misstep of the Animal Fable*), a rare allusion to the possibility of Gnostic return in his own time can be found: "How then is the worldly success of Gnosticism possible—the danger of Christian theology that continues until today in ever new forms, and whose extent has not yet been adequately assessed?"[106] Blumenberg never elaborated on this issue, but the fragment surely seemed to suggest that Gnosticism would keep on demanding new overcomings. In order to guarantee the continuing legitimacy of the modern age, modernity might need a new theodicy, and hence a "third overcoming of Gnosticism."[107] Is this third overcoming what Blumenberg actually attempted in *The Legitimacy of the Modern Age,* referring to the concepts of Gnosticism, divine absolutism, and theodicy? Blumenberg's abstract historical analyses of Western thought could indeed prove timelier than they initially appear. In spite of its seemingly modest scholarly pretensions, *The Legitimacy of the Modern Age* was

---

106. Hans Blumenberg, "Gnostischer Fehltritt der Tierfabel," Blumenberg Nachlass, DLA Marbach: "Wie konnte es dann zu dem in seiner Grösse noch gar nicht zureichend eingeschätzten Welterfolg der Gnosis kommen—der bis auf den heutigen Tag fortbestehenden Gefahr der christlichen Theologie in immer neuen Gestalten?"

107. Benjamin Lazier, *God Interrupted: Heresy and European Imagination between the World Wars* (Princeton: Princeton Unversity Press: 2008), 22.

more than just an intellectual history of the genesis of early modern thought. What was at stake in this book was the philosophical defense of the modern narrative after its limits had become frighteningly clear in the course of the twentieth century. And even more ambitiously, it can be read as an attempt to defend the legitimacy of the modern world itself—a theodicy, that is—at the moment that real evils had made any immediate investment in it extremely problematical.

Contra Adorno and Levinas, one could argue that precisely because of the Holocaust theodicy was necessary, no longer as an absolute rational justification of God but as a modest acceptance of the world. Theodicy, in this regard, would try to save the world from the destructive legacy of Auschwitz by showing that these evils have not corrupted reality in any absolute or Gnostic sense. Such a theodicy does not need God anymore because it no longer demands absolute justification. For Blumenberg and Marquard, the world did not need a divine vindication of all its single elements in order to be legitimate. What Blumenberg and Marquard paradoxically proposed was an atheological theodicy—a theodicy without God. This was a modest defense of the world at the moment that the belief in its creator was challenged in modernity. Without the need to defend God and justify his creation in absolute terms, it might even be easier to accept the world as it is. If there is no principle that bears absolute responsibility for the world, an absolute justification of reality and all its single elements is no longer necessary. This was at least what Blumenberg suggested in a range of comical *Atheistic Prayers* that can be found in his *Nachlass*, all addressing the impossibility of justifying and believing in God's existence.[108] It is hardly surprising that he even devoted one of them to Odo Marquard's *Philosophy of History*:

> Dear God, how beautiful would it be, if you existed. But how difficult would it then be to defend you. What a blessing that you are almighty,

---

108. See "Atheistengebet," "Gebet des Atheologen," "Fromme Atheisten," "Atheisten in der Kirche," "Gnostizismus der Atheismen," and "Die Theologie des Atheisten" in the *Götterschwund*-ordner, Blumenberg Nachlass, DLA Marbach.

otherwise you would not be able to make yourself not exist. Thus the world does not need to be the way it must have been if it had to be your work. No one has to carry the burden of justifying what exists. Not even once does man have to take on responsibility for it, because only he could have removed it from you, as it inevitably would be, if you existed, as Augustine and Marquard have proven. Thus I do not regret that I am an atheist. It is the only possibility not to be let down by you and remain assured of your love. Amen.[109]

---

109. Hans Blumenberg, "Letter to Odo Marquard of February 19, 1974," unpublished letter, Blumenberg Nachlass, DLA Marbach. :

Gebet eines Atheisten nach der Lektüre von Odo Marquards Geschichtsphilosophie.
Lieber Gott, Wie schön wäre es, wenn du existiertest. Aber wie schwer wäre es dann, dich zu verteidigen. Welches Glück also, dass du allmächtig bist, sonst hättest du nicht einmal bewirken können, dass du nicht existiert. So braucht die Welt nicht zu sein, wie sie sein müsste, wenn sie dein werk sein sollte. Es fällt auf niemanden, dass nicht zu rechtfertigen ist, was ist. Nicht einmal der Mensch braucht die Verantwortung dafür zu übernehmen, wie es unausweichlich wäre, wenn du existiertest, da nur er sie dir abnehmen könnte, wie Augustin und Marquard bewiesen haben. So bedauere ich nicht, dass ich ein Atheist bin. Es ist die einzige Möglichkeit, von dir nicht enttäuscht zu werden und deiner Liebe gewiss zu bleiben. Amen.

CONCLUSION

After being submerged in some kind of modern-Gnostic conspiracy, it almost comes as a surprise that most modern intellectuals did not see any connection between ancient Gnosticism and their own times. Realizing that there are other ways to make sense of the modern world feels like waking up from a dream dominated by "a mixed feeling of high anxiety and admiration" in which "the Gnostics have already taken hold of the whole world, and we are not aware of it," as Ioan Culianu phrased it.[1] This realization brings us back to the central question of this book: Why have so many thinkers used the notion of Gnosticism to make sense of the modern condition?

One of the book's main premises is that Gnosticism was increasingly used as a metaphor in the postwar German debates on

---

1. Ioan Culianu, "The Gnostic Revenge: Gnosticism and Romantic Literature," in *Gnosis und Politik,* ed. Jacob Taubes (Munich: Wilhelm Fink, 1984), 290.

modern Gnosticism. To make sense of the idiosyncratic uses of Gnosticism, the book asked how the concept of Gnosticism was increasingly metaphorized, and what the metaphor of Gnosticism then stood for. A final question remains, however: Why was such a metaphor needed in the first place? Answering this question could uncover the historical, political, and philosophical stakes of the Gnosticism debates. However pertinent these stakes were to the debaters themselves, they were shrouded in academic idiosyncrasies and metaphorical twists that often appear as nonsensical to the reader who is not familiar with the immediate German intellectual and historical contexts. Uncovering the metaphorics of Gnosticism therefore amounts to showing how the Gnosticism debates were related to the context of postwar German history, in general, and to the immediate German past and the heritage of the Second World War, in particular. At the same time, this strategy could uncover the intellectual and philosophical stakes of the Gnosticism debates, which are valuable in their own right, independently of conceptual and metaphorical idiosyncrasies and of the concrete historical contexts.

Gnosticism's Background Metaphorics and Metaphorization

Although Gnosticism has been approached in this book as a metaphor, it was never used as such by Jacob Taubes, Eric Voegelin, Hans Blumenberg, Hans Jonas, Odo Marquard, and Gershom Scholem. For these thinkers, Gnosticism was a historical concept that could be extended to designate certain theological and philosophical ideas that existed independently of the late ancient context in which Gnosticism historically flourished. However, this extension of the concept of Gnosticism beyond its initial historical scope eventually eroded its concrete meaning to such an extent that in postwar German thought it could mean virtually anything. Gnosticism became a pseudoconcept, or indeed a philosophical metaphor for a range of contemporary political and philosophical issues. The application of the concept of Gnosticism to historically unrelated phenomena proliferated its meanings to the point where it actually started functioning as a metaphor.

Hans Blumenberg himself studied the role of philosophical metaphors extensively throughout his career. In order to gain insight into the metaphorics of Gnosticism, a better understanding of how he interpreted the relation between concepts and metaphors might be rewarding. Blumenberg indeed granted that metaphorical connotations can operate in the background of discussions that initially appear purely conceptual or terminological. He aptly termed this "background metaphorics" (*Hintergrund-metaphorik*), adding that "metaphorics can also be in play where exclusively terminological propositions appear, but where these cannot be understood in their higher-order semantic unity without taking into account the guiding idea from which they were introduced and read off."[2] Gnosticism could be an example of such background metaphorics. Only by studying the metaphorics of Gnosticism can one really gain insight into the underlying ideas that had been obscured by terminological idiosyncrasies of the debate.

Blumenberg applied this concept of background metaphorics in his critical assessment of the German secularization debates in *The Legitimacy of the Modern Age*. He approached secularization here as a pseudoconcept with a specific metaphorical history. Interestingly, the German secularization debates not only coincided with the Gnosticism debates historically but also formed the intellectual background of these debates, as has been shown repeatedly throughout this book. For thinkers as diverse as Carl Schmitt and Karl Löwith, the concept of secularization traditionally designated the continuity between theological concepts and secular ideas. The idea of a Gnostic return in modernity is a specific instance of such a secularization thesis, as it conceives a continuity between Gnostic ideas and secular modernity. In this sense, Blumenberg also placed Marquard's, Voegelin's, and Taubes's thought under the same heading of secularization theory, in addition to Schmitt's and Löwith's. Despite the fact that all these thinkers used the same concept of

---

2. Hans Blumenberg, *Paradigms for a Metaphorology*, trans. Robert Savage (Ithaca: Cornell University Press, 2010), 62.

secularization, they actually had radically different philosophical agendas and even opposing interpretations of modernity. These differences notwithstanding, Blumenberg claimed that whenever the notion of secularization was used, specific implied meanings and connotations were unavoidable. These meanings and connotations, Blumenberg argued, were largely contingent upon the metaphorical history of the notion of secularization.

Secularization first came into being as a juridical concept around the end of the seventeenth century, designating the expropriation of ecclesiastical goods and territories by lay political authorities. At a later stage, this specific juridical concept was used as a metaphor for the relation between Christian ideas and modern culture, more generally. Although the conceptual history of secularization showed that its juridical and theoretical uses developed independently of each other, Blumenberg maintained that the initial metaphorical function of secularization inevitably influenced the formation of the concept in its theoretical sense. In short, secularization was no longer used as a metaphor, but its metaphorical background determined its current conceptual meanings and uses. Blumenberg described this specific role of metaphor in the formation of concepts as "a process of reference to a model that is operative in the genesis of a concept but is no longer present in the concept itself."[3]

Because of its background metaphorics, the concept of secularization had certain connotations that simply could not be dismissed, whatever its specific conceptual uses or meanings were. A first connotation of the secularization theorem that Blumenberg revealed was the narrative of identity and continuity. For Schmitt and Löwith, secularization implied the paradoxical identity of theology and modern secularism. Secularization merely designated the transfer of a specific idea or concept from the theological to the modern sphere. This connotation of identity was metaphorically in tune with secularization's juridical meaning. Here, secularization meant that a specific property is transferred from the ecclesiastical to the political sphere. In both cases, the content that has been

---

3. Hans Blumenberg, *The Legitimacy of the Modern Age*, trans. Robert Wallace (Cambridge, MA: MIT Press, 1983), 23. See also Blumenberg, *Paradigms*, 62–63.

transferred remains identical. From a rhetorical perspective, this claim that there are continuities between the traditional opposites of religion and secularism functioned as a provocation, according to Blumenberg. Indeed, such claims imply that modernity is not as modern or new as it thinks it is: modernity has fundamentally misunderstood itself. This connotation of the secularization thesis finally implied the "illegitimacy of the modern age": Schmitt and Löwith ultimately showed that modernity is not what it thinks it is, but that it is merely an inauthentic derivation of Christian thought. This rhetoric of illegitimacy and inauthenticity could also be derived from secularization's metaphorical history. Indeed, the juridical concept of secularization designated an expropriation of territories that originally belonged to the church. As a result of his metaphorological study of the concept, Blumenberg fiercely rejected secularization as a category that could adequately define the nature of modernity.

The concept of Gnosticism in postwar German thought had a comparable pseudo-conceptual status and metaphorical function as the notion of secularization. In spite of its heterogeneous conceptual meanings, Gnosticism had certain connotations that simply could not be dismissed and that were operative in the background of terminological uses. These connotations were even similar to those of secularization. Gnosticism often functioned as a category of illegitimacy that wanted to discredit modernity as heretical. These background metaphorics of Gnosticism were discussed extensively in chapter 3. However, the metaphorical trajectory of Gnosticism actually ran counter to that of secularization. It also implied some form of background metaphorics, but while secularization originated as a metaphor and was only later conceptualized by forgetting this metaphorical origin, Gnosticism was originally a concept that was later metaphorized unwittingly. In this regard, the uses of Gnosticism in postwar German thought could also be an instance of what Blumenberg termed *metaphorization,* designating the process in which a concept is increasingly used as a metaphor.

The process of Gnosticism's metaphorization shows similarities with a metaphor that Blumenberg studied in his book *The Genesis of the Copernican World*—namely, the Kantian metaphor of the Copernican turn. Kant used the name of Copernicus as a very specific metaphor for his own philosophical project, but almost immediately his readers and successors extended this metaphor beyond its intended meaning. The Copernican metaphor was soon used, without Kant's consent, to highlight the revolutionary nature of his transcendental philosophy. For Blumenberg, the appeal and significance of Kant's metaphor were so strong that it unwittingly contained an enormous potential for further metaphorization.[4] In complete opposition to Kant's intention, Copernicus's name could even become a metaphor for the decentered human being in Darwin's theory of evolution and Freud's theory of the unconscious. Blumenberg noted that this uncontrollable proliferation of a concept's or metaphor's meanings is a common process in intellectual history: "As so frequently happens in similar cases, the history of its influence has equipped the original casual coinage a weight of meaning that it did not originally possess."[5] The same held true for Hans Jonas's coinage of Gnosticism in the context of modern existential and nihilistic philosophy. As soon as Jonas made this metaphorical connection between Gnosticism and modern thought, there was no stopping the proliferation of this concept's meaning and applicability. Like Kant's Copernican metaphor in the eighteenth and nineteenth centuries, Gnosticism was increasingly metaphorized beyond its original scope in the course of the twentieth century.

If Gnosticism functioned as a metaphor in postwar German thought, the question is what the metaphor refers to and what it stands in for. What were Taubes, Voegelin, Blumenberg, Jonas,

---

4. See Hans Blumenberg, *The Genesis of the Copernican World,* trans. Robert M. Wallace (Cambridge, MA: MIT Press, 1987), 605: "So it is neither surprising nor reprehensible that a metaphor having the epochal importance that this one possesses sets the reader's constructive imagination in motion even before he has finished reading it. Kant is making use of a historical potential that seems, in the hindsight of historiography, to have been bound to become an independent force. This inevitability is, in turn, a symptom of the wealth of meaning that had become attached to Copernicus's name."

5. Blumenberg, *Genesis of the Copernican World,* 595.

Marquard, and Scholem actually discussing when they used the notion of Gnosticism? What legitimate historical, political, and philosophical concerns did the metaphor of Gnosticism stand in for? The different chapters in this book have tried to uncover some of these reference points of Gnosticism, which are as diverse as the nature of cultural crisis (chapter 1, "Crisis"), the problems of evil, pessimism, and salvation (chapter 2, "Eschaton"), the question of dissent and tradition (chapter 3, "Subversion"), the nihilistic confrontation with meaninglessness (chapter 4, "Nothingness"), the philosophy of history and the issue of periodization (chapter 5, "Epoch"), and the justification of God and the world (chapter 6, "Theodicy"). Obviously, the discourse on modern Gnosticism and its underlying metaphorics cannot be conceptualized completely. There is no final or absolute explanation for the meaning of the notion of Gnosticism in postwar German thought. This book has therefore often limited itself to exploring the many possible connotations of Gnosticism as well as the implied literary motifs, conceptual associations, and imaginative horizons of this metaphor of sorts. Nonetheless, a few questions remain unanswered: Why was such a metaphor needed in the first place? Why were legitimate concerns that could be discussed conceptually treated metaphorically? And additionally, why was this metaphorical treatment needed in Germany at this precise moment in history?

On this point, one can only speculate about why conceptual thought failed and the metaphor of Gnosticism had to stand in for it. One element, which has largely remained in the background of the book but surfaced toward the end of some chapters, could serve as a point of departure for such a speculation. This element is the experience of totalitarianism, which all thinkers discussed in this book have in common. More specifically, it is the philosophical legacy of the Second World War, and the impossibility of confronting the evils of the Holocaust through conceptual thought. Indeed, the Holocaust is the ultimate example of an event that defies philosophical understanding. The horrors of the Holocaust challenge the meaning of reality and the justification of history, God, tradition, and, most of all, the world as it is. Ultimately, the experience of the two world wars testified to the failure of conceptual thought to justify, defend, and give meaning to traditional values, beliefs, and truths.

Gnosticism, Totalitarianism, and the Holocaust

Given the place and the moment in history in which the Gnosticism debates took place (Germany, from the end of the 1940s until the 1970s), the immediate German past cannot be ignored if one wishes to make sense of the thinkers discussed in this book. Taubes, Scholem, Jonas, and Blumenberg were all German Jews whose lives and thought were fundamentally marked by the Second World War and by the event of the Holocaust. Taubes, Scholem, and Jonas left Germany before the war. Blumenberg stayed, but had to give up his studies, and was even imprisoned briefly at the end of the war as a so-called *Halbjude*. Voegelin, even though a Catholic, also had to flee Europe. He was fired from his job at the University of Vienna after the *Anschluss* because of his critical stance toward the NSDAP and just avoided being arrested by the Gestapo. Marquard, the youngest of these six thinkers, was only twelve when the war started and was hardly involved in it. At the end of the war, he joined the so-called *Volkssturm* and was briefly held as a prisoner of war for this reason.

It is hardly surprising that the topic of the Second World War was present in the work of these thinkers. Voegelin, as a political philosopher, studied totalitarianism extensively, although he never wrote on the Holocaust. Jonas's search for an ethics of responsibility in a technological age definitely has to be understood against the backdrop of totalitarianism. He was probably the only one of the thinkers discussed who addressed the problem of the Holocaust philosophically, in his essay "The Concept of God after Auschwitz." The Holocaust and totalitarianism were present in the work of Scholem too, albeit less structurally than in Voegelin and Jonas. In the case of Taubes, these issues remained implicit. Nonetheless, commentators have found tacit treatments of the Holocaust in Taubes's *Occidental Eschatology* as well as in *The Political Theology of Paul*—for example, in Taubes's assertion "Destruction exists" (*Es gibt Vernichtung*).[6] Blumenberg seems to be the exception here, as he never mentioned political issues in his published work. Recent discoveries in his *Nachlass*, however, revise this picture of Blumenberg as an apolitical thinker. Some recently published texts show that he was indeed very concerned with the legacy of totalitarianism.[7] Marquard, finally, was a representative of conservative antitotalitarianism, although his writings were arguably concerned more with the Cold War and with communism than with the immediate legacy of the Second World War.

In spite of the general presence of the Second World War in the writings of these thinkers, the Holocaust in particular was hardly treated as systematically and philosophically as in the work of their Jewish contemporaries, like Hannah Arendt or the members of the Frankfurt school. This is striking not only for historical but also for conceptual reasons. Significant thematic parallels exist between the German discussions of the Holocaust and the debates on modern Gnosticism. For one, the notion of Gnosticism that was applied in the German debates paralleled specific positions in Holocaust theology. The Holocaust paradigmatically challenged the traditional Jewish and Christian views of God. The existence of an omnipotent and caring God was simply irreconcilable with the evils of the Holocaust. Some theologians therefore rejected God's existence and proclaimed the death of God on theological grounds; others believed that God turned his face away from the world and was

---

6. Jacob Taubes, *The Political Theology of Paul*, trans. Dana Hollander (Stanford: Stanford University Press, 2004), 32. See Christoph Schmidt, *Die theopolitische Stunde: Zwölf Perspektiven auf das eschatologische Problem der Moderne* (Munich: Wilhelm Fink, 2009). For the topic of the Holocaust in *Occidental Eschatology*, see Martin Treml, "Nachwort," in Jacob Taubes, *Abendländische Eschatologie* (Munich: Matthes und Seitz, 2007).

7. Hans Blumenberg, *Präfiguration: Arbeit am Politischen Mythos*, ed. Angus Nicholls and Felix Heidenreich (Berlin: Suhrkamp, 2014); Angus Nicholls, *Myth and the Human Sciences: Hans Blumenberg's Theory of Myth* (New York: Routledge, 2014), 183–250; Angus Nicholls, "Hans Blumenberg on Political Myth: Recent Publications from the Nachlass," *Iyyun: The Jerusalem Philosophical Quarterly* 65 (2016): 3–33.

fundamentally absent from it during the Holocaust; still others, like Hans Jonas, argued that God's omnipotence should be given up.[8] These themes of divine nothingness, divine absence, and divine impotence arguably repeated leitmotifs from ancient Gnostic myths and were definitely in tune with the postwar debates on the Gnostic return in modernity.

The Holocaust left its mark not only on postwar theology but also on philosophy. Both the traditional conception of God and the moral and philosophical standard for understanding evil had been shattered at Auschwitz. In *The Origins of Totalitarianism,* Hannah Arendt famously coined the concept of "radical evil" to make sense of the horrors of the concentration camps. Evil was radical precisely because it "breaks down all standards we know."[9] For Arendt, the evil of Auschwitz was an unfathomable, thought-defying, and absolute force that "can no longer be deduced from humanly comprehensible motives."[10] By changing the locus of evil from moral intentions to an incomprehensible and abysmal void, Arendt transformed evil from something we can understand and conquer into something we cannot even hope to grasp, let alone control. Taken at face value, the notion of radical evil introduced a demonic, perhaps even Gnostic conception of evil. Such a Gnostic interpretation would nip every political or moral attempt to overcome evil in the bud, as it allowed only an abstract and transcendent hope to escape it. The confrontation with the concrete evils of the Holocaust would have metaphysical implications: the mere fact that such evils could exist denigrated the value of reality. In this view, the evils of the Holocaust could be the ultimate confirmation of the Gnostic-apocalyptic worldview. For a thinker like Taubes, the Holocaust itself could appear as the apocalyptic catastrophe

---

8. See, respectively, Richard Rubenstein, *After Auschwitz: Radical Theology and Contemporary Judaism* (Indianapolis: Bobbs-Merrill, 1966); Martin Buber, *Eclipse of God: Studies in the Relation between Religion and Philosophy* (New York: Humanity Books, 1952); Hans Jonas, "The Concept of God after Auschwitz: A Jewish Voice," *Journal of Religion* 67, no. 1 (1987): 1–13.

9. Hannah Arendt, *The Origins of Totalitarianism* (New York: Harcourt Brace, 1951), 459.

10. Arendt, *Origins of Totalitarianism*, 9.

par excellence, and even as the ultimate motivation for his Gnostic refusal to invest spiritually in the world as it is. Although he never put it like this, it would be perfectly reasonable for Taubes to reject a world in which the Holocaust was possible.

The problem of evil was of central importance in the discourse on modern Gnosticism as well, especially in the discussions on pessimism and theodicy (see chapters 2 and 6). However, the thinkers discussed in this book usually approached the problem of evil from a more distanced, historical point of view. They never tackled the problem philosophically, as Arendt did, let alone with reference to the Holocaust. In *Evil in Modern Thought,* Susan Neiman gives a convincing philosophical explanation for this fact. In stark contrast to the philosophical responses to the earthquake of Lisbon in 1755, she argued, "Auschwitz . . . evoked relative reticence."[11] Apparently, the confrontation with the evils of the Holocaust had been so horrific that the attempt to conceptualize them philosophically seemed futile. Neiman continued:

> Philosophers were stunned, and on the view most famously formulated by Adorno, silence is the only civilized response. In 1945 Arendt wrote that the problem of evil would be the fundamental problem of postwar intellectual life in Europe, but even there her prediction was not quite right. No major philosophical work but Arendt's own appeared on the subject in English, and German and French texts were remarkably oblique. Historical reports and eyewitness testimony appeared in unprecedented volume, but conceptual reflection has been slow in coming. It cannot be the case that philosophers failed to notice an event of this magnitude. On the contrary, one reason given for the absence of philosophical reflection is the magnitude of this task. What occurred in Nazi death camps was so absolutely evil that, like no other event in human history, it defies human capacities for understanding.[12]

If Neiman is right that the philosophical discourse on evil was both necessary and impossible after Auschwitz, it has to be possible to discover mediated and metaphorical treatments of the problem of evil in postwar German philosophy. The notion of Gnosticism

---

11. Susan Neiman, *Evil in Modern Thought: An Alternative History of Philosophy* (Princeton: Princeton University Press, 2002), 2.

12. Neiman, *Evil in Modern Thought*, 2.

could definitely function as a possible tool to achieve this, as the problem of evil was central to ancient Gnostic speculations and to the reflections on Gnostic return in modernity. Explicitly referring to Blumenberg, Marquard, and Taubes, Neiman stated that "post-war German history of philosophy . . . offered rich and significant work related to many aspects of the problem [of evil]."[13] There is little reason to believe that these thinkers consciously substituted the metaphor of Gnosticism for a more direct approach to the problem of evil. However, the use of this notion could bear witness specifically to the structural impossibility of discussing or even thinking evil in the traditional sense. It is telling that thinkers like Taubes and Blumenberg could not or did not want to talk about the immediate German past. The issue of the Holocaust was present in Taubes's work but always remained implicit; Blumenberg wrote about totalitarianism but explicitly refused to publish these writings.

Neiman suggested that Arendt, in contrast to her contemporaries, developed concepts of evil that allowed her to confront the issue of the Holocaust philosophically. It might not be mere coincidence, in this regard, that she did not refer to the notion of Gnosticism at all in her reflections on the modern condition. Since she knew most of the people involved in the Gnosticism debates personally, and since her critique of modernity as world-alienating suited Jonas's concept of Gnostic alienation (*Entweltlichung*), her thinking would have been perfectly amenable to a Gnostic interpretation of the modern age.[14] This indicates that the philosophical stakes of both

---

13. Neiman, 288–90.
14. Arendt was friendly with Gershom Scholem, with whom she corresponded extensively. As a German Jew, she had to leave Europe for the United States around the beginning of the Second World War, and not unlike fellow émigrés Jonas, Taubes, and Voegelin, she also continued her academic career at an American university. Jonas and Arendt studied together with Martin Heidegger in Germany and later taught at the New School in New York. For Arendt's debate with Voegelin on the nature of totalitarianism, see chapter 5. For a general discussion of the intellectual relation between Arendt and Blumenberg, see Hannes Bajohr, "The Unity of the World: Arendt and Blumenberg on the Anthropology of Metaphor," *Germanic Review: Literature, Culture, Theory* 90, no. 1 (2015): 42–59; Hans Blumenberg, *The Rigorism of Truth: Texts on Freud and Arendt*, trans. Joe Paul Kroll (Ithaca: Cornell University Press, 2018).

Arendt's interpretation of modernity and her philosophical account of evil were not dissimilar to those of the Gnostic interpretations of modernity. Nonetheless, her coinage of the notion of radical evil was definitely not meant as an endorsement of the Gnostic concept of evil. In order to avoid such Gnostic or demonic interpretations, she later even dismissed the notion of radical evil and replaced it with the provocative notion of the *banality of evil*.[15] In a letter to Scholem, Arendt explained the reason for this conceptual shift: "It is indeed my opinion now that evil is never radical, that it is only extreme, and that it possesses neither depth nor any demonic dimension. It can overgrow and lay waste the whole world because it spreads like a fungus on the surface. It is thought-defying, as I said, because thought tries to reach some depth, to go to the roots, and the moment it concerns itself with evil, it is frustrated because there is nothing. That is its banality."[16] More of a rhetorical tool than a new philosophical concept, the banality of evil did not replace her earlier understanding of radical evil.[17] Arendt's philosophical interpretation of evil did not fundamentally change, but the difference in connotation between "banality" and "radicalism" excluded the Gnostic/demonic interpretation of evil. If evil is banal, it is not too profound or mysterious for human imagination to grasp, but, on the contrary, almost too simple and superficial compared to its horrific implications.

Arendt's banality of evil actually functioned as an overcoming of Gnosticism. Neiman also hinted at this: "Arendt thought that Gnosticism would be the most dangerous, attractive and widespread heresy of the future. She therefore sought descriptions of

---

15. Hannah Arendt, *Eichmann in Jerusalem: A Report on the Banality of Evil* (New York: Penguin Books, 1977).

16. Hannah Arendt, "Letter to Gershom Scholem of July 24, 1963," in Hannah Arendt and Gershom Scholem, *Der Briefwechsel 1939–1964*, ed. Marie-Luise Knott (Berlin: Jüdischer Verlag im Suhrkamp Verlag, 2010). Arendt's provocative coinage of the term *banality of evil* in regard to Adolf Eichmann, one of the main organizers of the Holocaust, did not go down well with Scholem. Their disagreement on this point brought their friendship to an end.

17. See Richard Bernstein, *Radical Evil: A Philosophical Interrogation* (Cambridge: Polity Press, 2002), 218.

evil that resist the urge to give it satanic greatness, for such urges are both puerile and dangerous."[18] Arendt feared that a demonic-Gnostic interpretation of evil would be the easiest explanation for the horrors of the Second World War. Such demonization of the Nazi criminals, however, creates a radical political separation between "us and them," and hence a Gnostic dualism between good and evil. Moreover, such an interpretation makes evil into an unfathomable abyss that eventually threatens to corrupt reality. If such grave evils are able to exist, the world in which they are contained is no longer reliable. In such an interpretation of evil, the evils of the Holocaust corrupt the very roots of reality. This would essentially imply the return of Gnosticism's pessimistic cosmology. However, Arendt's interpretation of evil as banal countered this relapse into Gnosticism, according to Neiman: "If the forces that produce evil have neither depth nor dimension, then Gnosticism is false."[19]

In spite of some striking parallels between the Gnosticism debates and the discussions of the Holocaust, the Gnosticism debates cannot be reduced to a discussion of the Holocaust in disguise. The debaters clearly related themselves to the immediate German past and were concerned—either implicitly or explicitly—with relevant issues of political crisis or totalitarianism. It is crucial to relate the debates to their immediate political and historical context, but they should not be overly politicized either. Therefore, this book has mainly approached the Gnosticism debates as an intellectual phenomenon in their own right. Accordingly, it subscribes to the intellectual historian Peter Gordon's conviction "that there is something about the intellect that resists its wholesale reduction to a given social order."[20] Ideas are valuable in their own right, he argued, and studying ideas historically does not necessarily entail uncovering their sociopolitical context. Although the event of the Second

---

18. Neiman, *Evil in Modern Thought*, 302–3.
19. Neiman, 303.
20. Peter Gordon, "Contextualism and Criticism in the History of Ideas," in *Rethinking Modern European Intellectual History*, ed. Darrin McMahon and Samuel Moyn (Oxford: Oxford University Press, 2014), 50.

World War must have been in the back of these thinkers' minds, the Gnosticism debates were ultimately theoretical and academic and hardly ever dealt with real political issues. In a stupendous claim, Taubes even emphasized the fundamental irrelevance of political history and the Holocaust for his intellectual project: "Fascism, however, is much too uninteresting and episodic to concern this problem. It sacrificed 50 Million people, it created gas chambers, and still it remains an ultimately irrelevant episode."[21]

Another obvious reason why the role of the Second World War should not be overestimated is that the postwar Gnosticism debates continued a debate that started before the Second and even before the First World War. As the introduction and chapter 1 have shown, Gnosticism and Gnostic return in modernity were prominent topics of discussion in Germany from the beginning of the twentieth century onward. At the same time, tracing the topic of modern Gnosticism back to its roots highlights the fundamental conceptual differences between the pre- and postwar discussions of modern Gnosticism. The Second World War marked an important shift in the evaluation of Gnosticism in these debates. While Gnosticism was initially a source of fascination for German intellectuals in the interwar period, and hence generally considered a positive force, it increasingly became a category of illegitimacy with a generally negative connotation after the war. Although the Gnosticism debates as such can be understood independently from the immediate context of the Second World War, this shift itself can be explained only by an aggravated sense of crisis and hence by the traumatic experience of totalitarianism. The intellectual fascination with a mystical, nihilistic, subversive, and potentially irrational phenomenon like Gnosticism was hardly conceivable after the confrontation with extreme forms of irrationality during the war. While Gnosticism could still be considered as a solution for cultural and political crisis in the interwar period, immediately after the war Voegelin considered Gnosticism the very cause of totalitarian politics. This attempt to trace the religious roots of totalitarianism

---

21. "Jacob Taubes," in *Denken, das an der Zeit ist,* ed. Florian Rötzer (Frankfurt am Main: Suhrkamp, 1987), 319.

is of course a recurring leitmotif in postwar political thought.[22] This is another important parallel between the Gnosticism debates and the postwar discussions of totalitarianism.

To return, finally, to the question of Gnosticism's metaphorics, it is clear that Gnosticism did not function in postwar German thought as a metaphor for the world war, for totalitarianism, or for the Holocaust. Gnosticism did not function, certainly not exclusively, as a metaphorical attempt to overcome the past (*Vergangenheitsbewältigung*). However, Gnosticism was increasingly used after the war as a metaphor for exactly those issues that the experience of the world wars had made impossible to conceive in the traditional sense—the nature of cultural crisis, the problem of evil, the legitimacy of tradition, the confrontation with meaninglessness, the legitimacy of the modern age, and the justification of God—not surprisingly the respective topics of the six chapters of this book. What underlay the concern with all these specific issues is the more general failure to conceive of the meaning of the world in the traditional sense and, indeed, to have *spiritual investment in the world as it is*. Gnosticism was not a metaphor for the evils of the war, but for the philosophical problems that it left in its wake.

Thus, Taubes, Voegelin, Blumenberg, Jonas, Marquard, and Scholem were hardly concerned with Holocaust theology and with the ways in which Auschwitz challenged the traditional conception of the divine. Rather, they, like the philosopher Hannah Arendt, were concerned with the meaning and legitimacy of a world in which the Holocaust was possible. Totalitarianism challenged not only the traditional concept of God but also an understanding of the world itself. In *Lebenszeit und Weltzeit* (*Lifetime and World-time*), Blumenberg connected this issue of the world explicitly to an isolated reference to totalitarian politics, claiming that "Hitler had

---

22. See Jacob Talmon, *The Origins of Totalitarian Democracy*, 2 vols. (London: Secker and Warburg, 1952–60); Uriel Tal, "Structures of German 'Political Theology' in the Nazi Era," in *Religion, Politics, and Ideology in the Third Reich: Selected Essays* (London: Routledge, 2004), 87–129; Marcel Gauchet, *L'avènement de la démocratie*, vol. 3, *À l'épreuve des totalitarismes 1914–1974* (Paris: Gallimard, 2010).

no world."[23] The question for postwar German philosophy was how to continue living in a world that had produced Hitler and had made the Holocaust possible. Arendt, too, tried to defend the world's legitimacy against the legacy of Auschwitz. The question of the world and the "love of the world" were central philosophical concerns for her.[24] In *The Human Condition,* she developed the concept of *worldliness* relatively independent from the question of totalitarianism, arguing that the modern age is characterized by a loss of the world.[25] Modernity's distinguishing feature is its world alienation. Accordingly, the urgency of discussing the philosophical question of the world is related not only to the evils of the Second World War but to modernity as such.

The World as It Is

In spite of their recurring reference to the theological notion of Gnosticism, Taubes, Voegelin, Blumenberg, Jonas, Marquard, and Scholem were not doing theology but practicing philosophy. Their interest was not in Gnosticism's conception of divine absence as such but in the conception of a world from which the divine had radically withdrawn. For these thinkers, this withdrawal of the divine connected ancient Gnosticism to the modern disenchantment of the world, to the process of secularization, and to the death of God.

This question of the world and of God's gradual withdrawal from it highlights again the connection between the postwar German debates on modern Gnosticism and the debates on secularization that took place in Germany around the same time. The two debates cannot be strictly separated from each other, as the very same thinkers were involved. These debates coincided with each other, not only historically and geographically but also conceptually. The Gnostic readings of modernity, and the secularization theses, conceived

---

23. Hans Blumenberg, *Lebenszeit und Weltzeit* (Frankfurt am Main: Suhrkamp, 1986), 84.

24. See Hannah Arendt, *Love and Saint Augustine* (Chicago: University of Chicago Press, 1996).

25. Hannah Arendt, *The Human Condition* (Chicago: University of Chicago Press, 1958).

continuities between theology and modern secularism. Both debated the role of religion in modern thought and were concerned with the relation between Christianity or Judaism and modernity. Since the Gnosticism debates had a long intellectual history that stretched back to the early twentieth century, other reasons and contexts can obviously be given for the uses of this idiosyncratic notion of Gnosticism. The introduction and chapter 1 have referred to these typically German contexts, which ranged from radical theological speculations to the fascination with esoteric knowledge and messianism in German literature and philosophy. Yet, to understand the postwar debates on modern Gnosticism in their own right, the prominence of Gnosticism can be explained by relating these debates to the immediate context of the secularization debates. The appeal of Gnosticism in postwar German thought was that it could serve as a means to address the issue of secularization. The notion of Gnosticism, by way of an immense historical and metaphorical detour, could address the withdrawal of the divine from the world and the worldliness of a de-divinized world more pertinently than any other concept that was available at the time.

The German word for secularization—*Verweltlichung*—indicates that the same philosophical issue of the world is at stake in both debates. The postwar German interest in Gnosticism concerned the worldliness of a world from which the divine is absent. The status of this modern, disenchanted, secularized, or de-divinized world was all but evident. Just because we have lost our connection to a world beyond does not mean that we can simply fall back upon this one. In other words, the withdrawal of the divine from the world does not mean that we can now see the world for what it really is. Blumenberg made this very clear in the opening pages of *The Legitimacy of the Modern Age*: "The point is that 'the world' is not a constant whose reliability guarantees that in the historical process an original constitutive substance must come back to light, undisguised, as soon as the superimposed elements of theological derivation and specificity are cleared away."[26] Once the divine has withdrawn from the world, we still have to determine philosophically what the meaning of such a world could be exactly.

---

26. Blumenberg, *Legitimacy*, 8.

Because Gnosticism represented a similar situation where God was radically absent, its conception of the remaining value of this world could function as a point of reference for modernity. This point of reference was of course more metaphorical than historical. Gnosticism ultimately functioned as a metaphor for this condition of divine absence and worldly nihilism. Gnosticism's view of the world could either serve as a precedent for modernity, as it was for Taubes and Scholem, or be fiercely opposed, as it was by Voegelin, Blumenberg, Jonas, and Marquard.

In both cases, the crucial philosophical question for these thinkers was how to make sense of the world after the divine had withdrawn from it. Taken in a more existential and practical sense, the question was whether and how *spiritual investment in the world as it is* was possible in a modern, de-divinized world. It is only from the point of view of this shared question that the differences between these six thinkers discussed in this book can be highlighted once more.

One possible answer to this question remained fundamentally Gnostic. If the modern world is void of any spiritual or divine meaning, it could be reasonable to give up on it or abolish it altogether. For much the same reason, the world could be presented as radically evil. This position was epitomized in Taubes's apocalyptic attitude: "Let it all go down. *I have no spiritual investment in the world as it is.*"[27] By and large, Scholem shared this attitude. Interestingly, both wanted to save some form of spiritual investment without accepting the world as it is. Rather, their spiritual investment was one that ran counter to this world and prefigured another world of redemption.

A second answer rejected such a radical, revolutionary attitude and sought to reestablish spiritual investment in the world as it is. For more conservative thinkers like Voegelin, Jonas, and Marquard, saving the world from its modern-Gnostic meaninglessness had to be conceivable. They showed how the withdrawal of the divine that eroded the spiritual meaning of the world could be countered by revaluing the dignity of the cosmos. This could be done by

---

27. Jacob Taubes, "Appendix A: The Jacob Taubes-Carl Schmitt Story," in *The Political Theology of Paul,* trans. Dana Hollander (Stanford: Stanford University Press, 2004), 103.

retrieving premodern sources of meaning—the Platonic-Christian understanding of existence as being-in-between (*metaxy*), for Voegelin; the Greek conception of nature as *physis* that is fundamentally alive, for Jonas; the worldview of polytheism, for Marquard. A return to these systems could revive a spiritual investment in the world and legitimize the world as it is.

There is, however, another way to overcome the Gnostic abolishment of reality and save the world's legitimacy. This third possible answer was Blumenberg's. Rather than retrieving the old *spiritual* investments, he believed that modernity discovered new *nonspiritual* investments in the world as it is. As he did not want to save spiritual investment, Blumenberg's position is definitely the exception here. Because the world had lost its spiritual meaning, modern human beings could invest it with their own values, concepts, and projects. This investment in the world is characteristic of the modern program of self-assertion, according to Blumenberg. The burden of justifying and giving meaning to this world now lay with human beings. Without the need to justify its creator, the world hardly needed absolute meaning or legitimation. Although the modern world must not be the evil cosmos of Gnosticism, it did not have to be the harmonious cosmos of Greek philosophy, the kindhearted creation of Christianity, or the best possible world of Leibniz either. Although God's absence initially withdrew meaning from the world, it eventually made it easier for modern humanity to give it new meaning. Blumenberg's position was the genuinely modern solution to the question of meaning. As such, it entailed an overcoming of Gnosticism and of the entire premodern frame of reference, which had been applied over and over again to the modern condition. Blumenberg's position was convincing enough to put an end to the debates on modern Gnosticism. Although he definitely still belonged to this debate himself, and many of his contemporaries remained fascinated with his overcoming of Gnosticism for many years to come, no serious defense of the Gnostic nature of modernity appeared after Blumenberg's penetrating and nuanced critique. His overcoming of Gnosticism initiated the overcoming of the German Gnosticism debates themselves.

BIBLIOGRAPHY

Adorno, Theodor W. *Negative Dialectics*. Translated by Ernst Basch. New York: Continuum, 1983.

———. *History and Freedom: Lectures, 1964–1965*. Edited by Rolf Tiedemann and translated by Rodney Livingstone. Cambridge: Polity Press, 2006.

Agamben, Giorgio. *The Time That Remains: A Commentary on the Letter to the Romans*. Translated by Patricia Dailey. Stanford: Stanford University Press, 2005.

———. *The Kingdom and the Glory: For a Theological Genealogy of Economy and Government*. Translated by Lorenzo Chiesa. Stanford: Stanford University Press, 2011.

Altizer, Thomas. *Living the Death of God: A Theological Memoir*. Albany: SUNY Press, 2006.

Amslinger, Julia. *Eine neue Form von Akademie: "Poetik und Hermeneutik"—Die Anfänge*. Munich: Wilhelm Fink, 2017.

Aquinas, Thomas. *Summa Theologica: Volume I-Part I*. New York: Cosimo, 2007.

Arendt, Hannah. *The Origins of Totalitarianism*. New York: Harcourt Brace, 1951.

———. *The Human Condition*. Chicago: University of Chicago Press, 1958.

———. *Eichmann in Jerusalem: A Report on the Banality of Evil*. New York: Penguin Books, 1977.

———. *Love and Saint Augustine*. Chicago: University of Chicago Press, 1996.

Arendt, Hannah, and Gershom Scholem. *Der Briefwechsel 1939–1964*. Edited by Marie-Luise Knott. Berlin: Jüdischer Verlag im Suhrkamp Verlag, 2010.

Assmann, Jan. *Of God and Gods: Egypt, Israel, and the Rise of Monotheism*. Madison: University of Wisconsin Press, 2008.

Augustine, Aurelius. *On the Free Choice of Will, On Grace and Free Choice, and Other Writings*. Edited by Peter King. Cambridge: Cambridge Univeristy Press, 2010.

Bajohr, Hannes. "The Unity of the World: Arendt and Blumenberg on the Anthropology of Metaphor." *Germanic Review: Literature, Culture, Theory* 90, no. 1 (2015): 42–59.

Ball, Hugo. *Flight out of Time: A Dada Diary*. Translated by Ann Raimes and edited by John Elderfield. Berkeley: University of California Press, 1996.

Balthasar, Hans Urs von. *Apokalypse der deutschen Seele: Studien zu einer Lehre von letzten Haltungen*. 3 vols. Salzburg: Anton Pustet, 1937.

Barash, Jeffrey A. "The Sense of History: On the Political Implications of Karl Löwith's Concept of Secularization." *History and Theory* 37 (1998): 69–82.

Barth, Karl. *The Epistle to the Romans*. Translated by Edwin C. Hoskyns. Oxford: Oxford University Press, 1968.

Bataille, Georges. "Le bas matérialisme et la gnose." In *Oeuvres complètes* I, *Premiers écrits 1922–1940*, 220–27. Paris: Gallimard, 1970.

Baur, Ferdinand C. *Die christliche Gnosis: oder, die christliche Religionsphilosophie inihrer geschichtlichen Entwicklung*. Tübingen: Verlag von Osiander, 1835.

Benjamin, Walter. *Gesammelte Schriften*. Frankfurt am Main, Suhrkamp, 1977.

———. *Selected Writings*. Edited by Marcus Bullock, Howard Eiland, Michael W. Jennings, and Gary Smith. 4 vols. Cambridge, MA: Harvard University Press, 2003–6.

Benjamin, Walter, and Gershom Scholem. *The Correspondence of Walter Benjamin and Gershom Scholem, 1932–1940*. Translated by Gary Smith and Andre Lefevere. Cambridge, MA: Harvard University Press, 1992.

———. *Briefwechsel 1933–1940*. Edited by Gershom Scholem. Frankfurt am Main: Suhrkamp, 1997.

Bernstein, Richard. *Radical Evil: A Philosophical Interrogation*. Cambridge: Polity Press, 2002.

Biale, David. *Gershom Scholem: Kabbalah and Counter-History*. 2nd ed. Cambridge, MA: Harvard University Press, 1982.

———. "Gershom Scholem on Nihilism and Anarchism." *Rethinking History* 19, no. 1 (2015): 61–71.

Bielik-Robson, Agata. "Modernity: The Jewish Perspective." *New Blackfriars* 94 (2013): 188–207.

Bloch, Ernst. *Geist der Utopie*. Munich: Verlag von Duncker und Humblot, 1918.

———. *Thomas Münzer als Theologe der Revolution*. Munich: Kurt Wolff, 1921.

———. *The Spirit of Utopia*. Translated by Anthony A. Nassar. Stanford: Stanford University Press, 2000.

Blumenberg, Hans. *Die Legitimität der Neuzeit*. Frankfurt am Main: Suhrkamp, 1966.

———. *Die Genesis der kopernikanischen Welt*. Frankfurt am Main: Suhrkamp, 1975.

———. *Die Legitimität der Neuzeit*. 2nd rev. ed. Frankfurt am Main: Suhrkamp, 1976.

———. *Arbeit am Mythos*. Frankfurt am Main: Suhrkamp, 1979.

———. *The Legitimacy of the Modern Age*. Translated by Robert Wallace. Cambridge, MA: MIT Press, 1983.

———. *Work on Myth*. Translated by Robert M. Wallace. Cambridge, MA: MIT Press, 1985.

———. *Lebenszeit und Weltzeit*. Frankfurt am Main: Suhrkamp, 1986.

———. *The Genesis of the Copernican World*. Translated by Robert M. Wallace. Cambridge, MA: MIT Press, 1987.

———. *Paradigmen zu einer Metaphorologie*. Frankfurt am Main: Suhrkamp, 1997.

———. *Beschreibung des Menschen*. Frankfurt am Main: Suhrkamp, 2006.

———. *Paradigms for a Metaphorology*. Translated by Robert Savage. Ithaca: Cornell University Press, 2010.

———. *Präfiguration: Arbeit am Politischen Mythos*. Edited by Angus Nicholls and Felix Heidenreich. Berlin: Suhrkamp, 2014.

Blumenberg, Hans, and Carl Schmitt. *Briefwechsel 1971–1978*. Edited by Alexander Schmitz and Marcel Lepper. Frankfurt am Main: Suhrkamp, 2007.

Blumenberg, Hans, and Jacob Taubes. *Briefwechsel 1961–1981*. Edited by Herbert Kopp-Oberstebrink and Martin Treml. Berlin: Suhrkamp, 2013.

Bragagnolo, Celina María. "Secularization, History, and Political Theology: The Hans Blumenberg and Carl Schmitt Debate." *Journal of the Philosophy of History* 5 (2011): 84–104.

Brumlik, Micha. *Die Gnostiker: Der Traum von der Selbsterlösung des Menschen*. Frankfurt am Main: Eichborn, 1992.

Buber, Martin. *Eclipse of God: Studies in the Relation between Religion and Philosophy*. New York: Humanity Books, 1952.

Buch, Robert, and Daniel Weidner, eds. *Blumenberg Lesen*. Berlin: Suhrkamp, 2014.

Bultmann, Rudolf. *Geschichte und Eschatologie*. Tübingen: J.C.B. Mohr, 1958.

———. *Primitive Christianity in Its Contemporary Setting.* Minneapolis: Fortress Press, 1975.

———. *"New Testament and Mythology," and Other Basic Writings.* Edited and translated by Schubert M. Ogden. Minneapolis: Fortress Press, 1984.

Camus, Albert. *L'homme revolté.* Paris: Gallimard, 1951.

Carlebach, Elisheva. *The Pursuit of Heresy.* New York: Columbia University Press, 1990.

Caygill, Howard. "The Apostate Messiah: Scholem, Taubes, and the Occlusions of Sabbatai Zevi." *Journal of Cultural Research* 13, nos. 3–4 (2009): 191–205.

Chappel, James. "Nihilism and the Cold War: The Catholic Reception of Nihilism between Nietzsche and Adenhauer." *Rethinking History* 19 (2015): 95–110.

Cloots, André. "Modernity and Christianity: Marcel Gauchet on the Christian Roots of the Modern Ways of Thinking." *Milltown Studies* 61 (2008): 1–30.

Cohn, Norman. *The Pursuit of the Millennium: Revolutionary Millenarians and Mystical Anarchists of the Middle Ages.* London: Pimlico, 1957.

Corngold, Stanley. *Lambent Traces: Franz Kafka.* Princeton: Princeton University Press, 2004.

Culianu, Ioan. *The Tree of Gnosis: Gnostic Mythology from Early Christianity to Modern Nihilism.* Translated by H. S. Wiesner. San Francisco: Harper Collins, 1992.

Derrida, Jacques. "The Eyes of Language: The Abyss and the Volcano." In *Acts of Religion,* edited by Gil Anidjar, 189–22. New York: Routledge, 2002.

Descartes, René. *The Philosophical Writings of Descartes.* Volume 1. Translated by John Cottingham, Robert Stoothoff, and Dugald Murdoch. Cambridge: Cambridge University Press, 1985.

Dickey, Laurens. "Blumenberg and Secularization: Self-Assertion and the Problem of Self-Realizing Teleology in History." *New German Critique* 41 (1987): 151–65.

Dickinson, Colby, and Stéphane Symons, eds. *Walter Benjamin and Theology.* New York: Fordham University Press, 2016.

Engel, Amir. *Gershom Scholem: An Intellectual Biography.* Chicago: University of Chicago Press, 2017.

Faber, Richard. *Politische Dämonologie: Über modernen Marcionismus.* Würzburg: Königshausen und Neumann, 2007.

Faber, Richard, Eveline Goodman-Thau, and Thomas Macho, eds. *Abendländische Eschatologie: Ad Jacob Taubes.* Würzberg: Königshausen und Neumann, 2001.

Fuhrmann, Manfred, ed. *Terror und Spiel: Probleme der Mythenrezeption.* Munich: Wilhelm Fink, 1971.

Funkenstein, Amos. *Heilsplan und natürliche Entwicklung: Formen der Gegenwartsbestimmung im Geschichtsdenken des hohen Mittelalters.* Munich: Nymphenburg, 1965.

Gauchet, Marcel. *The Disenchantment of the World: A Political History of Religion.* Translated by Oscar Burge. Princeton: Princeton University Press, 1999.

———. *L'avènement de la démocratie.* Vol. 3, *À l'épreuve des totalitarismes 1914–1974.* Paris: Gallimard, 2010.

Géréby, György. "Political Theology versus Theological Politics: Eric Peterson and Carl Schmitt." *New German Critique* 35, no. 3 (2008): 7–33.

Geulen, Eva. "Passion in Prose." *Telos* 158 (2012): 8–20.

Gogarten, Friedrich. *Despair and Hope for Our Time.* Translated by Thomas Wieser. Philadelphia: Pilgrim Press, 1970.

Gold, Joshua R. "Jacob Taubes: Apocalypse from Below." *Telos* 134 (2006): 140–56.

Gordon, Peter. "Jacob Taubes, Karl Löwith, and the Interpretation of Jewish History." In *German-Jewish Thought between Religion and Politics,* edited by Christian Wiese and Martina Urban, 349–70. Boston: De Gruyter, 2012.

———. "Weimar Theology: From Historicism to Crisis." In *Weimar Theology: A Contested Legacy,* edited by Peter Gordon and John McCormick, 150–78. Princeton: Princeton University Press, 2013.

———. "Contextualism and Criticism in the History of Ideas." In *Rethinking Modern European Intellectual History,* edited by Darrin McMahon and Samuel Moyn, 32–55. Oxford: Oxford University Press, 2014.

Grafton, Anthony. "The Magician." *New Republic,* March 3, 2003.

Grimstad, Kirsten J. *The Modern Revival of Gnosticism and Thomas Mann's "Doktor Faustus."* Rochester: Camden House, 2002.

Harnack, Adolf von. *Marcion: Das Evangelium vom Fremden Gott.* Leipzig: J.C. Hinrichssche Buchhandlung, 1924.

———. "Fünfzehn Fragen an die Verächter der wissenschaftlichen Theologie unter den Theologen." In *Aus der Werkstatt des Vollendeten,* 51–54. Giessen: A. Töpelmann, 1930.

Hegel, G. W. F. *Faith and Knowledge.* Translated by Walter Cerf and H. S. Harris. Albany: SUNY Press, 1977.

———. *Introduction to the Philosophy of History.* Translated by Leo Rauch. Cambridge: Hackett, 1988.

Heidegger, Martin. "Nietzsche's Word: God Is dead." In *Off the Beaten Track,* translated by Julian Young and Kenneth Haynes, 157–99. Cambridge: Cambridge University Press, 2002.

Heidenreich, Felix. *Mensch und Moderne bei Hans Blumenberg.* Munich: Wilhelm Fink, 2005.

Heidgen, Michael, Matthias Koch, and Christian Köhler, eds. *Permanentes Provisorium: Hans Blumenbergs Umwege.* Munich: Wilhelm Fink, 2015.

Horkheimer, Max, and Theodor Adorno. *Dialectic of Enlightenment.* Translated by Edmund Jephcott. Stanford: Stanford University Press, 2007.

Hotam, Yotam. "Gnosis and Modernity: A Postwar German Intellectual Debate on Secularisation, Religion, and 'Overcoming' the Past." *Totalitarian Movements and Political Religions* 8, nos. 3–4 (2007): 591–608.

———. *Modern Gnosis and Zionism: The Crisis of Culture, Life Philosophy, and Jewish National Thought.* London: Routledge, 2009.

Hume, David. *Dialogues Concerning Natural Religion, and Other Writings.* Edited by Dorothy Coleman. Cambridge: Cambridge University Press, 2007.

Idel, Moshe. *Old Worlds, New Mirrors: On Jewish Mysticism and Twentieth-Century Thought.* Philadelphia: University of Pennsylvania Press, 2010.

———. "Messianic Scholars: On the Early Israeli Scholarship, Politics, and Messianism." *Modern Judaism* 32 (2012): 22–53.

Ifergan, Pini. "Cutting to the Chase: Carl Schmitt and Hans Blumenberg on Political Theology and Secularization." *New German Critique* 37 (2010): 149–71.

Iser, Wolfgang, ed. *Immanente Ästhetik, ästhetische Reflexion: Lyrik als Paradigma der Moderne; Kolloquium Köln 1964: Vorlagen und Verhandlungen.* Munich: Wilhelm Fink, 1966.

Jacobson, Eric. *Metaphysics of the Profane: The Political Theology of Walter Benjamin and Gershom Scholem.* New York: Columbia University Press, 2003.

Jauss, Hans Robert, ed. *Die nicht mehr Schönen Künste: Grenzphänomene des Ästhetischen.* Munich: Wilhelm Fink, 1968.

Jay, Martin. "Review of *The Legitimacy of the Modern Age.*" *History and Theory* 24 (1985): 183–96.

Jonas, Hans. *Gnosis und spätantiker Geist.* 2 vols. Göttingen: Vandenhoeck und Ruprecht, 1934–54.

———. "Gnosticism and Modern Nihilism." *Social Research* 19 (1952): 430–52.

———. *The Gnostic Religion: The Message of the Alien God and the Beginnings of Christianity.* Boston: Beacon Press, 1958.

———. "Response by Hans Jonas." In *The Bible in Modern Scholarship: Papers Read at the 100th meeting of the Society of Biblical Literature, December 28–30, 1964,* edited by J. Philip Hyatt, 279–93. Nashville: Abingdon Press, 1965.

———. "Life, Death, and the Body in the Theory of Being." In *The Phenomenon of Life,* 7–37. New York: Harper and Row, 1966.

———. "Delimitation of the Gnostic Phenomenon: Typological and Historical." In *Le origini dello Gnosticismo: Colloquio di Messina 13–18 Aprile 1966,* edited by Ugo Bianchi, 90–108. Leiden: Brill, 1967.

———. *The Imperative of Responsibility: In Search of an Ethics for the Technological Age.* Chicago: University of Chicago Press, 1984.

———. "The Concept of God after Auschwitz: A Jewish Voice." *Journal of Religion* 67, no. 1 (1987): 1–13.

———. "Heidegger's Resoluteness and Resolve." In *Martin Heidegger and National Socialism,* edited by G. Neske and E. Kettering, 197–203. New York: Paragon House, 1990.

———. *Memoirs*. Translated by Krishna Winston. Lebanon, NH: University Press of New England, 2008.

Jung, Carl G. *The Gnostic Jung*. Edited by Robert A. Segal. London: Routledge, 1992.

Kant, Immanuel. "On the Miscarriage of All Philosophical Trials in Theodicy." In *Religion and Rational Theology*, translated by Allen Wood and George Di Giovanni, 17–30. Cambridge: Cambridge University Press, 1996.

Katz, Jacob. *A House Divided: Orthodoxy and Schism in Nineteenth-Century Central European Jewry*. Translated by Ziporah Brody. Lebanon, NH: University Press of New England, 2005.

King, Karen L. *What Is Gnosticism?* Cambridge, MA: Harvard University Press, 2003.

Klossowski, Pierre. *Sade mon prochain*. Paris: Seuil, 2002.

Klossowski, Pierre, and Jean-Maurice Monnoyer. *Le peintre et son démon*. Paris: Flammarion, 1985.

Kopp-Oberstebrink, Herbert. "Die Subversion der Reformation der Revolution: Jacob Taubes' Bermerkungen zur Kleinschreibung." *Trajekte* 23 (2011): 27–32.

———. "Between Terror and Play: The Intellectual Encounter of Hans Blumenberg and Jacob Taubes." *Telos* 158 (2012): 119–34.

Lazier, Benjamin. "Overcoming Gnosticism: Hans Jonas, Hans Blumenberg, and the Legitimacy of the Natural World." *Journal of the History of Ideas* 64, no. 4 (2003): 619–37.

———. *God Interrupted: Heresy and the European Imagination between the World Wars*. Princeton: Princeton University Press, 2008.

———. "On the Origins of Political Theology: Judaism and Heresy between the World Wars." *New German Critique* 35 (2008): 143–64.

Lebovic, Nitzan. "The Jerusalem School: The Theopolitical Hour." *New German Critique* 35 (2008): 97–120.

Lee, Philip J. *Against the Protestant Gnostics*. Oxford: Oxford University Press, 1993.

Leibniz, Gottfried W. *Theodicy: Essays on the Goodness of God, the Freedom of Man, and the Origin of Evil*. Translated by E. M. Huggard. La Salle: Open Court, 1985.

Leisegang, Hans. *Die Gnosis*. Leipzig: A. Kröner, 1924.

Levinas, Emmanuel. "Useless Suffering." In *The Provocation of Levinas: Rethinking the Other*, edited by Robert Bernasconi and David Wood, 156–67. London: Routledge, 1988.

Lilla, Mark. *The Stillborn God: Religion, Politics, and the Modern West*. New York: Vintage Books, 2008.

Löwith, Karl. *Von Hegel zu Nietzsche: Der revolutionaire Bruch im Denken des neunzehnten Jahrhunderts*. Zurich: Europa, 1941.

———. "Nietzsche's Doctrine of Eternal Recurrence." *Journal of the History of Ideas* 6, no. 3 (1945): 273–84.

———. *Meaning in History: The Theological Implications of the Philosophy of History.* Chicago: University of Chicago Press, 1949.

———. *Weltgeschichte und Heilsgeschehen: Die theologischen Voraussetzungen der Geschichtsphilosophie.* Stuttgart: W. Kohlhammer, 1953.

———. *Heidegger and European Nihilism.* Edited by Richard Wolin and translated by Gary Steiner. New York: Columbia University Press, 1995.

———. *Nietzsche's Philosophy of the Eternal Recurrence of the Same.* Translated by Harvey Lomax. Berkeley: University of California Press, 1997.

Lukács, Georg. *Die Theorie des Romans: Ein geschichtsphilosophischer Versuch über die Formen der großen Epik.* Berlin: Cassirer, 1920.

Macho, Thomas, and Peter Sloterdijk, eds. *Weltrevolution der Seele: Ein Lese- und Arbeitsbuch der Gnosis von der Spätantike bis zu der Gegenwart.* Vol. 2. Lahnau: Artemis und Winkler, 1991.

Maciejko, Pawel. *The Mixed Multitude: Jacob Frank and the Frankist Movement, 1755–1816.* Philadelphia: University of Pennsylvania Press, 2011.

Marquard, Odo. "Idealismus und Theodizee." *Philosophisches Jahrbuch* 73 (1965): 33–47.

———. *Schwierigkeiten mit der Geschichtsphilosophie.* Frankfurt: Suhrkamp, 1973.

———. *Abschied vom Prinzipiellen: Philosophische Studien.* Stuttgart: Reclam, 1981.

———. *Apologie des Zufälligen.* Stuttgart: Reclam, 1986.

Mendes-Flohr, Paul. " 'To Brush History against the Grain': The Eschatology of the Frankfurt School and Ernst Bloch." *Journal of the American Academy of Religion* 51, no. 4 (1983): 631–50.

Möller, Melanie, ed. *Prometheus gibt nicht auf: Antike Welt und modernes Leben in Hans Blumenbergs Philosophie.* Munich: Wilhelm Fink, 2015.

Moltmann, Jürgen. *The Coming of God: Christian Eschatology.* Translated by Margaret Kohl. London: SCM Press, 1996.

Monod, Jean-Claude. *La querelle de la sécularisation: Theologie politique et philosophies de l'histoire de Hegel à Blumenberg.* Paris: Vrin, 2012.

Mosès, Stéphane. "Gershom Scholem's Reading of Kafka: Literary Criticism and Kabbalah." *New German Critique* 77 (1999): 149–67.

———. *The Angel of History: Rosenzweig, Benjamin, Scholem.* Translated by Barbara Harshav. Stanford: Stanford University Press, 2009.

Muller, Jerry Z. "Reisender in Ideeen: Jacob Taubes zwischen New York, Jerusalem, Berlin und Paris." In *"Ich staune, dass Sie in dieser Luft atmen können": Deutsch-jüdische Intellektuelle in Deutschland nach 1945,* edited by Monika Boll and Raphael Gross, 40–61. Frankfurt am Main: Fischer Taschenbuch, 2013.

Myers, David. "The Scholem-Kurzweil Debate and Modern Jewish Historiography." *Modern Judaism* 6, no. 3 (1986): 261–86.

Nadler, Steven. *The Best of All Possible Worlds: A Story of Philosophers, God, and Evil.* Princeton: Princeton University Press, 2010.

Nancy, Jean-Luc. *Dis-enclosure: The Deconstruction of Christianity*. Translated by Bettina Bergo, Gabriel Malenfant, and Michael B. Smith. New York: Fordham University Press, 2008.

Neiman, Susan. *Evil in Modern Thought*. Princeton: Princeton University Press, 2002.

Nicholls, Angus. *Myth and the Human Sciences: Hans Blumenberg's Theory of Myth*. New York: Routledge, 2014.

———. "Hans Blumenberg on Political Myth: Recent Publications from the Nachlass." *Iyyun: The Jerusalem Philosophical Quarterly* 65 (2016): 3–33.

Nieli, Russel. "Eric Voegelin's Evolving Ideas on Gnosticism, Mysticism, and Modern Radical Politics." *Independent Journal of Philosophy* 5 (1988): 93–102.

Nietzsche, Friedrich. *On the Genealogy of Morality*. Cambridge: Cambridge University Press, 2007.

Ohana, David. "J. L. Talmon, Gershom Scholem, and the Price of Messianism." *History of European Ideas* 34, no. 2 (2008): 169–88.

O'Regan, Cyril. *Gnostic Return in Modernity*. Albany: SUNY Press, 2001.

Pankakoski, Timo. "Reoccupying Secularization: Schmitt and Koselleck on Blumenberg's Challenge." *History and Theory* 52 (2013): 214–45.

Pauen, Michael. *Dithyrambiker des Untergangs: Gnostizismus in Ästhetik und Philosophie der Moderne*. Berlin: Akademie, 1994.

Potter, Julian. "Meaning in Eternity: Karl Löwith's Critique of Hope and Hubris." *Thesis Eleven* 110 (2012): 27–45.

Puech, Henri-Charles. *En quête de le gnose*. Paris: Gallimard, 1978.

Rabinbach, Anson. "Between Enlightenment and Apocalypse: Benjamin, Bloch, and Modern German Jewish Messianism." *New German Critique* 34 (1984): 78–124.

———. *In the Shadow of Catastrophe: German Intellectuals between Apocalypse and Enlightenment*. Berkeley: University of California Press, 1997.

Reitzenstein, Richard. *Die hellenistischen Mysterienreligionen: Nach ihren Grundgedanken und Wirkungen*. Stuttgart: B.G. Teubner, 1927.

Rubenstein, Richard. *After Auschwitz: Radical Theology and Contemporary Judaism*. Indianapolis: Bobbs-Merrill, 1966.

Ruyer, Raymond. *La gnose de Princeton: Des savants à la recherche d'une religion*. Paris: Fayard, 1974.

Schmidt, Christoph. *Die theopolitische Stunde: Zwölf Perspektiven auf das eschatologische Problem der Moderne*. Munich: Wilhelm Fink, 2009.

Schmitt, Carl. *Political Theology: Four Chapters on the Concept of Sovereignty*. Translated by George Schwab. Chicago: University of Chicago Press, 1985.

———. *The Concept of the Political*. Translated by George Schwab. Chicago: University of Chicago Press, 1996.

———. *The Nomos of the Earth in the International Law of Jus Publicum Europaeum*. Translated by G. L. Ulmen. New York: Telos Press Publishing, 2006.

———. *Political Theology II: The Myth of the Closure of Any Political Theology*. Translated by Michael Hoelzl and Graham Ward. Cambridge: Polity Press, 2008.

Schmitt, Eugen H. *Die Gnosis: Grundlagen der Weltanschauung einer edleren Kultur*. Vol. 2, *Die Gnosis des Mitteralters und der Neuzeit*. Jena: Eugen Dietrichs, 1907.

Scholem, Gershom. *Major Trends in Jewish Mysticism*. New York: Schocken Books, 1946.

———. *Jewish Gnosticism, Merkabah Mysticism, and Talmudic Tradition*. New York: The Jewish Theological Seminary Press, 1960.

———. *Judaica 1*. Frankfurt am Main: Suhrkamp, 1963.

———. "Reflections of the Possibility of Jewish Mysticism." *Ariel* 26 (1970): 43–52.

———. *The Messianic Idea in Judaism and Other Essays on Jewish Spirituality*. New York: Schocken, 1971.

———. *Judaica 3*. Frankfurt am Main: Suhrkamp, 1973.

———. *Sabbatai Zevi: The Mystical Messiah, 1626–1676*. Princeton: Princeton University Press, 1973.

———. *Judaica 4*. Frankfurt am Main: Suhrkamp, 1984.

———. "Une lettre inédite de Gerschom Scholem à Franz Rosenzweig: À propos de nôtre langue, une confession." *Archives des Sciences Sociales des Religions* 60, no. 1 (1985): 83–84.

———. *Briefe: 1948–1970*. Edited by Thomas Sparr. Munich: C.H. Beck, 1995.

———. *Briefe: 1971–1982*. Edited by I. Shedletzky. Munich: C.H. Beck, 2000.

———. *A Life in Letters*. Edited and translated by Anthony David Skinner. Cambridge, MA: Harvard University Press, 2002.

———. "Reflections on Jewish Theology." In *On Jews and Judaism in Crisis*, 261–97. Philadelphia: Paul Dry Books, 2012.

Schultz, Wolfgang. *Dokumente der Gnosis*. Jena: Eugen Diedrichs, 1910.

Schweitzer, Albert. *Das Messianitäts- und Leidensgeheimnis: Eine Skizze des Lebens Jesu*. Tübingen: J.C.B. Mohr, 1956.

Silber, Michael. "The Emergence of Ultra-Orthodoxy: The Invention of a Tradition." In *The Uses of Tradition: Jewish Continuity in the Modern Era*, edited by Jack Wertheimer, 23–84. New York: Jewish Theological Seminary of America, 1992.

Spengler, Oswald. *Der Untergang des Abendlandes: Umrisse einer Morphologie der Weltgeschichte*. 2 vols. Munich: C.H. Beck, 1922.

———. *The Decline of the West*.Translated by Francis Atkinson. 2 vols. New York: A. Knopf, 1926–28.

Steinmetz-Jenkins, Daniel. "French Laïcité and the Recent Reception of the German Secularization Debate into France." *Politics, Religion, and Ideology* 12, no. 4 (2011): 433–47.

Strauss, Leo, and Eric Voegelin. *Faith and Political Philosophy: The Correspondence between Leo Strauss and Eric Voegelin, 1934–1964*. Translated and edited by Peter Emberly and Barry Cooper. Columbia: University of Missouri Press, 2004.

Tal, Uriel. *Religion, Politics, and Ideology in the Third Reich: Selected Essays.* London: Routledge, 2004.

Talmon, Jacob. *The Origins of Totalitarian Democracy.* 2 vols. London: Secker and Warburg, 1952–60.

———. *Political Messianism: The Romantic Phase.* London: Secker and Warburg, 1960.

Taubes, Jacob. *Abendländische Eschatologie.* Berlin: Matthes und Seitz, 1947.

———, ed. *Der Fürst dieser Welt: Carl Schmitt und die Folgen.* Munich: Wilhelm Fink, 1983.

———, ed. *Gnosis und Politik.* Munich: Wilhelm Fink, 1984.

———. *Ad Carl Schmitt: Gegenstrebige Fügung.* Berlin: Merve, 1987.

———. "Jacob Taubes." In *Denken, das an der Zeit ist,* edited by Florian Rötzer, 305–19. Frankfurt am Main: Suhrkamp, 1987.

———. *Die politische Theologie des Paulus.* Edited by Aleida Assmann and Jan Assmann. Munich: Wilhelm Fink, 1993.

———. *Vom Kult zur Kultur: Bausteine zu einer Kritik der historischen Vernunft; Gesammelte Aufsätze zur Religions- und Geistesgeschichte.* Edited by Aleida Assman et al. Munich: Wilhelm Fink, 1996.

———. *The Political Theology of Paul.* Translated by Dana Hollander. Stanford: Stanford University Press, 2004.

———. *Der Preis der Messianismus: Briefe von Jacob Taubes an Gershom Scholem und andere Materialen.* Edited by Elletra Stimilli. Würzburg: Königshausen und Neumann, 2006.

———. *Occidental Eschatology.* Translated by David Ratmoko. Stanford: Stanford University Press, 2009.

———. *From Cult to Culture: Fragments toward a Critique of Historical Reason.* Edited by Charlotte E. Fonrobert and Amir Engel. Stanford: Stanford University Press, 2010.

———. *To Carl Schmitt: Letters and Reflections.* Translated by Keith Tribe. New York: Columbia University Press, 2013.

———. *Apokalypse und Politik: Aufsätze, Kritiken und kleinere Schriften.* Edited by Herbert Kopp-Oberstebrink and Martin Treml. Munich: Wilhelm Fink, 2017.

Taubes, Jacob, and Carl Schmitt. *Briefwechsel mit Materialen.* Edited by Herbert Kopp-Oberstebrink, Thorsten Palzhof, and Martin Treml. Munich: Wilhelm Fink, 2012.

Taubes, Jacob, and Eric Voegelin. *Briefwechsel.* Edited by Herbert Kopp-Oberstebrink. Munich: Wilhelm Fink, forthcoming.

Taubes, Susan. "The Gnostic Foundations of Heidegger's Nihilism." *Journal of Religion* 34, no. 3 (1954): 155–72.

———. *Die Korrespondenz mit Jacob Taubes 1950–51.* Munich: Wilhelm Fink, 2011.

Taylor, Charles. *A Secular Age.* Cambridge, MA: Harvard University Press, 2007.

Tishby, Isaiah. "The Messianic Idea and Messianic Trends in the Growth of Hasidism." *Zion* 32 (1967): 1–45.

Treml, Martin. "Nachwort." In Jacob Taubes, *Abendländische Eschatologie.* Munich: Matthes und Seitz, 2007.

———. "Reinventing the Canonical: The Radical Thinking of Jacob Taubes." In *Escape to Life: German Intellectuals in New York; A Compendium of Exile after 1933,* edited by Eckhart Goebel and Sigrid Weigel, 457–78. Berlin: De Gruyter, 2013.

Vanheeswijck, Guido. "De dubbele Franciscaanse Erfenis: Een ontbrekende Schakel in het Löwith-Blumenberg-debat." *Tijdschrift voor Filosofie* 74, no. 1 (2012): 11–44.

Vattimo, Gianni. *Belief.* Stanford: Stanford University Press, 1999.

Voegelin, Eric. *The New Science of Politics: An Introduction.* Chicago: University of Chicago Press, 1952.

———. "The Oxford Political Philosophers." *Philosophical Quarterly* 11, no. 3 (1953): 97–114.

———. "Review of *The Origins of Totalitarianism.*" *Review of Politics* 15 (1953): 68–76.

———. *Order and History.* Vol. 4, *The Ecumenic Age.* Columbia: University of Missouri Press, 2000.

———. "The Political Religions." In *The Collected Works of Eric Voegelin,* vol. 5, *Modernity without Restraint,* edited by Manfred Henningsen, 19–73. Columbia: University of Missouri Press, 2000.

———. "Science, Politics, and Gnosticism: Two Essays." In *The Collected Works of Eric Voegelin,* vol. 5, *Modernity without Restraint,* edited by Manfred Henningsen, 243–313. Columbia: University of Missouri Press, 2000.

———. *Order and History.* Vol. 1, *Israel and Revelation.* Madison: University of Missouri Press, 2001.

———. *Selected Correspondence: 1950–1984.* Columbia: University of Missouri Press, 2007.

Waldstein, Michael. "Hans Jonas' Construct 'Gnosticism': Analysis and Critique." *Journal of Early Christian Studies* 8 (2000): 341–72.

Wallace, Robert M. "Progress, Secularization, and Modernity: The Löwith-Blumenberg Debate." *New German Critique* 22 (1981): 63–79.

Weber, Max. *Gesammelte Aufsätze zur Religionssoziologie.* Tübingen: J.C.B. Mohr, 1920–21.

Weigel, Sigrid. *Walter Benjamin: Images, the Creaturely, and the Holy.* Translated by Chadwick Truscott Smith. Stanford: Stanford University Press, 2013.

———. "In Paul's Mask: Jacob Taubes Reads Walter Benjamin." In *Theological Genealogies: Reflections on Secularization in 20th-Century German Thought,* edited by Stéphane Symons and Willem Styfhals. Albany: SUNY Press, forthcoming.

Wetters, Kirk. "Working over Philosophy: Hans Blumenberg's Reformulations of the Absolute." *Telos* 158 (2012): 100–118.

Wetz, Franz Josef, and Hermann Timm, eds. *Die Künst des Überlebens: Nachdenken über Hans Blumenberg*. Frankfurt am Main: Suhrkamp, 1999.

Wiese, Christian. " 'For a time I was privileged to enjoy his friendship . . .': The Ambivalent Relationship between Hans Jonas and Gershom Scholem." *The Leo Baeck Institute Yearbook* 49, no. 1 (2004): 25–58.

Williams, Michael. *Rethinking "Gnosticism": An Argument for Dismantling a Dubious Category*. Princeton: Princeton University Press, 1999.

Wiser, James L. "From Cultural Analysis to Philosophical Anthropology: An Examination of Voegelin's Concept of Gnosticism." *Review of Politics* 42 (1980): 92–104.

Wolin, Richard. *Heidegger's Children: Hannah Arendt, Karl Löwith, Hans Jonas, and Herbert Marcuse*. Princeton: Princeton University Press, 2001.

INDEX

CPSIA information can be obtained
at www.ICGtesting.com
Printed in the USA
LVHW091753020419
612710LV00004B/509/P

9 781501 731006